THE GREAT POWERS

Jim Cannon M.A. Dip. Ed.

Principal Teacher of Modern Studies,
Craigmount High School, Edinburgh

Bill Clark M.A.

Depute Principal,
Wester Hailes Education Centre, Edinburgh

George Smuga M.A. Dip. Ed.

Depute Head Teacher,
Beeslack High School, Penicuik

Oliver & Boyd

Contents

PART 4 China Today

Introduction

This book is about the Great Powers – the USA, the Soviet Union and China – three powerful countries in the modern world whose actions influence the lives of tens of millions of people. The book is divided into four parts: The Great Powers, the USA Today, the Soviet Union Today and China Today.

In Part 1 we define what is meant by a 'great power' and illustrate their main characteristics as well as explaining the main ideological differences between the three Great Powers in the modern world. In this part of the book there is a special emphasis on the use of stimulating visual and statistical material to illustrate the ways in which the Great Powers are involved in and influence world affairs. We hope that you will find Part 1 an interesting general introduction to the more detailed study of the three countries which follows.

Parts 2, 3 and 4 have a common structure of four chapters in which we first study the people of each country and their lifestyles, followed by details of each country's economic organisation and performance. We then examine the political system and government of each country and conclude with a study of their involvement in world affairs. Each of the four chapters concludes with an examination of recent issues which are of special importance or interest. For example, the chapter on the Soviet economy concludes with three issues: the problems of Soviet agriculture, the development of Siberia's vast resources, and industrial technology, each of which is, in its own way, of vital importance to the Soviet economy both at present and in the future.

The text is designed to be followed through chapter by chapter within each part, but within each chapter the units are self-contained and can be largely understood without necessarily having studied previous units. At appropriate points there are questions based on the text or on the statistics, cartoons and photographs which accompany the text. These questions are designed to ensure understanding of the basic points in the text and to develop skill in using visual material. Also included are case studies which illustrate the meaning and impact of the events you are studying at a personal level. Some are fictional, but based on fact (for example, the five lifestyles described in the USA Lifestyles unit); others are factual (for example, the watch repairer and the Ch'ens in the China Economy in Action unit).

At the end of the book you will find a Glossary and Who's Who to help you understand some of the terms used and highlight some of the principal figures who have helped to influence the development of the Great Powers. Words and names in these lists appear in bold in the text when they first appear in a chapter. A time chart for each of the three countries is also included to give a brief chronological timetable of the most important social, economic and political events together with important events in international affairs in which they have been involved.

Events and personalities in the Great Powers will inevitably change. It is up to you to keep up to date by studying outside the text-book – by use of newspapers, magazines, radio and television. A book of 176 pages cannot cover all the crucial issues in the three Great Powers nor do full justice to the complexities of the issues described but we hope it will give an insight into these three powerful countries.

PART 1

The Great Powers

1. Defining the Great Powers

The Great Powers

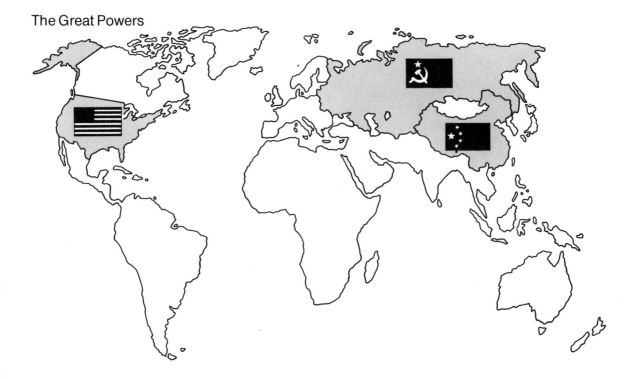

The countries highlighted in the map above are often referred to as 'Great Powers'. In this chapter the aim is to illustrate those aspects of the three countries which lead to them being considered 'Great Powers'. One such aspect is the power or ability they have to influence world affairs, that is, international involvement.

INTERNATIONAL INVOLVEMENT

An example which illustrates this particularly well occurred in 1979 when the USSR intervened militarily in its neighbouring State of Afghanistan. The USA showed great concern at these events. China also criticised the USSR's actions.

PRESTEL
AFGHANISTAN CRISIS

24-27 Dec. 1979 ... 350 Soviet aircraft land at Kabul Airport.

27 Dec. 1979 ... Pro-Soviet President Hafizullah Amin shot dead. Replaced by Babrak Karmal.

28 Dec. 1979 ... Afghan capital, Kabul, completely in Soviet hands.

29-31 Dec. 1979 ... Twin-pronged invasion by Soviet ground forces.

1 Jan. 1980 ... Estimated 50000 Soviet troops in Afghanistan.

Afghanistan: Great Power interest and involvement

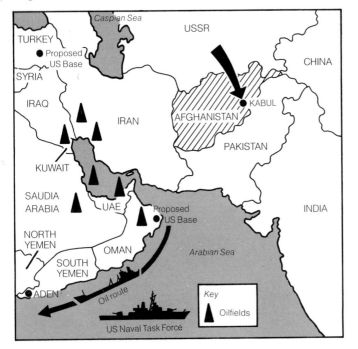

USSR

1. Afghanistan is a border neighbour.
2. The USSR had supported the Government of Afghanistan before 1979 and supported the new Government led by Babrak Karmal.
3. Afghanistan is close to huge Middle East oil supplies for the USA and the West.
4. The USSR was afraid that a revolution in Afghanistan might lead to a Muslim, Islamic Revolution similar to the one which changed Iran's Government. Islamic revolutionary ideas might even spread to the USSR's Muslim population of roughly 40 million.

USA

1. Afghanistan is a neighbour of Iran, with whom the USA had close links before the removal of the Shah in the Islamic Revolution.
2. Afghanistan is close to the Middle East oilfields which supply some of the USA's oil needs.
3. The USA fears an increase in Soviet power in the Middle East.
4. The USA was afraid of Soviet advance towards the Arabian sea for southern 'warm water' ports for the Soviet navy.

China

1. Afghanistan is a border neighbour.
2. China had been supplying military aid to Pakistan, Afghanistan's neighbour.
3. Chinese advisers had been working in Pakistan.
4. China was afraid that its own large neighbour, the USSR, was advancing its power and influence in areas close to China.

Great Power Reactions to the Afghanistan Crisis

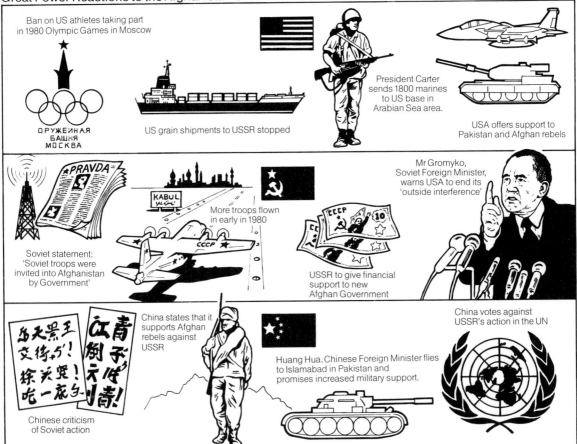

Military strength

	USA	USSR	China
Armed forces on active duty	2.09 million	4.84 million	4.3 million
Nuclear warheads	7192	6302	500
Long-range missiles	1628	2384	2
Warplanes	3988	4885	5500
Tanks	11 560	48 000	11 000
Aircraft carriers	13	2	0
Other major surface warships	210	266	25
Submarines	121	370	92

We have looked at one aspect of the Great Powers, that is, the scale on which they are prepared to become involved internationally to defend or advance their own interests. There are several other aspects common to the Great Powers.

MILITARY STRENGTH

One aspect is the extent to which each of them can develop its military strength. The table above indicates the military strengths of the three Great Powers.

ECONOMIC STRENGTH

A third aspect of a Great Power is economic strength. The largest companies in the USA are **multinationals** with branches in many other countries. The biggest company is General Motors which in 1978 had sales worth $63 221 million and employed over 800 000 people. The power of these industrial giants can be seen by comparing their sales with the wealth produced in several countries throughout the world.

POPULATION

A fourth aspect of a Great Power is population size.

Economic strength

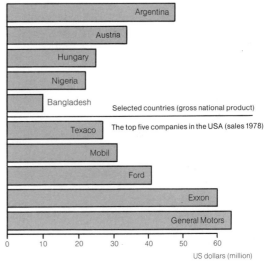

Selected countries (gross national product)

The top five companies in the USA (sales 1978)

US dollars (million)

Population

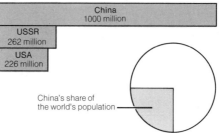

China 1000 million

USSR 262 million

USA 226 million

China's share of the world's population

The following quotations provide two views on the importance of China's large population.

'What is a true bastion of iron? It is the masses, the millions of people who genuinely support the Revolution. That is the real bastion which it is impossible, and absolutely impossible for any force on earth to smash.'

(*Mao Zedong*)

'There were not enough machines, there was no cement, no mortar and other building materials. Hundreds of thousands of inhabitants of Peking set out to . . . [build a dam]. In eight hour shifts they worked day and night without a break. They scratched away the earth from the surrounding hills often with no more than their fingernails, they split stones with the most primitive tools, and carried earth and stone in little baskets on carrying-poles to the river bed, where more thousands stood and stamped the stones and earth flat with their feet . . . In six months the dam was built. It is 2088 feet high and 38.2 feet wide at its base.'

(*Hugo Portisch*, a journalist, describing how a dam was built in China in 1958)

Military strength	USA	USSR	China
Military spending in relation to GNP	6%	12%	9%
Armed forces	2.09 million	4.84 million	4.3 million
Nuclear warheads	7192	6302	500
Nuclear submarines	70	85	1

Industrial strength	USA	USSR	China
GNP ($US billions)	2100	1200 (est)	444 (est)
Steel (million tonnes)	135	166	34
Oil (million tonnes)	474	629	110
Computers in use	340 000	30 000	2 000
Percentage of workforce in agriculture	3.3	25	85

Size and Population	USA	USSR	China
Area (km²)	9 million	21 million	10 million
Population (millions)	226	262	1000
Average life expectancy (years)	73	69	65
Percentage of population aged under 20	35	37	40–45

THE DEFINITION OF A GREAT POWER

A Great Power is a country which has the economic and military strength to defend its own interests when these are challenged, and above all the strength to exert its influence on other areas throughout the world.

Size (area), population and wealth are all indicators of a country's economic strength. A country's size is likely to be related to the number of resources that might be available to that country. Population is important as it provides the potential workforce and the consumers. The GNP (gross national product) is an indicator of the extent to which a country has used its resources to develop its potential economic strength.

Military strength is also important as an indicator of power and can be measured in terms of armed forces and types of conventional and nuclear weapons.

Questions

1. Give four reasons why the USA, USSR and China can be considered 'Great Powers'.
2. Why were the three Great Powers involved in the Afghanistan crisis?
3. What effect did this involvement have on
   (*a*) the 1980 Olympic Games;
   (*b*) USA–USSR trade;
   (*c*) Chinese relations with the other two Powers?
4. Study the statistics above. What conclusions do you draw about the comparative strengths of the three Great Powers?

2. Ideological Differences

The three Great Powers have different political, economic and social systems. To a large extent the reason for these differences can be traced to historical backgrounds, or to geographical and economic factors, such as the availability of resources. But a large part is also due to the different political, economic and social values which the Powers hold. These values and beliefs about the political system, about the way the economy should be run and about the way society should be structured are known as *ideologies*. The USA follows the ideology and model of **capitalism**. The USSR and China are both examples of *communist* societies, although they differ in their interpretation of **communism**.

What are these different ideologies which the major powers profess, and what views do they have of each other? Here are the views you might hear from an American, a Soviet and a Chinese official speaking about their own country.

Speaking for the USA

The United States of America is founded on capitalism and democracy. These twin ideals are basic to the American way of life and have been since the USA declared its independence from Britain in 1776 with these famous words:

'We hold these truths to be self-evident, that all men are created equal, that they are endowed by their Creator with certain unalienable rights. Among these are Life,

Liberty and the Pursuit of Happiness. To secure these rights Governments are instituted among Men, deriving their just powers from the consent of the governed.'

(Declaration of Independence)

Our democratic political system is founded on these ideals. It is 'government of the people, by the people, for the people'. The US **Constitution** is a model of political freedom and an example to the world of the democratic process. It establishes an elected government which serves for a limited term. One-person-one-vote and a choice of political parties are essentials. In few other countries are there so many elected offices. Our Government is limited, since no one branch of government can become too powerful. The Constitution guarantees our individual rights: the right to free speech, free press, free assembly and freedom from arrest without charge. Our capitalist system is based upon freedom. We believe in the right of private ownership of property in an open competitive economic system. It is open to anyone to invest money and labour in business or land so that its value can increase and thereby create wealth. This acts as a great incentive to work harder, and ultimately the whole of society benefits. Freedom of the individual to choose is also important: hospitals, colleges and so on are all privately owned and competition between them for customers ensures the best services for all.

The Government should interfere in people's lives as little as possible. Thomas Jefferson, author of the Declaration of Independence and one of our early Presidents, summed this up by saying 'that government is best which governs least'.

And our system works. The USA is the wealthiest and most powerful country in the world. It has provided a home for millions of oppressed people from all over the world. The USA has given them the opportunity to find political freedom and the means to build a good life.

We are opposed to communism because it stands for the opposite of all we believe in. The USSR and China are one-party States in which human rights are suppressed. There is no democracy in these countries. Without a choice of political party, elections are a farce. Nor is there a classless society in these countries. This is especially so of the USSR where a small elite enjoy a life of privilege denied to the rest of the people. Their economic system does not work. They cannot provide their people with an adequate standard of living and can only encourage them to work harder by offering material incentives. Competition will eventually prove indispensable.

Speaking for the USSR

The USSR is a socialist country, which is working towards the ideal state of communism. Our political and economic system is founded upon the ideas of Marxism–Leninism. **Karl Marx** showed history to be a series of struggles between different social classes. Capitalism is only one stage in this and just as feudalism gave way to capitalism so must capitalism give way to socialism. Capitalism contains the seeds of its own destruction because it depends upon a privileged class exploiting the mass of the people who actually produce the wealth. Lenin showed how revolution would bring about the change from capitalism to socialism, and in 1917 the Communist (Bolshevik) Party, led by Lenin, seized power and signalled a new era in world history by making the Soviet Union the world's first socialist State.

Under socialism there are no class divisions caused by the unequal distribution of wealth. There is no private ownership of property. All the resources – land, buildings, factories – are owned by the State on behalf of the people. All citizens are guaranteed the right to work, to free education and medical treatment, and to be cared for in times of illness, disability and old age.

Socialism guarantees real freedom of the individual. The Soviet system completely eliminates oppression and exploitation. It establishes equality of all peoples. It is based on the principle: 'From each according to his ability, to each according to his work.' As socialism develops, it reaches its final stage: communism. Public wealth becomes abundant and provides a basis for the realisation of our ultimate aim, 'From each according to his ability, to each according to his needs.'

All power in the country belongs to the people and they exercise this power through the Soviets, councils which are freely elected by the citizens of the USSR. The Communist Party is the leading force in Soviet society and it unites and guides the people.

And our system works. We have made remarkable progress since 1917, despite having almost no industrial base to build upon and despite being devastated during World War 2. We are the world's second greatest industrial power and our people's living standards are continually improving. This is a tribute to our system of Government planning and is only possible under socialism.

We believe that capitalism is doomed to failure. The USA preaches about freedom and democracy but these are useless without equality. What freedom do the blacks, the poor and other oppressed groups in the USA have? Freedom of choice is only freedom for the rich and for the privileged. Real human rights mean equal treatment and opportunities for all.

Speaking for China

The People's Republic of China is also a socialist country. We too based our political, economic and social system upon the ideas of Marxism–Leninism. But we should not be seen as a copy of the USSR. The Soviet Union looks to Lenin as its great revolutionary leader and thinker. We look to **Mao Zedong** (Mao Tse-Tung) as our founding figure. He led the Communist Party to power in 1949 and directed China along its own road to socialism. We have added Maoism to Marxism–Leninism and have provided a lead to all oppressed peoples in the Third World, who are trying to escape from imperialism and feudalism. It must be remembered that China was, and to a large extent still is, an agricultural country, and no successful transformation to socialism can come about without the support of the peasantry. Before the Revolution in 1949, communism grew among the peasants and built up from there. One of Mao's great achievements was in waging a revolutionary guerrilla war by using the peasants as a base.

After the Revolution in 1949, our form of socialism began to develop differently from that of the USSR. It became increasingly clear to us that the Soviet Union could not provide us with a model to follow. Our socialism is based upon developing both the countryside and the cities. The People's Communes are the basis of socialism in the Chinese countryside. They provide the means by which political, economic and social equality can be reached. Socialism in the USSR has gone wrong. It has revised 'Marxism–Leninism' and lost the true path to a classless society. The Soviet Union has become a bureaucratic dictatorship in which Party officials and other leaders have become divorced from the people. It has become an imperialist power like the USA.

And our system works. We know only too well the evils of capitalism and imperialism from our own recent history. Before 1949, China was ravaged by foreign powers and ruled by a privileged minority who cared little for the lives of the masses of the people. Since then we have made huge strides to create an equal society in which the ordinary people have benefited greatly. This has all been accomplished in a predominantly agricultural country without any major industrial base. Now, under our present leadership, we are poised to embark upon a programme of modernisation to make us into a major industrial power.

These three statements are designed to introduce you to the values of the three Great Powers and their perceptions of each other. Once you have studied the three Powers in more depth, you can look back and see how closely they have been able to put their ideologies into practice.

3. The Great Powers and World Affairs

Rival Aims in Foreign Policy

USA
Statements by Great Power leaders
USSR

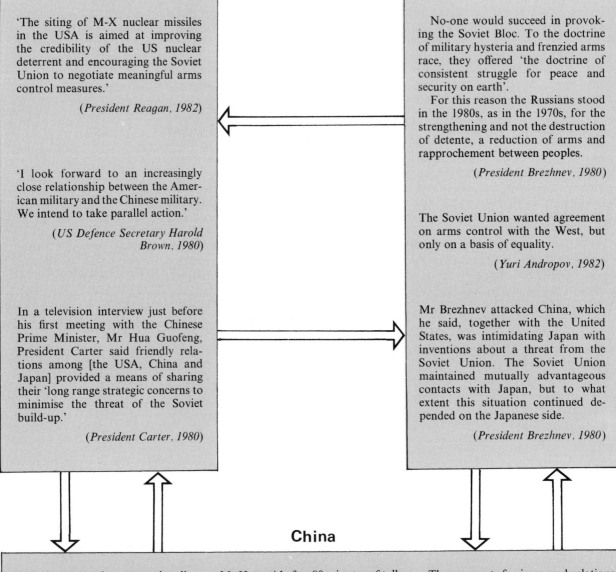

'The siting of M-X nuclear missiles in the USA is aimed at improving the credibility of the US nuclear deterrent and encouraging the Soviet Union to negotiate meaningful arms control measures.'

(*President Reagan, 1982*)

'I look forward to an increasingly close relationship between the American military and the Chinese military. We intend to take parallel action.'

(*US Defence Secretary Harold Brown, 1980*)

In a television interview just before his first meeting with the Chinese Prime Minister, Mr Hua Guofeng, President Carter said friendly relations among [the USA, China and Japan] provided a means of sharing their 'long range strategic concerns to minimise the threat of the Soviet build-up.'

(*President Carter, 1980*)

No-one would succeed in provoking the Soviet Bloc. To the doctrine of military hysteria and frenzied arms race, they offered 'the doctrine of consistent struggle for peace and security on earth'.

For this reason the Russians stood in the 1980s, as in the 1970s, for the strengthening and not the destruction of detente, a reduction of arms and rapprochement between peoples.

(*President Brezhnev, 1980*)

The Soviet Union wanted agreement on arms control with the West, but only on a basis of equality.

(*Yuri Andropov, 1982*)

Mr Brezhnev attacked China, which he said, together with the United States, was intimidating Japan with inventions about a threat from the Soviet Union. The Soviet Union maintained mutually advantageous contacts with Japan, but to what extent this situation continued depended on the Japanese side.

(*President Brezhnev, 1980*)

China

'China's unswerving external policy has been to oppose hegemonism and preserve world peace.' Mr Hua said. 'Acts of aggression and expansion have become more unscrupulous in the attempt to seize important sources of raw materials, strategic bases and control sea lanes.'

(*Premier Hua, 1979*)

Mr Hua said after 80 minutes of talks with Mr Carter that he was satisfied with China's growing relations with the US. It was important for world peace for China to develop them further, as well as her ties with Japan, Western Europe and the Third World.

(*Premier Hua, 1980*)

The prospects for improved relations between China and the USSR depend on whether the Soviet Union acts to remove the "threat" against China's borders.

(*Prime Minister Zhao Ziyang, 1982*)

Great Power Relations

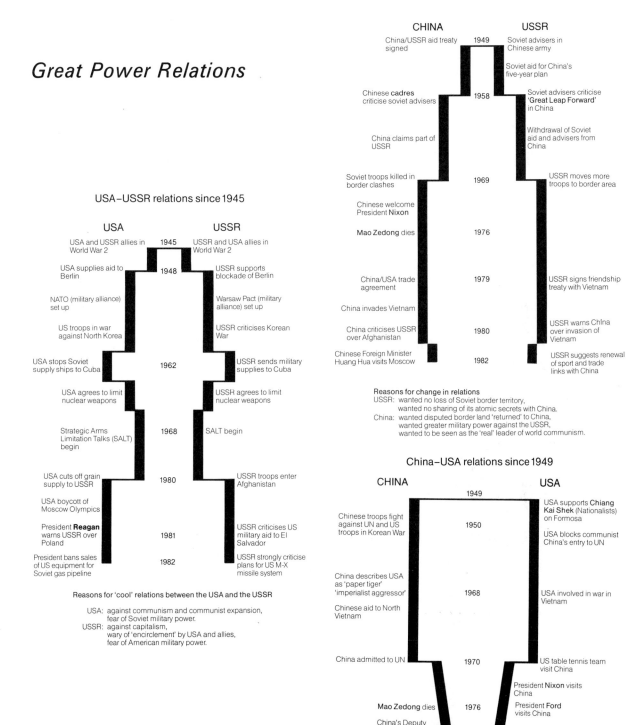

Sino-Soviet relations since 1949

CHINA		USSR
China/USSR aid treaty signed	1949	Soviet advisers in Chinese army
		Soviet aid for China's five-year plan
Chinese **cadres** criticise soviet advisers	1958	Soviet advisers criticise **'Great Leap Forward'** in China
China claims part of USSR		Withdrawal of Soviet aid and advisers from China
Soviet troops killed in border clashes	1969	USSR moves more troops to border area
Chinese welcome President **Nixon**		
Mao Zedong dies	1976	
China/USA trade agreement	1979	USSR signs friendship treaty with Vietnam
China invades Vietnam		
China criticises USSR over Afghanistan	1980	USSR warns China over invasion of Vietnam
Chinese Foreign Minister Huang Hua visits Moscow	1982	USSR suggests renewal of sport and trade links with China

Reasons for change in relations

USSR: wanted no loss of Soviet border territory,
wanted no sharing of its atomic secrets with China.
China: wanted disputed border land 'returned' to China,
wanted greater military power against the USSR,
wanted to be seen as the 'real' leader of world communism.

USA–USSR relations since 1945

USA		USSR
USA and USSR allies in World War 2	1945	USSR and USA allies in World War 2
USA supplies aid to Berlin	1948	USSR supports blockade of Berlin
NATO (military alliance) set up		Warsaw Pact (military alliance) set up
US troops in war against North Korea		USSR criticises Korean War
USA stops Soviet supply ships to Cuba	1962	USSR sends military supplies to Cuba
USA agrees to limit nuclear weapons		USSR agrees to limit nuclear weapons
Strategic Arms Limitation Talks (SALT) begin	1968	SALT begin
USA cuts off grain supply to USSR	1980	USSR troops enter Afghanistan
USA boycott of Moscow Olympics		
President **Reagan** warns USSR over Poland	1981	USSR criticises US military aid to El Salvador
President bans sales of US equipment for Soviet gas pipeline	1982	USSR strongly criticise plans for US M-X missile system

Reasons for 'cool' relations between the USA and the USSR

USA: against communism and communist expansion,
fear of Soviet military power.
USSR: against capitalism,
wary of 'encirclement' by USA and allies,
fear of American military power.

China–USA relations since 1949

CHINA		USA
	1949	USA supports **Chiang Kai Shek** (Nationalists) on Formosa
Chinese troops fight against UN and US troops in Korean War	1950	USA blocks communist China's entry to UN
China describes USA as 'paper tiger' 'imperialist aggressor'	1968	USA involved in war in Vietnam
Chinese aid to North Vietnam		
China admitted to UN	1970	US table tennis team visit China
		President **Nixon** visits China
Mao Zedong dies	1976	President **Ford** visits China
China's Deputy Premier, **Deng Xiaoping** visits USA		USA opens embassy in China
Chinese trade exhibition in San Francisco (California)	1980	60 US firms set up in China
USA restricts Chinese textile sales to USA	1982	US arms sales to Taiwan

Reasons for change in relations

China: wanted to modernise industry and military quickly,
wanted US support against the USSR.
USA: wanted an end to the Vietnam war,
wanted Chinese support against the USSR,
wanted trade with a potential large customer.

World Pressure Points

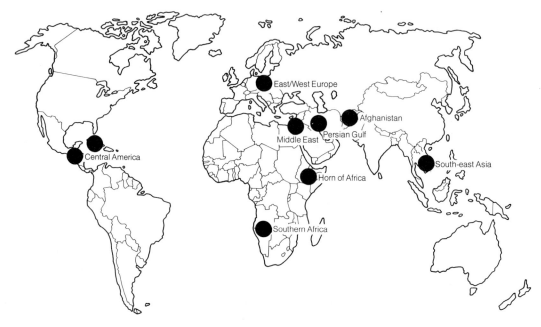

East/West Europe

Afghanistan

Middle East

Persian Gulf

Central America

Horn of Africa

South-east Asia

Southern Africa

How the Great Powers Influence World Affairs

		USA	USSR	China
Economic aid		Israel	Cuba	Tanzania
Military aid		Saudi Arabia	Ethiopia	Egypt?
Alliances		NATO (Military)	Warsaw Pact (Military)	Friendship Treaties e.g. with Japan
Political pressure		Guatemala	Poland	Taiwan
Military intervention		El Salvador	Afghanistan	Vietnam
Covert (Secret) intervention		Chile?	Namibia?	Kampuchea?

PART 2

The USA Today

1. The People of the USA

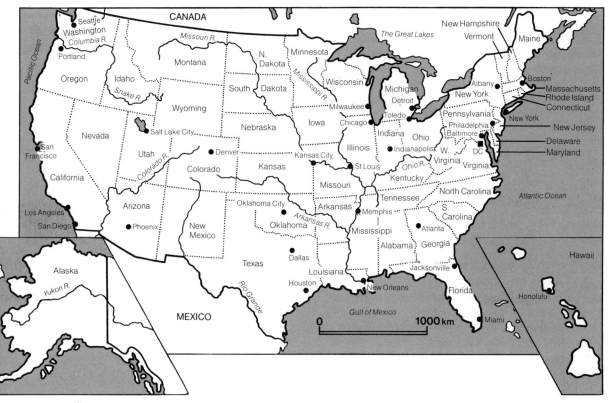

Population Survey: People on the Move

IMMIGRATION

The USA, often thought of as a land of immigrants, has had a long tradition of accepting many immigrants as part of its population policy. During the early part of this century as many as 1 million immigrants, mainly Europeans, arrived in the USA each year. This immigration reached a peak just before the outbreak of World War 1 in 1914.

In the late 1970s and early 1980s another peak of nearly 1 million immigrants a year was reached; this time the incomers were mainly people from Central America, the Caribbean, and South-east Asia.

Average annual legal immigration into the USA

From:
Europe 91.6%
Asia 3.7%
N. & S. America 4.1%

From:
Europe 18.4%
Asia 35.3%
N. & S. America 43.5%

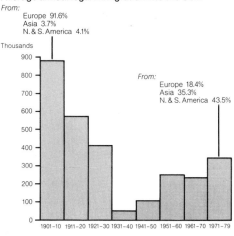

Who are the New Immigrants?

Many of these new immigrants are, like many of the early European immigrants (Irish, Italian, German, Russian), fleeing from their own countries to avoid poverty and persecution. The reasons may vary from group to group, and even from family to family.

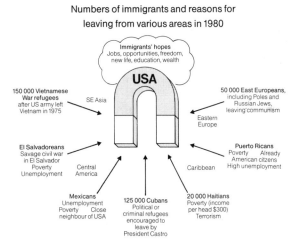

Numbers of immigrants and reasons for leaving from various areas in 1980

Immigrants' hopes
Jobs, opportunities, freedom, new life, education, wealth

USA

150 000 Vietnamese War refugees after US army left Vietnam in 1975 — SE Asia

50 000 East Europeans, including Poles and Russian Jews, leaving communism — Eastern Europe

El Salvadoreans Savage civil war in El Salvador Poverty Unemployment — Central America

Puerto Ricans Poverty Already American citzens High unemployment — Caribbean

Mexicans Unemployment Poverty Close neighbour of USA

125 000 Cubans Political or criminal refugees encouraged to leave by President Castro

20 000 Haitians Poverty (income per head $300) Terrorism

Illegal Immigrants

A number of the immigrants who enter the USA each year do so illegally, without proper documents or official permission. The US Census Bureau estimates that over $\frac{1}{4}$ million illegal immigrants have entered the country each year over the last ten years, and that in total there are about 5 million illegal 'aliens' living in the USA at present. Many of these illegal immigrants suffer difficulties and hardship in their efforts to enter the USA.

> 13 illegal immigrants from El Salvador, including nine women and a 14 year old boy, died when border smugglers left them without water in the blazing heat of the Arizona Desert in the USA. Police in helicopters reported finding 12 survivors. The survivors said the smugglers had led them across the Mexican–American border, had stolen their money, and deserted them.

(*Reuter News Agency Report*, July 1980)

Along the Mexican border, many thousands of illegal aliens are captured by American border immigration guards each year, but many others get into the USA without being caught. Most 'border crossers' are Mexicans although about a tenth are from El Salvador, Guatemala, and Ecuador. Many are imprisoned in detention camps, then sent back over the border in special buses or, as in the case of the El Salvadoreans, about 50 per day are flown back to El Salvador. Many of those deported start the journey back again towards the USA as soon as possible. They will try again and this time hope to avoid the border guards and settle secretly in the USA.

What do the Immigrants do in the USA?

Most of the immigrants hope to find work in the USA but, with US unemployment figures fairly high, employment is not always easy to find. Often the only jobs immigrants can find are poorly paid: as farm workers, bus and subway workers, clothes makers, and restaurant kitchen workers.

Immigrant (Mexican) farm workers in California

Reactions in the USA to Immigrants

People living in the USA have different reactions to the continuing flow of immigrants into the country. Here are the views of some Americans, speaking for or against immigration.

For more immigration

'The USA has always welcomed refugees'
'The USA is a nation of immigrants'
'They do jobs other Americans don't want to do.'
'Their work helps the US economy'

'Ours is a country of refugees. We'll continue to provide an open heart and open arms to refugees.'

(*President Carter, 1980*)

Against more immigration

'The USA can't take more refugees'
'Many are illegal immigrants'
'They take jobs from American workers and
keep wages down'
'They just claim hand outs'

'On present trends, immigration will add
about 35 million people by year 2000.
Where are we going to find the resources
of food, water, energy, and land?'
(Senator Huddleston (Kentucky), 1980)

Immigration Laws

Give me your tired, your poor,
Your huddled masses yearning to breathe free.
The wretched refuse of your teeming shore.
Send these, the homeless, tempest-tost to me.
I lift my lamp beside the golden door.

(Poem carved on the base of the
Statue of Liberty, New York Harbour)

For many refugees all over the world the hope is that the message of this poem may still be true and that they will be able to enter the USA without difficulty. However, even as early as 1924, there was a rise of American opinion against large numbers of immigrants and an Immigration Act was passed to restrict their numbers. Between 1960 and 1980 the total population increased by 46 million. The increasing flow of immigrants again roused opposition in the USA, and a poll in 1980 showed that 80% of Americans were in favour of reducing immigration. Already there have been outbreaks of violence against Vietnamese shrimp fishermen in parts of the USA and the **Ku Klux Klan** has threatened violence and organised protest marches against Cuban refugees.

Many Americans are agreed that the laws need to be reformed but it is difficult to see how this can be done without annoying one country or another. In 1965 a Refugee and Family Ties Act was passed which declared that fixed limits did not apply to refugees ('people who are unable and unwilling to return to their homeland because of political, racial, religious, or other persecution'). When this law was passed, however, it was not foreseen how vast the numbers of refugees coming in from Vietnam, Cuba, and Mexico would be. In 1980, a proposal was put forward to limit the numbers of

Mexicans, but the Mexican Government and Mexican Americans were against it. The welcoming open door of the USA continues to let many people in to the country, but some Americans feel the time has come to close it. They would like to rewrite the poem on the Statue of Liberty so that it began 'Do not give me your tired, your poor . . . .

Melting Pot or Salad Bowl

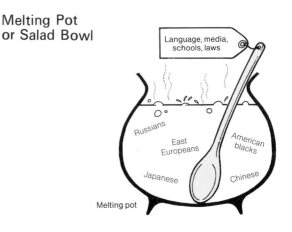

The mixture of different racial and ethnic groups in the population of the USA has been termed the 'melting pot'. The original idea was that the different groups of immigrants would eventually integrate with each other in the USA and would become 'American' citizens. This would be brought about by the fact that all citizens would be under the same US laws, go to the same schools, speak English as their language, and look at American television programmes, magazines and newspapers.

A more recent description of the mixture of immigrants in the USA, however, is the 'salad bowl' where different groups live in one country, but keep their own identities, customs and beliefs. It may be that this is a better description than 'melting pot' since many groups, for

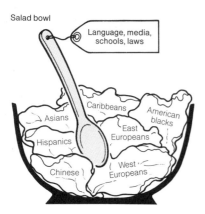

Salad bowl

Language, media, schools, laws

Caribbeans
American blacks
Asians
East Europeans
Hispanics
West Europeans
Chinese

INTERNAL MIGRATION

Within the borders of the USA, there are also movements or 'migrations' of people. Since the beginning of this century many Americans, especially blacks, migrated to the large industrial cities of the north and north-east in the hope of finding work. In recent years, however, this has changed. The 1980 Census has highlighted two new trends in population movement in the USA: a move of people to 'sunbelt' areas to find work; and a move of people out of cities.

example, Cubans, Mexicans, or black Americans, have not mixed or been integrated entirely into the US population. Most of the **Hispanics** (Spanish speakers), especially from Mexico, keep close links with Mexico and its language. They often send money back to their homeland, and make little effort to learn English. Language is a main stumbling block for many first-generation Americans, and there is a shortage of special language teachers to cope with almost 70 different languages.

Movement to the 'Sunbelt' Areas

Many people are leaving the north and north-east to seek employment in the 'sunbelt' States. This is shown by the much greater increases in population in these areas than elsewhere in the USA. In recent years the older industries of north and north-east USA, such as the car and steel industries, have faced difficulties because of declining sales. As a result, unemployment has risen in some of these northern cities, and this has caused people to move to the west and

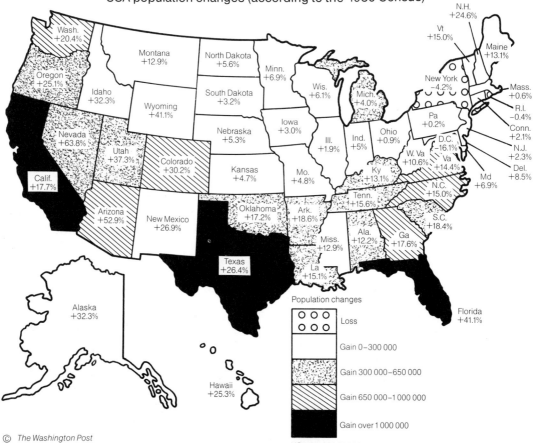

USA population changes (according to the 1980 Census)

Wash. +20.4%
Oregon +25.1%
Idaho +32.3%
Montana +12.9%
North Dakota +5.6%
Minn. +6.9%
Wis. +6.1%
Mich. +4.0%
N.H. +24.6%
Vt +15.0%
Maine +13.1%
New York –4.2%
Mass. +0.6%
R.I. –0.4%
Conn. +2.1%
Nevada +63.8%
Utah +37.3%
Wyoming +41.1%
South Dakota +3.2%
Nebraska +5.3%
Iowa +3.0%
Ill. +1.9%
Ind. +5%
Ohio +0.9%
Pa +0.2%
N.J. +2.3%
Del. +8.5%
Colorado +30.2%
Kansas +4.7%
Mo. +4.8%
Ky +13.1%
W. Va +10.6%
Va +14.4%
D.C. –16.1%
Md +6.9%
Calif. +17.7%
Arizona +52.9%
New Mexico +26.9%
Oklahoma +17.2%
Ark. +18.6%
Tenn. +15.6%
N.C. +15.0%
S.C. +18.4%
Miss. +12.9%
Ala. +12.2%
Ga +17.6%
Texas +26.4%
La +15.1%
Alaska +32.3%
Hawaii +25.3%
Florida +41.1%

Population changes

○○○ / ○○○ Loss
Gain 0–300 000
Gain 300 000–650 000
Gain 650 000–1 000 000
Gain over 1 000 000

US total: 226 505 000 (+12.3%)

south-west where jobs are available in factories, transport, building trades, and oil-related work.

Unemployment Figures (1980)

North-east	South (sunbelt)
Detroit 23%	Dallas 4%
Flint (Michigan) 17%	Houston 3%

Newspaper seller, Detroit, Michigan

This movement of people from the north-east has both economic and political effects. Economically, the move means that some States lose skilled workers, and taxpayers. Cities such as Philadelphia and Detroit have less money available. States that are losing population therefore find difficulty in paying for their social services, while those that are gaining population have enough money but cannot build new schools, hospitals, and roads quickly enough.

Politically, the movement of people could have a major effect since, although the US Senate has two members from each State, the US House of Representatives (see page 49) has its membership based on a proportion of the population of each State. In the 1976 and 1980 Presidential elections many States in the western USA had **Republican** majorities. The movement of people from the north-east (which is mainly **Democratic**) could benefit the Republican Party because the increased population level in the western States would mean they had more seats in the House of Representatives.

Flight from the Cities

The second trend highlighted in the 1980 Census is that, although 70% of Americans are still living in cities, there has been an increase in population in rural areas and small towns in the USA. There is a migration from large urban areas to smaller towns, as many Americans seek the benefits of small-town life: safe surroundings for children, a slower pace of life, peaceful retirement. Already this move has brought protests from the residents of some small towns and from environmentalists who fear that rural USA might be overwhelmed.

· Questions

1. From which countries do many of the USA's recent immigrants come?
2. What are the main reasons why they move to the USA?
3. Explain what is meant by
   (a) the 'melting pot',
   (b) the 'salad bowl'.
4. Describe two effects of the movement of people away from the north-east of the USA.

Lifestyles

Is there such a thing as 'the American way of life'? Is there any comparison between, for example, the lifestyle of the prosperous young business executive and the family of the poor Hispanic immigrant? Any attempt to generalise about lifestyles in the USA today would be misleading, because there are so many variations. In the next few pages you will read a number of case studies which are fictitious but based on fact. They cover a wide spectrum and are *not* typical of the majority of people in the USA. Together with a selection of items from the US and British media they are designed to help you to learn about the great variety and unpredictability of 'the American way of life'.

CASE STUDIES

Lucy Andrews

Hi! My name's Lucy Andrews. I'm fifteen years old and I live in the town of Newport Beach between Los Angeles and San Diego in California. I attend the local high school where

'Minnesota Twins' baseball player
Ken Landreaux in action

my favorite subjects are math, science and social studies. But I really enjoy school most because of the sports like basketball, tennis and swimming. I'm glad our school doesn't suffer from the problems I've heard about in some of the city schools. Sure, some of my friends skip classes now and again, and a few have tried drugs, but we don't have the violence they have in LA.

I usually watch breakfast TV before setting off for school in the morning, especially if there's a cartoon or sports program on. My mom drives me to school in our new Japanese car which my dad bought this year because our old Chevy was too expensive to run. After school I like to put on my Walkman and go to the local roller-disco, or in summer go swimming or surfing in the bay. I suppose my real heroes are in sports – Tracy Austin is my favorite, and my tennis coach thinks I might win a tennis scholarship to UCLA if I work hard and keep practising. Who knows, I might play against her some day!

Our house is quite big – my two brothers and myself each have a room to ourselves. We have our own small swimming pool and at weekends mom and dad sometimes have a barbecue to which I am allowed to invite some of my school friends. There are all the usual labor-saving gadgets in the house, everything from a food mixer to an automatic crushed-ice dispenser. My parents have their own personal computer which they use to work out our monthly budget and they recently bought a new video-disc machine. Maybe that's why our house has been broken into twice during the last six months.

Harry Johnstone

My name is Harry Johnstone. I was born in Detroit forty-six years ago and have lived in the city ever since. My parents were Scots who came to the USA in the 1920s. After leaving school I worked for the giant Chrysler Corporation, first as a trainee in the assembly plant and later as foreman engineer supervising a production line. A few years ago I became unemployed for the first time in my life and I see no hope of ever finding a job in the auto industry again. I'm really scared about what I'll do when my unemployment benefit runs out. I feel just like another statistic – one of 200 000 laid off by the auto industry in Detroit in the last few years. The only advice my union gives me is 'give up, leave town and try to find work in some other city'. Trouble is, I can't afford to go or stay.

I used to blame the Japanese for the problems of the auto industry in Detroit. Now I'm not so sure. You can't really blame them for taking advantage of the demand for smaller cars. The American car bosses should have been prepared for the change to smaller cars, and our Government should have done something much sooner to stop the Japanese flooding the market.

Whoever's to blame, I've found it difficult to adjust my standard of living. I can no longer even think about taking my wife and two kids on our usual holiday to the west coast or Miami. My wife has far less to spend on her weekly visit to the supermarket and the ice-box is no longer as full as it used to be. My wife has been so deeply affected by the changes in our life that she has had to make regular visits to the psychoanalyst during the last few months.

Ernie Williams

I was born twenty-two years ago in the Brownsville area of Brooklyn, New York. I never knew who my father was, and my mother survived by a combination of welfare handouts and drink. I haven't seen her these past twelve years. I remember my childhood clearly – Brownsville is one of those areas of the Big Apple you don't see in the tourist brochures, neglected by the politicians for as long as anybody can remember: shuttered shops, derelict slums, rat-infested garbage piled high in the alleys and scattered by the packs of wild dogs roaming the streets, and the heroin traders on every street corner. It's no wonder I had to become 'street-wise' before I reached my teens.

I learned a lot at school of course, like how to make a fast buck, the art of street hustle, and how to deal in narcotics. Our school was a real disaster – teachers who couldn't teach, barred and bricked windows and barbed wire to stop rival gangs breaking in, and security guards patrolling the corridors to make sure we didn't rape or murder the teachers. Like most others I just stopped going. I guess I was lucky to get a part-time job as delivery boy for a grocery store when I left school. Now I drive the delivery truck myself and make a reasonable and honest living, but I still live in Brownsville.

I'm sure glad I stayed out of serious trouble with the cops when I was younger. Some of my school friends have been in the best reformatories and prisons in the State. Crime's the only real 'job' some of them have ever had. Blacks may have more chances to be successful in the States today, but not blacks born in Brownsville! Some of my old school friends say that those black guys who have made it have sold out to the whites, and they hate them all. And people say that things will get worse for blacks under Reagan because of social security and welfare cuts.

Jane Henson

My name is Jane Henson. I'm thirty-two years old and divorced. I work as a freelance journalist, contributing articles on politics mainly to newspapers like the *Washington Post* and the *New York Daily News*. I've also done some short stories for magazines like the *Reader's Digest*. Recently I've done some work in television and have been involved in programs for a number of local cable-TV stations as well as programmes syndicated nationwide by CBS and ABC. I'm based in Washington DC, at the heart of the political life of the nation, where I have a fourth-floor air-conditioned apartment. In the last year I've covered stories in New York, Atlanta, Houston and San Francisco – whenever possible I travel by air; it's the only way, with such large distances involved. My favorite city is New York – I love going to the theatre on Broadway or simply strolling through Greenwich Village. But I also like getting away from city life once a year and enjoy sailing in the Florida Keys in summer.

I'm a strong supporter of the Women's Movement because I believe in total equality of the sexes. One of the reasons for the breakup of my marriage was that my husband, a successful business executive with the Xerox corporation,

couldn't accept my right to have a career of my own. My strong views often lead to arguments with editors and producers who, even today, are usually male. I've noticed an increase in the number of women in management and executive jobs in the last ten years, but there's still a long way to go.

I am deeply concerned about my country's problems. The newspapers I contribute to are dominated by headlines and stories about crime, unemployment, the recession and the nuclear threat. I know I have a high standard of living, but I'm very aware that the 'American dream' has turned sour for millions of citizens. I can only hope that things will improve when the recession ends.

Roy Little Bull

My name is Roy Little Bull. I was born and brought up on the Hungry Horse Reservation of the Blackfeet tribe in the shadow of the Rocky Mountains in Montana, near the Canadian border. Until recently, life was very hard for me and my family. For many years I managed to scrape a living by working as a ranch hand in summer on one of the huge ranches near the Reservation. My wife made a few dollars selling leather moccasins and rubber tomahawks to the tourists from a souvenir stand beside the main highway to Browning. But winter was always hard. The heavy winter snowfalls and freezing temperatures meant there was no work anywhere. We had to live on the little we had saved from the summer and often depended on Federal Government handouts for survival.

In the last few years things have improved thanks to the head of our tribe, Chief Earl Old Person. In 1970 he went to Washington to raise money to start up a factory. The Blackfeet Indian Writing Company was launched in 1971, making cheap pencils and plastic pens. It was difficult breaking into the market at first but now we sell our products to many of America's biggest companies. Even the giant Sears department store advertises our pens in its mail order catalogues and sold over 8 million last year. One of our biggest customers is the US Army and Air Force who use our pens and pencils all over the world.

Now almost 100 of us have jobs working for the company, but many of my fellow Blackfeet are not so lucky. Unemployment is still around 50% on our reservation and is even higher on other reservations in Oregon and Idaho. But at least we have managed to restore a little of the pride of the Indian nation which has been almost totally destroyed by the white people.

Well this is life! This is prime time!
This is livin' in the USA,
Well this is life! This is prime time!
This is livin' the American way . . .

(Don McLean)

Brooke Shields   Mohammed Ali

John McEnroe   Diana Ross

'Dallas' is where the big bucks are – both in the oil fields and on the spectacularly successful TV series! Number one money-maker on the show is archvillain J.R. Ewing, played by 49-year-old Larry Hagman, who picks up an incredible $85,000 for each of 22 episodes – a total of $1870,000.

'Recently, Hagman was paid an incredible $250,000 for an afternoon's work on a whiskey ad,' said the source.

(*National Enquirer*, 23 June 81)

WOMAN JUDGE

WASHINGTON, Tuesday – The Senate Judiciary Committee, by a vote of 17–0, recommended today that Mrs Sandra Day O'Connor be confirmed as the first woman judge of the Supreme Court.

WASHINGTON, Monday. – President Reagan was shot and seriously wounded by a gunman in an assassination attempt outside a Washington hotel this afternoon.

US doctors operate on baby in womb

SAN FRANCISCO, Sunday – A University of California medical team have performed the world's first known successful surgical treatment on an unborn child, a twin now 11 weeks old and healthy, doctors reported today.

Drug abuse

Almost half the American soldiers and sailors based in Europe have taken drugs or alcohol while on duty, according to a US Congressional study.

A survey of nearly 2000 low-ranking troops found that almost 43 per cent of soldiers, and nearly 50 per cent of sailors, had taken drugs or alcohol during duty in the month before they had been interviewed.

It's enough to Make you Feel Ill

It's the kind of service you will not find on the National Health. Some United States hospitals, competing for patients, have started offering steak and champagne dinners and Mediterranean cruises to attract new 'customers'.

What's on TV?
(Daytona Beach, Florida area)

All this before breakfast!

9	Marcus Welby, MD	5:00
17	Mission: Impossible	
ESPN	WIBC Bowling	
9N	News	5:04
17	Rat Patrol	5:15
9N	Voyage to the bottom of the Sea	5:30
6	Summer semester	
17	World at Large	5:45
12	Living Words	5:50
17	World at Large	
2	Daily Devotional	5:55
9	Daily Word	
12	Jim Bakker	
2	Today in Florida	6:00
6	Black Awareness	
9	Sunrise	
17	Hollywood Report	
35	Jim Bakker	
4	Media Roundtable	6:11

9N	News	6:30
6	Exercise with Ed Allen	
4	Kutana	6:41
7 24	a.m. Weather	6:45
9	Good Morning Florida	6:55
12	Hi, neighbor	
2	Today	7:00
4 6	Morning with Charles Kuralt	
9N	Jimmy Swaggart	
7	Sesame Street (R) (CC)	
9 12	Good Morning America	
17	Funtime	
24	Villa Alegre (R)	
35	Birdman and the Galaxy Trio	
ESPN	Sports Center	

'I was ridin' on the subway in the afternoon,
I saw some kids a-beatin' out a funky tune,
The lady right in front of me was old and brown,
The kids began to push her, they knocked her down.
I tried to help her out but there was just no way,
Life ain't worth a damn on the street today,
I passed the ambulance and the camera crews,
I saw the instant replay on the evening news.
So this is life, this is prime time,
This is livin' in the USA

(Don McLean)

1. Compare the lifestyle of Lucy Andrews with that of Ernie Williams or Roy Little Bull.
2. Explain why there are such differences between their lifestyles.
3. Using the information on pages 19 to 23 write a paragraph entitled 'The American way of life'.

Race Relations

ISSUE

The 1960s were a major period of civil unrest in the USA with demonstrations and violent riots in Watts, Detroit, Newark and many other cities. President **Johnson** appointed the Kerner Commission to examine the causes of these disturbances. The Commission reported in 1968 that:

> 'Our Nation is moving towards two societies, one black, one white – separate and unequal ... White racism is essentially responsible for the explosive mixture which has been accumulating in our cities ... The events of the summer of 1967 are in large part the culmination of 300 years of racial prejudice.'

The 1970s were a much calmer period. The riots subsided and race relations seemed to fade from the major issues of domestic problems. What had changed? Had race relations improved? Had the blacks in the USA at last begun to improve their social, political and economic position and share in the 'American dream'?

THE BEGINNINGS

Although the USA is a land of immigrants, the blacks have always differed from the others in that they were 'forced immigrants', having been brought to America as slaves. As slaves they had no human rights at all and were bought and sold like cattle.

NEGROES FOR SALE – A negro woman, 24 years of age, and her two children, one eight and the other three years old. Said negroes will be sold SEPARATELY or together, as desired. The woman is a good seamstress. She will be sold low for cash or exchanged for groceries. For terms apply to Mathew Bliss & Co.

(Advertisement in a New Orleans newspaper, 1830)

Ku Klux Klansmen protesting against Cuban immigrants

After the Civil War, slavery was abolished, but life for blacks in the USA did not improve, even although they were now free people. In the south where the bulk of the black population lived, the whites kept their supremacy through violent intimidation by the Ku Klux Klan, through ingenious tests which prevented black people from using their vote and through the 'Jim Crow' laws which kept blacks and whites rigidly segregated in all aspects of life.

During the twentieth century there has been a massive movement of the black population from the south to the large cities of the north and later to the west to California. In the cities they concentrated in the poorer parts of the inner-city. Areas such as Harlem in New York and Watts in Los Angeles became black **ghettoes**, where the blacks suffered widespread poverty and discrimination.

CIVIL RIGHTS AND BLACK POWER

The late 1950s saw the beginning of a drive by black people to improve their position in American society. This was spearheaded by the **Civil Rights Movement** under the leadership

Martin Luther King

of **Martin Luther King**. They campaigned, particularly in the south, for an end to segregation, an end to the barriers which kept blacks from voting, and for equal civil rights with white people. The methods were those of non-violent protest. Boycotts of segregated transport, restaurants, etc. were organised.

'There comes a time that people get tired. We are here this evening to say to those who have mistreated us so long that we are tired – tired of being segregated and humiliated. . . . But in our protest there will be no cross burnings. No white person will be taken from his home by a hooded Negro mob and brutally murdered. . . . Our method will be that of persuasion. In spite of the mistreatment that we have confronted we must not become bitter and end up by hating our white brothers'

(*Martin Luther King, 1955*)

The Civil Rights Movement had major successes. In 1954 the Supreme Court ruled that segregated schools were unconstitutional and ordered that all schools were to be mixed. In 1964 the Civil Rights Act was passed, prohibiting racial discrimination, and in 1965 a Voting Rights Act was passed which made illegal the barriers to blacks voting.

However, despite these measures, the position of blacks in the USA did not seem to be improving. This was especially so in the ghettoes where poverty and social inequality were still the lot of black people. A new type of black protest movement was developing. This became known as 'Black Power' and became associated with such groups as the Black Panthers, the Black Muslims and such leaders as **Malcolm X**. Impatient with

Martin Luther King's non-violent methods, they rejected his vision of blacks integrating into white society. Instead they claimed that blacks would have to learn to defend themselves against white America which was basically racist and evil.

'How can I love the man who raped my mother, killed my father, enslaved my ancestors . . . and keeps me cooped up in the slums? I'd rather be tied up in a sack and tossed into the Harlem river first.'

(*Malcolm X*)

'People were just filling the streets, and they weren't singing no freedom songs. They were mad. People would try and strike up a freedom song but it wouldn't work. All of a sudden you heard this 'Black Power, Black Power'. People felt what was going on. They were tired of this whole non-violent bit. They were going to do something.'

(*Student demonstrator, 1968*)

The murder of Martin Luther King in 1968 sparked off a fresh wave of violence and it appeared that the USA was to be ripped apart by civil unrest and revolution.

BLACK POLITICS

As noted earlier, the civil unrest eventually faded away. The 1970s did see real progress on political rights. Taking advantage of the opportunities opened up by the Voting Rights Act, blacks began to register as voters and use their political power wherever they were in a majority. In 11 southern States the number of black voters doubled between 1967 and 1974. In terms of elected officials, the large gains came in State **legislatures** where blacks could use their large numbers, and in city elections where a number of large cities such as Los Angeles, Detroit and Washington were run by black mayors. At national level, in **Congress**, the number of black politicians is still small: only one black Senator and 18 members of the House of Representatives (see page 49). Blacks still hold only 1% of all elected posts in the USA although they make up 12% of the population.

A BLACK MIDDLE CLASS

In addition to progress in politics, there has been some economic progress. Of the 26 million black Americans, about one-third are now in an economic sense middle class, being white-collar workers in professional occupations. One-quarter of the black working population earns over $18 000 (1981) a year and the number employed in skilled trades has increased greatly.

THE WORSENING GHETTOES

Ghetto street scene: Harlem, New York

However, the improvements experienced by some blacks only highlight the worsening problems of the majority of blacks who remain in the ghettoes. To be black in the USA still means usually to be poor. The average income of black families in 1980 was $15 806 compared with $24 939 for whites. Unemployment is far higher for blacks than for whites and when the US economy started to face problems during the latter part of the 1970s the black community suffered the most. The proportion of black unemployed teenagers went above 30% in 1971 and has remained there ever since. Within the inner-city areas, which are becoming predominantly black as whites move out to the suburbs, crime, violence and social problems are widespread. Health and housing remain serious problems.

Forty per cent of American black families are headed by a single female parent, life expectancy for blacks is lower than for whites, crime rates are higher for blacks than for whites. A life of crime and drug-taking is common for many young black teenagers.

> 'The changes have been immense, but not enough. If you just examine the statistics – the infant mortality rate, family income, life expectancy – these figures for black people reflect that we are still at the bottom of the economic totem pole in this country.'
>
> (*Julian Bond, Senator for Georgia State*)

BUSING

Despite the desegregation of education, many black children, especially in the large city areas, still go to predominantly black schools. The reason for this is housing patterns. As white people congregate in the largely white suburbs, the inner-city areas become predominantly black areas and as a result the local schools are themselves predominantly black. This led the Government in the 1970s to introduce 'busing': an attempt to achieve racially mixed schools by taking white children by bus to black schools and vice-versa. This has aroused massive opposition from both white and black parents and has been challenged by politicians and in the courts. It now seems doubtful whether busing will ever solve the problem of integrating schools.

OTHER MINORITY GROUPS

In addition to blacks there are other minority groups who suffer from racial discrimination. The American Indians have long been the forgotten people of the USA and during the 1970s their cause was highlighted and championed by people such as the film actor Marlon Brando.

The largest group next to the blacks are the Hispanic Americans. There are believed to be some 12 million Spanish-speaking people in the USA, 3.5 million Puerto Ricans and possibly 7 million illegal immigrants, mainly from Mexico. The Hispanics suffer similar problems to the blacks, with more than one-fifth living below the poverty line, and an unemployment rate almost double that of white Americans. Since the birth rate of Hispanics is double that of whites, the problems are bound to increase.

THE 1980s?

During 1980 there were serious race riots in Miami. These pointed out the harsh fact that unemployment, poverty and racial tension still existed and that despite the gains which had been made, the USA was a long way from healing the divide between the 'two separate but unequal nations' that the Kerner Commission had warned of in 1968.

'AMERICA'S TWILIGHT WORLD'

An insight into life in the ghettoes in the 1980s can be had from these extracts from a series of articles in *The Guardian* written in August 1981.

The unemployed black young, the biggest sufferers in the present inflation-recession, probably hold the answer to what might erupt in the near future. To learn their current mood, I have talked with the families of people I have known since the early days of the civil rights movement. I have also spent much of the last three months in the ghettoes . . .

All the majority want is a sense of acceptance as themselves and not as a racial stereotype – and above all a feeling of hope that the future is going to be much better.

This feeling of hope was stimulated through the seventies by job programmes, aid in completing school and going on to university, and in the very extensive unemployment and welfare relief subsidies. Much of this is now being cut – and hope along with it.

As one young black, aged 21, told me in New York (and he spoke for a great many I talked with across the country), 'I had a night job as a security guard, but got laid off before I was eligible for unemployment. I also went back to school during the day and I graduate in March, but now there's no chance of going on to college. There are no grants or loans. I've got three daughters, aged from six to three months, but my wife can't get welfare. Where am I supposed to get the rent money?'

Unable to find another job, his only answer was to go to midtown Manhattan, where the money is, and earn a few dollars any way he could, by selling drugs or any other form of hustling he could get into. Hope was certainly fading in his case as it is with a great many others in the ghettoes. If only a comparatively few turn to violence, that can mean great trouble as the recent British riots have shown, but the big difference is that guns and other deadly weapons are ready to hand on the American scene.

(W.J. Weatherby, *The Guardian*, 24 August 1981)

Questions

1. What did the Kerner Commission claim was the main cause of the racial problem in the USA?
2. Briefly summarise the background history of blacks in the USA.
3. Describe the Civil Rights Movement: refer to leadership, aims, methods and achievements.
4. How did the 'Black Power' movement differ from the civil rights campaign?
5. Describe and account for the political progress made by black Americans since the late 1960s.
6. Describe what life is like for those who live in the ghettoes of the big cities. You should make use of the extract from *The Guardian* newspaper.
7. What is busing and how successful has it been?
8. Which other minority groups in the USA have suffered from prejudice and discrimination?
9. Study the quotations used in this section and explain what each reveals about race relations in the USA.

Wealth and Poverty

AFFLUENT AMERICA

Buying for show has always been as American as apple pie, especially in Beverly Hills where there are almost as many gold-plated Cadillacs as there are heart-shaped swimming pools.

But even in that golden ghetto there are no homes to rival ones being built along a mile of road leading from the suburb of Westwood into Beverly Hills.

In the next couple of years 21 luxury apartment buildings will have risen into the smog-filled sky to make Wiltshire Boulevard the most costly strip of residential property in the world.

The starting price for these flats is a 'bargain' £100,000 for one-bedroom – and rises to £7 million for an eight-bedroom penthouse.

For that the owner will get goldplated bathroom fittings shaped like porpoises, a 24-hour pet walking service, masseuses, and secretaries – and a 'free' Rolls-Royce with a personalised number plate.

There is no shortage of would-be buyers. They include film stars, doctors, psychiatrists and an airline owner.

(*Daily Express*, 15 August 1981)

The 17-mile drive through California's Del Monte Forest is said to be the most spectacular in America and it is world famous.

It has nothing on Scotland's Trossachs, but what puts the icing on the cake is the fact that it is a conclave of the very wealthiest in a very wealthy part of the world.

The privileges enjoyed by the residents of this privately owned stretch, who include film stars like Clint Eastwood, demonstrates the sort of amenities that you can enjoy if you have the sort of money to buy your little piece of paradise on what is probably the most expensive piece of real estate in the US.

To cater for the residents in the spectacularly palatial residences that dot the area, there are no fewer than six golf courses along the route, including the famous Pebble Beach, home of the Crosby Pro-Am tournament. The Crosby family have a home nearby.

(Edinburgh Evening News,
11 April 1981)

As the news extracts show, there are some very wealthy (affluent) people in the USA. These include managers of big business firms such as Ford Motor Company, or Exxon Oil Corporation. Also among the very wealthy are some lawyers, film stars and pop stars, and the President. President **Ronald Reagan**, for example, is a millionaire with property and investments worth about $4 million. He owns a $1 million 700-acre ranch in California. Past Presidents **Jimmy Carter**, **Gerald Ford**, **Richard Nixon**, **Lyndon Johnson** and **John F. Kennedy** were all millionaires.

The fact that some Americans are very wealthy has been a feature of American Society for a long time. In 1980, the number of millionaires grew by 10.3% to 574 342 and the wealthiest top 1% of Americans owned about 25% of the USA's privately owned wealth. This top 1%, about 2 million people, all together received more money in one year than the poorest 50 million Americans did.

'PRIVATE AFFLUENCE – PUBLIC SQUALOR'

In describing the unequal distribution of wealth in the USA, Professor John K. Galbraith, an American economist, used the phrase 'private affluence – public squalor'. By this he meant that some people have great private wealth while at the same time there is not enough money for public services such as trains, city subways, roads, medical care, housing, and schools. Many of these public services are in such poor condition that the US economy could be in difficulties in the future.

Percentage of population in different income groups

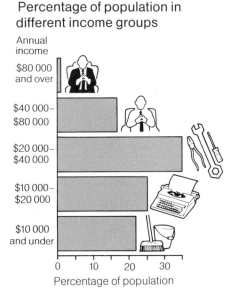

(Newsweek: Christopher Blumrich)

POOR AMERICA

The landscape looks unlived in, bare to the horizon. Trees are scarce, crooked, and parched. Civilisation is a wooden shack. A family of eight in two big rooms. Stove at one end of the shack and tin bath at the other. An old-fashioned shotgun on the wall.

The parents are in their early thirties, look 10 years older. The six children all patter round in bare feet, shoes are saved for school. No television, no radio, no newspapers. They live isolated from the 1980s except for what their teachers bring to them. Nobody knows where India is or Egypt. The three Rs are only half grasped. I mention Carter and Reagan. Never heard of them. 'Who do they play for?' asks the eldest boy with a grin. Not for them apparently.

This is rural Mississippi, the shock of whose poverty Robert Kennedy never recovered from. It hasn't changed much. The kids still don't seem to get enough to eat in areas like this; their minds, too, are still deprived. This is America's Third World at home.

(W.J. Weatherby, *The Guardian*, 9 November 1980)

The poor whites of America: Harlan County, Kentucky

In the dusty, narrow lanes of the Lower East Side ... visitors never notice the trucks stopping and starting on their routes along the bustling streets, delivering bales of cut fabric, collecting thousands of newly sewn and pressed garments. Who spares a second glance for the tired faces of immigrant workers scurrying from doorways at dusk, as much prisoners and victims of the sweatshop as their forefathers were in the 1900s?

Ten years ago, there were probably no more than 200 garment factory sweatshops left in New York City. Today there are at least 3000. In tiny spaces, always uncomfortable, often dangerous, more than 50 000 people work long hours for $15 a day that may be paid late or never be paid at all. They are immigrants, usually penniless, lonely, afraid. To whom would they complain? Those who are here legitimately can find no other jobs. Those who are here illegally fear being turned over to the authorities.

(Linda Blandford, *The Guardian*, 26 July 1981)

Who are the Poor in the USA?

The two quotations above show that some of the people in the USA are very much at the lower end of the 'ladder'. Indeed, it has been said that some of the poor are 'not even on the bottom rung'. According to US Government estimates there are about 25 million Americans (15% of the population) below the poverty line which in

Percentages of whites and blacks below the poverty line

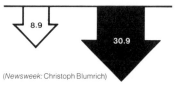

8.9

30.9

(*Newsweek*: Christoph Blumrich)

1980 was set at a level of $8380 a year for a family of four. Most of these low-income Americans receive aid from US Federal Funds. Workers earning low wages, as well as the unemployed, can usually make claims for aid and benefits from the Government, based on the poverty line. The poor in the USA come from a wide range of racial groups and age groups, and include whites, blacks, Hispanics, and Asians. Many of them are recent immigrants, legal and illegal, who are prepared to work long hours (over 60 a week in some cases) for a little as $60 a week: in the clothes industry, in agriculture, and in cafe/restaurant jobs. The effects of serious poverty can be seen in the following comment,

'Millions of black children lack self-confidence, feel discouragement, despair, numbness or rage as they try to grow up in islands of poverty, ill health, inadequate education, squalid streets, with dilapidated housing, crime, and rampant unemployment in a nation of boastful affluence'

(*Marion Edelman, President of USA Children's Fund 1981*)

Government (Federal) Aid to the Poor

A selection of population groups and industries affected by unemployment

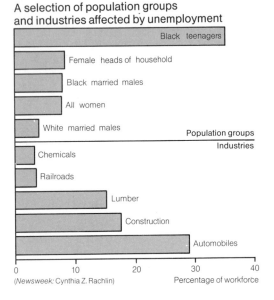

(*Newsweek*: Cynthia Z. Rachlin)   Percentage of workforce

Federal aid programmes to help the poor have been increasing in number and finance for several years, especially since President Lyndon Johnson's aim to create a 'greater society' which would give more help to the poor sectors of society. From 1970 to 1981, aid rose from $76 billion (US) to $295 billion. In 1981, however, President Reagan, with the support of Congress, announced plans to cut back national public spending by billions of dollars by 1984. These cutbacks have serious effects on the aid programmes, and on the thousands of low-income Americans who received them.

Reagan's cuts in Government spending

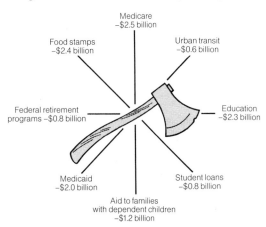

Medicare
–$2.5 billion

Food stamps
–$2.4 billion

Urban transit
–$0.6 billion

Federal retirement programs –$0.8 billion

Education
–$2.3 billion

Medicaid
–$2.0 billion

Student loans
–$0.8 billion

Aid to families with dependent children
–$1.2 billion

ISSUE

Questions

1. What is meant by 'private affluence – public squalor'?
2. Which groups of people in the USA are very poor?
3. Who are the affluent members of society in the USA?
4. What effects could President Reagan's financial cuts have on the poor?

Violent America

> ## Who shot J.R.?
> 'J.R. Ewing, of the Ewing Oil Company in Dallas, was shot last night in his office by an unknown attacker.'

This incident from the television series 'Dallas' caused great interest not only in the USA, but also in Britain and many other countries where the series was shown.

In real life, however, the shooting of one person in the city of Dallas, where in one year more people are shot than in the whole of Britain, would be unlikely to hit the headlines.

Watts: Los Angeles ghetto

So Watts has come full circle, from its post-riot hopes of 15 years ago when bureaucrats and black leaders shared a sense of urgency and purpose in a drive to create something like real social justice, to today's relapse into a gang-ridden, police-encircled ghetto-of-no-escape. Portion out the blame as you will, the lessons Watts offers are all negative, the warnings grim.

Watts, like poor black neighbourhoods elsewhere, is 'imploding', labouring to self-destruct. Its frustration, the sense of helplessness, are reflected in soaring gang-war figures. Police put the total strength of Southern California's 700 youth gangs at more than 50 000, and blame them for a third of the 2000 murders in Los Angeles county last year. Now, with their home turf so thoroughly picked over, the marauders are foraying out from the inner city to prey on the wealthy white suburbs.

(*Observer*, 19 July 1981)

Freedom... and fear

We do not cower in distant suburbs afraid to come to the city for dinner. In fact we all live in cities, and have evolved over time a certain pride in urban survival.

And yet something has changed.

Maybe it was the 13-year-old son held up on the way home from school by 17-year-old boys. Maybe it was the fourth time the car window has broken and the third time the stereo was stolen. Maybe it was the purposeful murder of John Lennon or the random murder of Dr Michael Halberstam. Or maybe there are simply too many incidents too close to home to brush off anymore.

I don't mean to suggest that we are obsessed, that we quake in fear. We don't. But our guard is up more often in more places.

On the street, we may fantasize a plan of self-defense. In the elevator, in the ladies room, in the subway, an image of danger may flit across our consciousness for just a moment.

It isn't just the criminal offensive that affects our lives, it is our own growing defensive. When we learn to turn on the alarm, put the jewelry in the refrigerator, push down the buttons in the car, think twice about walking down a street, our lives are diminished.

The man looks at the burglar alarm keys in his hand. He hates them. I tuck the chain inside my pocket-book and resent it. The woman is escorted to her room and feels smaller. All of us are somehow less free.

(© 1981, The Boston Globe Newspaper Company/reprinted with permission.)

Over a hundred years ago, President Lincoln said that 'internal violence' was the USA's biggest problem. In September 1981 President Reagan said 'Crime is an American epidemic. It takes the lives of 23 000 Americans, touches a third of American households, and it results in at least $8800 million a year in financial losses.'

CRIME STATISTICS

Violent crime

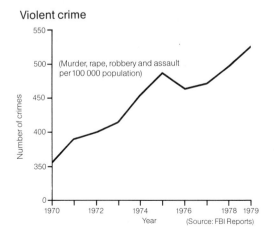

(Murder, rape, robbery and assault per 100 000 population)

Number of crimes

Year

(Source: FBI Reports)

Serious crimes are increasing in the USA, to a point where many people become involved either as victims or as criminals. It is estimated, for example, that across the whole country a house is burgled every 10 seconds, and a murder is committed every half-hour (about 400 per week). Although many of the murders and serious crimes are committed in cities, there is also concern at the spread of crime beyond urban areas. In Southern Florida, for example, Dade County, which includes the city of Miami, had a 70% increase in its murder rate from 1979 to 1980. In fact, Miami is quickly becoming the 'murder capital' of the USA.

Increases in crime in some US cities
(number per 100 000 population)

San Francisco

	Murder	Rape	Robbery
1972	11.4	71.0	642.8
1975	20.8	82.3	855.2
1980	16.6	112.6	1116.6

Los Angeles

	Murder	Rape	Robbery
1972	17.3	76.2	491.9
1975	20.3	64.8	535.0
1980	34.6	96.2	870.7

Houston

	Murder	Rape	Robbery
1972	22.5	36.9	390.8
1975	25.6	43.3	473.3
1980	41.2	68.6	717.7

Chicago

	Murder	Rape	Robbery
1972	21.3	45.9	705.9
1975	26.4	53.5	715.4
1980	29.1	42.2	550.4

Miami

	Murder	Rape	Robbery
1972	22.6	28.7	740.8
1975	26.9	48.8	728.0
1980	70.1	100.0	1995.6

(*Newsweek:* Greg Kauffman)

ASSASSINATION

When there is such a high crime rate in the USA, it is inevitable that well-known people such as politicians, film stars, and pop stars are particularly at risk. Assassinations are the worst threat. Presidents are obvious targets: past murders include those of Abraham Lincoln in 1865, William McKinley in 1901 and John F. Kennedy shot in Dallas in 1963. In 1972, President Gerald Ford had two separate attempts made on his life, both by women, and President Ronald Reagan had a narrow escape in 1981. Famous politicians such as Robert Kennedy (John Kennedy's brother) and Martin Luther King (black civil rights leader) were killed by assassins' bullets, as was pop star John Lennon. To protect themselves, many entertainers and film stars have heavily guarded homes, while some, like pop star David Bowie, are protected day and night by several armed guards.

The shooting of President Reagan: British
press headlines

WHY VIOLENCE?

John Lennon shot dead

John Lennon (40) one of the founders of the
Liverpool pop group The Beatles, was shot dead
as he was returning to his Manhattan apartment
with his wife Yoko Ono on Monday night. A
25-year-old man from Hawaii has been charged
with his murder. He had apparently had his copy
of Lennon's new record autographed earlier in
the day but accosted the singer as he got out of his
car. There was an argument and Lennon was shot
five times.

(*Guardian Weekly*, 14 December 1980)

There are many reasons why there is such a high
level of violence in some areas of the USA. It is
partly because there are slum ghetto areas where
poverty and frustration lead to violence. Another
reason is the high unemployment among certain
groups, such as blacks, whose unemployment
rate is double that of whites. Violence can also
result when there are large sudden inflows of
immigrants, such as the Cubans into Florida.
Increasingly, drugs are a cause of violence, either
directly or because of the need for money to buy
them. In 1980 12 785 cases of heroin addiction
were reported to US hospitals, and illegal drugs

are sold for a total of about $60 billion a year. The
most important reason for the high level of
violence, however, is that guns of all types are
easily available. The USA has the highest murder
by guns rate in the world, and it is estimated
there are about 55 million guns in the USA.

GUN CONTROLS/LAWS

Although some States have laws against the
illegal possession of handguns, and others have
gun ownership licensing laws, guns are easily
available from pawnshops and gunshops in most
States in the USA. The Gun Control Act of 1968,
and dozens of State and local laws, are meant to
make it difficult to obtain a gun, but there is a
large trade in illegal handguns. It is often
possible to walk into a pawnshop and buy a gun,
without too many questions being asked. Many
shops advertise openly.

Why then are the laws not stricter? Many
Americans are against gun sales but others believe they have a right to self-protection by
owning a handgun. The Second Amendment to
the US Constitution guarantees citizens 'the
right to bear arms', and that is strongly defended
by powerful groups, such as the National Rifle
Association. Even President Reagan, the victim
of a gun attack in March 1981, stated later than
he was against more controls on the ownership
of handguns. It is paradoxical that in allowing
guns as self-protection the USA has become a
more dangerous country to live in.

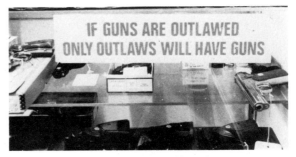

Guns on display in a New Jersey
sporting goods store

Questions

1. To what extent is crime a serious problem in
   the USA?
2. Which well-known Americans have been the
   victims of gun attacks?
3. What are the reasons for the high level of
   crime and violence in many parts of the USA?
4. Give the main points for and against stricter
   controls on gun ownership in the USA.

2. The Economy

The Wealthiest Country in the World

The USA is the wealthiest country in the world and the majority of its people enjoy a very high standard of living. This great wealth is the result of a combination of factors.

Firstly, the United States has large quantities of natural resources such as coal, oil, water, iron ore, and vast areas of fertile agricultural land. Some of these resources, particularly iron ore and oil, have been used up to such an extent during the twentieth century that reserves are now dwindling, but many of the raw materials needed by manufacturing industry are still available in large quantities. The rich grainfields of the Mid West and the abundant supplies of fresh and processed fruit and vegetable products from the Californian 'market garden' enable the USA to be virtually self-sufficient in food.

Secondly, the USA's industries have been developed during the twentieth century along the lines of mass production based on the use of a wide variety of labour-saving machines. Men like Henry Ford, founder of the giant Ford Motor Company, established this system of producing large quantities of goods faster, cheaper and more efficiently than ever before. In recent years, the application of technology to industrial production has been taken a stage further by developments in automation – based on computers and robots – which increase efficiency even further. The application of modern technology to the farming industry has enabled American farmers to become the most efficient producers in the world. Many American manufacturing companies are well-known as world leaders in their field: Boeing, Ford, IBM (Computers) and Coca Cola are just a few in an endless list of companies whose products are sold and used world-wide.

Most Americans live in comfortable houses, can afford to eat well, have luxury goods such as cars, televisions, stereos, etc, and can take a holiday in another part of the United States or abroad if they choose to do so. There are, of course, exceptions to this general pattern. The blacks in the **ghettoes**, the Hispanic immigrants recently arrived in the USA, and the unemployed of all races and colours do not have an equal share of the nation's 'cake'. Nevertheless, the American poor are less poor than those in many other countries.

US crop production 1980

		Harvested production
Maize (Corn)	(million bushels)*	6 648
Wheat	(million bushels)*	2 370
Oats	(million bushels)*	458
Barley	(million bushels)*	359
Rice	(million kg)	6 579.9
Cotton	(million bales)	11.1
Dry beans	(million kg)	1 183.9
Potatoes	(million kg)	13 653.6
Peanuts	(million kg)	1 000.6
Sugar beet	(thousand short tonnes)	23 275

*A bushel is equal to 25.4 kg for maize, 27.2 kg for wheat; 14.5 kg for oats; 21.8 kg for barley. A bale of cotton is 226.8 kg gross, 217.7 kg net.

Billboard on a California highway, about 1936

WORLD'S HIGHEST STANDARD OF LIVING

There's no way like the American Way

The American economy: 'recipe for success'

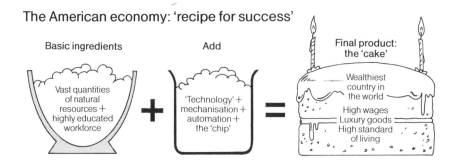

Basic ingredients: Vast quantities of natural resources + highly educated workforce

Add: 'Technology' + mechanisation + automation + the 'chip'

Final product: the 'cake' — Wealthiest country in the world. High wages. Luxury goods. High standard of living

THE CAPITALIST SYSTEM

The US economy is organised along capitalist lines. The United States is the world's leading capitalist nation and many other nations have copied the way its economy is organised.

What is **capitalism**?

In a capitalist economy all industry, business and agriculture is owned by private individuals and companies. Competition between privately owned factories, shops and farms should result in the lowest possible prices for consumers, fair wages for workers, and a reasonable amount of profit for the owner. Capitalist economies depend a great deal on freedom. The Government should not interfere in the working of the economy, but leave the running of the economy to 'market forces'.

The theory of supply and demand is the most important of these market forces. When factories produce more of a product than the public want to buy, the price of the product will have to fall in order to encourage consumers to buy more. If a product is in short supply compared with the demand by consumers, the public will pay higher prices to get it and more businesses will be encouraged to start making the product. Whatever happens, there will be a balance (or equilibrium) between supply and demand which benefits both the consumers and the producers. Sometimes the mechanism does not work quite as smoothly as this, and annual sales, loss leaders and price-cuts are used in order to achieve the balance between supply and demand.

Another important factor in the capitalist theory is the profit motive. Capitalists believe that men and women should be allowed to start up and develop their own businesses, employ other people as workers, and keep the profits for themselves. The right to make, and keep, profits is an important incentive which encourages people to start up businesses, always with an eye on efficiency to ensure profit rather than loss.

Like most theories, the theory of capitalism when applied in practice has been amended to take into account the particular circumstances in which it is applied. Total non-intervention by government, for example, is unrealistic in the modern world. Some level of government interference in the economy – through taxation, aid to struggling industries (such as the car industry), and help for the unemployed and poor – is inevitable. The smooth running of the economy also depends on the development of infrastructure: transport systems, housing, communications systems, which are also dependent on government aid. In recent years the **Federal** Government in Washington has increasingly extended its influence in the US economy although President Reagan has given notice of his intention to reduce the Federal Government's role significantly.

In spite of the steady increase in government intervention during the twentieth century, the US economy resembles very closely the

Features of capitalism

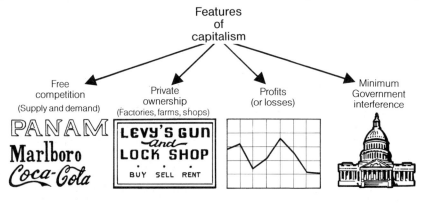

Free competition (Supply and demand) — Private ownership (Factories, farms, shops) — Profits (or losses) — Minimum Government interference

theoretical model described above. The vast majority of businesses are privately owned, employ workers, make a profit or a loss, and sell their products in competition with other businesses. There is no direct control of wages, prices and output as is found in **communist** countries. Government intervention is kept to the minimum possible. The Government's role is to oil the machinery of the economy when necessary, then reduce its activities as soon as possible after the market forces have begun to work smoothly again.

However, the economies of all the major industrial nations are closely linked through international trade and commerce and are therefore affected by world-wide events. In view of this it seems likely that the Federal Government will play an important part in the US economy in the future.

Questions

1. Why is the USA such a wealthy country?
2. How do the majority of American people benefit from their country's wealth?
3. Describe the main features of a capitalist economy.
4. How closely does the US economy resemble the model of a capitalist economy?
5. What is the role of the Federal Government in the US economy?

The Economy in Action

MULTINATIONAL INDUSTRIES

The *Wall Street Journal*, an American financial newspaper, told the following story:

A businessman checks out of his room at the Sheraton Hotel, gets into a car hired from Avis Rent-a-Car, drives to his stockbroker's to discuss his shares in Hamilton Mutual Fund, then goes to his office where he posts a cheque to pay his quarterly premium for his American Mutual Life Assurance policy, sends a telegram to Britain and then checks on financing some equipment through the Kellog Corporation. A routine morning's work, dealing with a variety of matters. But in fact all these different dealings have been with one company: the International Telephone and Telegraph Corporation (ITT).

This story highlights the nature of much of American business and industry. Its key feature is 'bigness'. These huge enterprises are known as corporations, conglomerates or **multinationals**. At the beginning of the twentieth century there were some two thousand large corporations who owned the bulk of the manufacturing industries of the USA; by the middle of the century there were about one thousand large corporations; by the 1970s only two hundred corporations owned two-thirds of the manufacturing assets of the USA. Many of these private corporations have larger assets and more resources than some independent countries. These huge companies do not just confine their activities to the USA but are world-wide concerns.

By the end of the 1970s the biggest companies in the USA were as given in the following table.

Company	1978 Sales ($ million)	Main industries	Employees
General Motors	63 221	cars, lorries	839 000
Exxon	60 334	oils, chemicals	130 000
Ford Motor	42 784	cars, lorries	506 531
Mobil	34 736	oil	407 700
Texaco	28 607	oil	67 841
Standard Oil	23 232	oil, chemicals	37 575
IBM	21 076	computers	325 517
General Electric	19 653	electrical goods	401 000
Gulf Oil	18 069	oil	58 300
Chrysler	16 340	cars, lorries	157 958
ITT	15 261	telecommunications	379 000
Standard Oil (Indiana)	14 961	oil	47 011
Atlantic Richfield	12 298	oil	50 716
Shell Oil (Houston)	11 062	oil	34 974
US Steel	11 049	iron and steel	166 848
El du Pont	10 584	chemicals	132 140
Western Electric	9 525	electrical	161 000

The large multinationals dominate in the car industry, the oil industry, chemicals, computers and electronics, and steel. The car industry is dominated by three companies: General Motors, Ford and Chrysler. The steel industry is dominated by about six companies and the aerospace industry by three main companies.

In addition to dominating the industry with which they are associated many of these huge companies – as in the example of ITT – have branched into other concerns. General Motors produce washing machines and televisions as well as cars. Gulf and Western Industries began by manufacturing car bumpers and branched out by buying Paramount Pictures Corporation, several huge farms and companies which made such different products as fertilisers, zinc, electric organs and cigars.

The large multinationals have grown by producing more and more products, but they have also grown by swallowing up or merging with rival companies. General Motors grew by taking over many smaller car producers such as Buick, Pontiac, Oldsmobile and Cadillac. Similar takeovers happen when the multinationals have branched out into other unrelated industries.

Takeovers and mergers ($2 billion and more), announced in 1981

		Value (billions)
Du Pont	Conoco	$7.3
Elf Aquitaine	Texasgulf	$4.3
Fluor Corporation	St Joe Minerals	$2.7
Kraft	Dart Industries	$2.4
Freeport Minerals	Mc MoRan Oil and Gas	$2.3
Nabisco	Standard Brands	$2.0
Standard Oil (Ohio)	Kennecott	$2.0

Many business people see this increase in the size of companies as inevitable and worthwhile. The bigger the company the more efficient and profitable it can be. Others have expressed concern about this concentration of power into the hands of fewer and fewer companies. It is argued that this eliminates competition and prevents smaller companies from developing, and the US Government has passed several Acts such as the Sherman Act and the Clayton Act to control the growth of these monopolies.

Questions

1. Explain the point of the story told by the *Wall Street Journal*.
2. Write a definition of a 'multinational industry'.
3. Draw a bar graph showing the main US multinational companies; grade them according to sales, and colour code them according to product.
4. Find out if Britain has any multinational companies, who they are and what they produce.
5. What are the advantages and dangers of the trend towards multinational companies?

AGRICULTURE OR AGRIBUSINESS
The Changing Pattern of Farming in the USA

'Old Macdonald had a farm
Ee i ee i o!
and on that farm he had some cattle
Ee i ee i o!'

The farmer Macdonald in the old folk song may have had cattle grazing on his farm but his farming methods would be very different from the modern high-technology business methods used by some present-day American farmers such as Pat Benedict in Minnesota.

For tall, burly Pat Benedict, 44, the day begins early. . . . By 6 a.m. he is breakfasting with some neighbors at the Double D Diner. For an hour or so, he trades community gossip, argues about politics and drops casual remarks about crops and prices designed to feel out what his fellow farmers are doing. . . . Then off to the fields – and into the computer age.

Benedict makes a quick trip by pick-up truck around his 3500 acres of wheat and sugar beets. . . . By 8 a.m. he is heading home to start the most important part of his day: several hours spent at a roll-top desk in his small study. There Benedict goes over computer print-outs analyzing his plantings acre by acre: inputs of seed, fertilizer, irrigation water, machine time; output in bushels and dollars. He draws up precise operating schedules for his half-million dollars' worth of machinery; after all, every gallon of fuel saved adds a few more cents to profit. His print-outs also help him ponder marketing strategy (when should he time the sale of his crops to get the best price?) and financial problems (how can he distribute the stock in his family corporation so that his wife and seven children pay the lowest estate taxes?).

Although all farmers in the USA are not as 'industrialised' as Pat Benedict, nevertheless one of the main reasons why American farming produces so much is that mechanisation and technology are widely used. The USA's agricultural production is significantly higher than any other country in the world.

HOW THEY GROW

Number of people fed per farmer

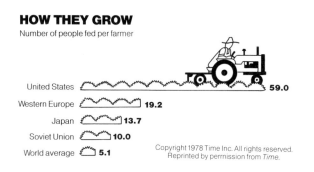

United States	59.0
Western Europe	19.2
Japan	13.7
Soviet Union	10.0
World average	5.1

Main farming areas

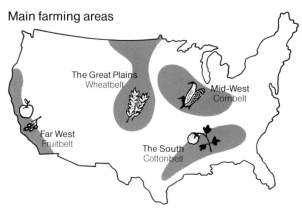

The Great Plains
Wheatbelt

Mid-West
Cornbelt

Far West
Fruitbelt

The South
Cottonbelt

Some Modern Farming Methods

Many cattle are now fattened in 'feedlots' where machines bring food and water to the cattle who stay in pens. This feeding system is called zero-grazing. Also, many calves, chickens and pigs are reared in sheds which have automatic controls for food supply, lighting and temperature. In crop growing there are seed-planting machines fitted with sensors to measure the exact amount of seed, fertiliser and pesticide going into the soil. Over a quarter of grain crops in the USA are produced with the aid of pipeline irrigation. In the cotton plantations, machines are now used to pick the cotton crop, while even some fruit crops are gathered by a machine which 'shakes' the tree and collects the falling fruit. Many tractors on farms are fitted not only with anti-roll cabs and power steering but also with stereophonic radios and air-conditioning.

Problems for Modern Agriculture

Increasing mechanisation has led to a decline in the number of people working on farms in the USA (down from 30.5 million in 1940 to about 10 million in 1980). Not only does the use of machinery cause farm workers to be made unemployed but also many smaller-farm owners are forced out of business because of the high cost of energy and machines. Mexican American farm workers in California have struggled amid increasing change on the fruit farms.

Despite mechanisation, the weather can still cause problems and, as recently as 1980, a serious drought destroyed crops and thousands of cattle in the States of Texas, Kansas, and North Dakota.

There is also increasing concern by environmentalists over the vast quantities of chemical sprays and pesticides used in American farming. In 1973 tens of thousands of cattle in the State of Michigan were poisoned by contaminated food and had to be destroyed.

The Importance of Agriculture in the USA

Farming in the USA is one of the most important and successful industries, for the following main reasons.

1. *Food supply*. Farming provides a wide variety of foods which more than meets the demands of the American home market.

2. *Trade* (**balance of payments**). Exports of agricultural products are double the agricultural imports, which leaves more money available to buy foreign goods such as oil. (In 1978–9 the USA's net surplus in agricultural products was $15.8 billion.)

3. *Trade* (other countries). Agricultural exports from the USA form an important trade link with countries such as Japan, Netherlands, West Germany, Canada, and the USSR.

4. *Employment*. Although the number of people employed in farming is declining, agriculture is still a major source of employment with more workers than either the steel industry or car industry.

5. *Politics*. American farmers form a powerful political 'lobby' and no politician can entirely ignore their demands. For example, the halting of grain sales to the USSR in 1980 led to protests by farmers, and in 1981 sales were resumed against the wishes of some of the President's Government officials.

Questions

1. Give some examples of 'high-technology' farming methods in the USA.
2. What problems have been caused by the rapid changes in farming methods?
3. How important are agricultural products in terms of the USA's trade with other countries?
4. In what ways are the political views of American farmers important?

Industrial Relations

ORGANISATION

The USA has about 20 million workers who are members of trade unions. Some 13 million of these workers are in unions which belong to the major labour organisation in the USA: the AFL–CIO (American Federation of Labour and the Congress of Industrial Organisation). The AFL–CIO merger took place in 1955 and, under the presidency of George Meaney, the AFL–CIO dominated American trade unions during the 1960s and 1970s.

The 6 million union members who are outside the AFL–CIO include members of the largest and most important individual unions:

(a) the International Brotherhood of Teamsters with a membership of over 2 million;

(b) the United Mineworkers with a membership of some 160 000.

CHARACTERISTICS

To a large extent the trade union movement in the USA, as with unions elsewhere, is concerned with improving wages, hours and working conditions through collective bargaining with employers. But an outstanding feature of trade unionism in the USA, which distinguishes it from trade unionism in Europe, is its commitment to the capitalist system. Unlike trade unions in the United Kingdom, American trade unions do not put forward any firm political ideology to change the economic system or to help bring about socialism. There has been no real attempt by major American trade unions to build the equivalent of the British Labour Party. This feature of American trade unionism was summed up by George Meaney, President of the AFL–CIO when he said that, 'I believe in the capitalist system just as much as anyone. This economy we have in this country is a capitalist economy and the trade union movement is part of this economy.' This does not mean that trade unions have no political power or that they are uninvolved in political activity. They are very active at city, State and national levels where they help to organise campaigns to promote the election of a President and legislators who will be sympathetic to trade unions. In addition to this the unions have always acted as very powerful pressure groups on **Congress** and State **legislatures** (see pages 49 and 59).

In most cases the trade unions support the Democratic Party but not to the same extent as trade unions in Britain support the Labour Party. Support for Presidential candidates varies and in 1972 President Nixon, the **Republican** candidate, received more support from trade union members than did the Democratic candidate. Again George Meaney summed up this more neutral, opportunistic stance when he said that 'the Republican Party stinks and the Democratic Party is almost as bad.'

CORRUPTION

Another feature which has periodically marked trade unionism in the USA has been accusations and charges of political corruption and criminal activities.

The Teamsters were expelled from the AFL–CIO in 1957 after a Senate committee had revealed a huge network of corruption. In 1964, Jimmy Hoffa, leader of the Teamsters, was sentenced to eight years in jail for bribing jury members and to a further five years for using union funds for his personal gain. Hoffa remained president of the union even while he was in jail and in fact had a salary increase. After being released from jail, Hoffa disappeared under circumstances which gave rise to speculation about gangland murder.

Another example of union corruption and violence occurred in the United Mineworkers when Tony Boyle, president of the union, was convicted of the murder of Joseph Yablonski, the man who had challenged him in 1972 for leadership of the union. Yablonski had accused Boyle of corruption in running the union and had tried to gain the leadership in order to bring about reform. After an election campaign which was marked by corruption and violence, a gang had broken into Yablonski's home and shot Yablonski, his wife and daughter.

STRIKES

The amount of strike activity varies in the USA from year to year and from industry to industry. Recent years have seen a rise in militancy among white-collar public service workers such as teachers, fire fighters, nurses, air traffic controllers and even the police. Extreme militancy is hindered, however, by the fact that, in certain ways, American unions operate under difficult circumstances. The Taft-Hartley Act (passed in 1947) outlaws the closed shop, secondary picketing and allows the President to

Picketing during the Air Traffic Controllers' strike, 1981

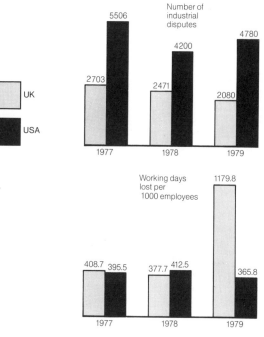

(Source: *Department of Employment Gazette and ILO*)

Questions

1. Describe the organisation of trade unions in the USA.
2. Explain the main points of similarity and difference between trade unions in the USA and in Europe.
3. Study the graphs above and explain what they show about industrial relations in the USA and UK.
4. Outline the difficulties facing trade unions in the USA: refer to legislation, employer resistance and declining membership.

intervene in disputes which threaten to 'imperil the national health or safety'. President Carter used this Act to intervene in a long and bitter coal strike by ordering the miners to go back to work for a 'cooling-off' period while negotiations continued.

Employers in the USA are more prepared to take action against unions; some parts of the southern States of America are anti-union and workers have great difficulty in establishing unions in workplaces. President Reagan showed another aspect of this tough action when in 1981 he took financial and legal action against the air traffic controllers and dismissed those who went on strike.

A further problem for US trade unions has been a relative decline in union membership. Of more than 100 million Americans in the workforce, less than 25 million are union members. In general it is the better-off workers who are union members; black unskilled workers and migrant agricultural workers, for example, are not usually union members.

Energy Crisis

ENERGY UNLIMITED

The USA has a great many oilfields which for a long time provided a cheap and plentiful supply of oil. This led Americans to be exceptionally wasteful in their use of energy and oil products. Electricity from oil-fired power stations was widely used in factories and for lighting. Oil-fired air conditioning, cooling, and heating systems were used in shops, offices, and homes. Oil-based synthetic goods such as cloth, plastic goods, and wrappers became popular. Even

New York at night

more popular were the very large American cars whose engines used a lot of petrol ('gasoline').

In the 1970s, however, so much oil was being used that the USA, although a huge producer of oil, had to import up to 25% of its oil to meet demand.

CRISIS!

The US energy crisis arose in the 1970s because of increasing dependence on imported oil. Two events elsewhere in the world led to steep rises in the price of oil. Firstly, oil prices were dramatically increased in 1973–4 by the governments of several members of **OPEC** (Organisation of Petroleum Exporting Countries), some of whom had nationalised their own oil. In a three-month period, prices rose four times, and they continued to rise (less steeply) throughout the 1970s.

The second event which caused oil prices to rise was the Iranian Revolution in 1979. The Shah of Iran was overthrown and that ended the USA's links with Iran. Iranian oil supplies to the USA were cut off and the USA was then dependent on other oil producers, who raised their prices considerably.

During the 1970s the USA was unable to switch quickly to other energy sources. As a result, its total bill for imported oil rose dramatically during this time from $5 billion in 1972 to about $80 billion in 1980, and $100 billion in 1981.

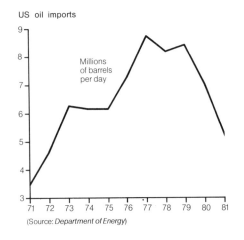

US oil imports

Millions of barrels per day

(Source: *Department of Energy*)

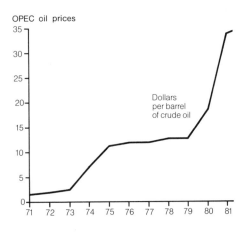

OPEC oil prices

Dollars per barrel of crude oil

REACTIONS AND EFFECTS IN THE USA

At first many Americans were unwilling to believe how serious the effects of the increased oil prices would be. In 1977, President Carter's plan, to save fuel by putting a tax on imported oil and on 'gas-guzzling' vehicles, was defeated in Congress after protests by truck drivers and car drivers.

Gradually, however, as prices continued to rise, the USA was directly affected. Fuel costs for average Americans affected family budgets significantly. Sales of big cars slumped and unemployment increased, especially in the car-producing areas (see Problems of the Auto Industry). The Government encouraged people to 'conserve' energy, and as a result the level of oil imports fell slightly. There was an increased interest in foreign policy affairs to protect US oil import routes and supplies from the Middle East. A $20 billion project to build an 8000-kilometre oil and gas pipeline from Alaska to the USA was encouraged, while there was renewed oil exploration at greater depths within the USA itself. Government permission was also granted to 'open up environmental areas' to firms prospecting for coal and oil. Some major oil firms, such as Exxon, began to develop oil products from coal while others began to 'mass produce' solar cells for electricity. Indeed, oil companies now have control of 80% of the US solar energy programme.

OTHER SOURCES OF ENERGY

Coal
Coal supplies about 20% of US energy needs at present, and it is estimated that the USA has enough coal reserves to last for the next 250 years! Both President Ford and President Carter encouraged the increased use of coal. Already there have been experiments with powdered coal and coal fuels.

Problems
Coalmining could become more expensive because the remaining coal seams are deeper or more broken. Coal is difficult to transport and dirty to use. Environmental control laws on coal mining are firmer than before.

Nuclear Power
Nuclear power supplies about 10% of US electricity needs from about 60 nuclear power stations. It has the potential to increase considerably, since uranium supplies are available in the USA. This would provide a relatively cheap source of power.

Problems
Public protest about leaks at a nuclear power station in Pennsylvania in 1979 caused a major slow-down in nuclear energy production. Only seven nuclear power stations have been built since then because of new safety laws and public protests. A further problem is what to do with the radioactive nuclear waste. Several States are trying to have a complete ban on nuclear power.

Alternative ('Renewable') Energy

Solar Power

Although early experiments in solar power were not always successful, many big oil companies are now investing in methods of turning the sun's rays into usable energy by means of silicone 'wafers', especially in sunbelt States. Energy, in future, could be beamed back to earth from orbiting space stations.

Problems

The technology is not yet suitable for large-scale production of energy, though by the year 2000 solar energy could be a large industry. The cost of experiments is high: for example $20 million to collect solar energy stored for ponds of salt water in California.

Wind Power

New lightweight windmills have been developed which use wind as a readily available source of power. In a few States, such as New Mexico and Massachussets some homes are supplied by electricity generated from windmills.

Problems

As with solar energy, the technology is still not fully developed and there are problems over the numbers of windmills which would be required at present to produce electricity on a large scale.

Questions

1. In what ways have Americans used oil lavishly?
2. Which two events led to steep increases in the price of oil in the USA in the 1970s?
3. How did these increases affect the USA?
4. State the arguments for and against increasing nuclear power capacity in the USA.

ISSUE The Economy: Problems and Solutions

The wealthiest country in the world is in trouble. Since the late 1970s and early 1980s the United States has been faced with a number of major economic problems which are likely to continue to pose difficulties for some time to come.

President Reagan has stated that, together with improvements in the USA's military strength, he regards the tackling of these economic problems as a major priority. His proposed solution is a two-pronged attack:

The President's main priority is to slow down inflation and end the stagnation which has been crippling the US economy. His programme was set out in a 281-page volume called *American's New Beginning – A Programme for Economic Recovery*. The main proposals included reductions in Federal spending of $467 billion and tax savings for individuals and businesses of $709 billion between 1981 and 1986. Over-all, the aim of the Reagan administration is to reduce the involvement (or interference) of the Federal Government in people's lives by reducing taxes, spending less, reducing social welfare and education programmes and shifting more responsibility on to the States and cities.

As a result of these plans, fewer people will qualify for welfare benefits, social security, unemployment compensation, subsidised school meals and other social services. The Federal departments of Education and Energy have been scrapped. President Reagan hopes that the tax cuts will lead to more savings, investment and the incentive to work harder, all of these leading to more healthy economic growth.

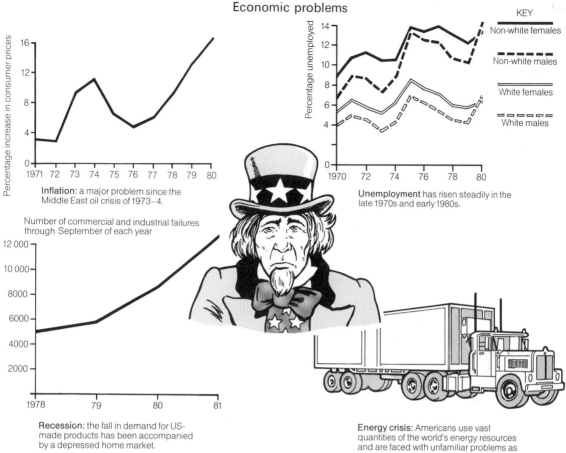

Economic problems

Inflation: a major problem since the Middle East oil crisis of 1973–4.

(Chart: Percentage increase in consumer prices, 1971–80)

Unemployment has risen steadily in the late 1970s and early 1980s.

(Chart: Percentage unemployed, 1970–80)

KEY
— Non-white females
- - - Non-white males
═══ White females
- - - White males

Number of commercial and industrial failures through September of each year

(Chart: 1978–81)

Recession: the fall in demand for US-made products has been accompanied by a depressed home market.

Energy crisis: Americans use vast quantities of the world's energy resources and are faced with unfamiliar problems as these resources run out.

Unfortunately, they might also lead to increased Government debts or lead to a consumer spending spree, both of which might result in higher inflation. The President is, however, hoping for a psychological change in the outlook of the American people which would convince them that they must support him in his attack on these problems.

The results will not be achieved immediately.

The problems may, in time, be reduced. It is unlikely they will be solved.

Questions

1. Describe the four main economic problems facing the USA in the 1980s.
2. What policies has President Reagan introduced to tackle these problems?

Economic solutions

Cuts in public expenditure (to ensure a balanced budget)

and

Tax cuts (to put more money in people's pockets, encouraging them to save and invest)

US CITIES AND THEIR PROBLEMS

The USA contains many large cities. According to the latest census, three in every four Americans live in city areas. No two cities are the same: there are great contrasts between the older northern cities such as New York, Philadelphia and Chicago and the spreading modern cities of the south such as Atlanta and Dallas.

The Major US Cities (Metropolitan Areas)

	Number of people
New York	9 175 777
Los Angeles	7 208 583
Chicago	7 021 758
Philadelphia	5 597 632
Detroit	4 395 229
San Francisco/Oakland	3 241 210
Washington D.C.	3 011 183
Dallas/Forth Worth	2 794 342
Houston	2 669 447

Many of the older urban areas of the USA today suffer from serious economic and social problems. Obsolete industries, disintegrating schools, derelict housing, streets without lights or police patrols, and the flight of population are some of the major difficulties. The financial problems are largely the result of the dwindling populations. Many people have left the decaying inner-city areas to move to the more pleasant suburbs.

Because of the system of local taxation in the USA, people who move to the suburbs do not pay the city taxes which are needed to pay for all the services provided by the city council: schools, police, public transport, for example. Many of the suburban dwellers continue to work and shop in the cities and therefore use these services. The result is that the city councils have to try to keep their services running efficiently, but have less money coming in to pay for them.

The financial problems of the cities are made worse because the people who remain in the inner-city areas are, to a large extent, poor, unemployed or old, and therefore contribute little in the way of taxes. In St Louis, for example, more than 16% of the people are on welfare (the equivalent of social security), the unemployment rate is over 8% (46% of the people are black) and old people over the age of 65 account for 18% of the population. This is a great drain on the city's resources.

The most visible result of these financial problems is that the services provided in many of the cities have deteriorated considerably. Housing is a major problem in many cities. Areas of Harlem, the Bronx and Brooklyn in New York have become very run down: decay and derelict slums are everywhere. In St Louis, one of the worst areas, 25% of the city's houses have been abandoned as uninhabitable since 1950 and it is said that some areas of the city resemble a ghost town. Perhaps the most notorious example of urban decay is the Pruitt-Igoe public housing

Demolition of the Pruitt-Igoe public housing blocks in St Louis·

project. This huge high-rise complex, built in St Louis by the Federal Government in the mid 1950s at a cost of $21.5 million, rapidly fell into decay and became a high-crime area, with the result that the buildings were dynamited in the early 1970s after a life span of less than 20 years. The 55-acre site is now covered in grass, and St Louis still has a major housing shortage.

There are also problems with public transport in many American cities. It is estimated that nearly 30 million people travel by bus, subway or commuter train every day of the week in the USA. Subways and mass-transit railways are especially vital to the economic and business life of the cities. In New York (5 million transit system users each day) and Chicago (1 million travellers) the overburdened systems are suffering from lack of investment, leading to old rolling stock, breakdowns, higher fares and increasing frustration among delayed passengers. New York's subway (run by the Metropolitan Transportation Authority: MTA) is dirty and graffiti-covered, the trains run late, and the whole system is notorious for crime (18 murders, 12 000 muggings and other crimes in 1980). The MTA is deeply in debt, running at a loss and falling into decay, yet it is vital to the city: during a 10-day strike of the MTA in 1980 New York businesses estimated they lost $100 million in sales each day.

Curtis 'The Rock' Sliwa (seated) founder of the Guardian Angels, with some of his 'Angels' aboard a New York subway car

'These major economic problems are accompanied by similarly difficult social problems. Cities which contain large numbers of people who depend on welfare handouts for their existence, and live in overcrowded slum conditions, are natural breeding grounds for all kinds of crime (see Violent America).

During the last few years there have been some signs of improvement in several cities, including New York. Mayor Ed Koch, who has been mayor of New York since 1978, has managed to balance the city's budget for the first time in many years, and the prospect of the city going bankrupt is much less likely now than it was in the 1970s. But even he has not solved some of the major problems. Financial success has been achieved mainly by cutting services such as welfare and education which have deteriorated as a result. Crime has become worse, and the problems of the MTA are no nearer solution. The likelihood of them being solved is even more remote in view of President Reagan's determination to reduce the amount of money to the cities by the Federal Government.

Questions

1. Describe the main social and economic problems of American cities today.
2. In what way have attempts to solve New York's difficulties created both benefits and problems for its citizens?
3. Why is it unlikely that the major problems of US cities will be solved in the foreseeable future?

Problems of the Auto Industry

ISSUE

For several decades, the large 'gas-guzzling' automobile has been one of the most visible signs of the prosperity of the USA and the high living standards of its people. Detroit was established as the car-making capital of the world, and one in every five Americans owed their living directly or indirectly to the automobile industry. Most American families owned at least one automobile, and two-car or three-car families were a common feature of US society. The 'big three' motor manufacturing companies – General Motors, Ford, and Chrysler – with their high US sales and their overseas markets controlled through subsidiaries brought a great deal of prosperity to the USA.

The US car industry in the 1980s

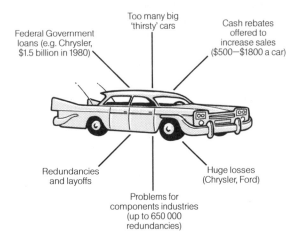

Federal Government loans (e.g. Chrysler, $1.5 billion in 1980)

Too many big 'thirsty' cars

Cash rebates offered to increase sales ($500—$1800 a car)

Redundancies and layoffs

Huge losses (Chrysler, Ford)

Problems for components industries (up to 650 000 redundancies)

By the start of the 1980s, however, huge problems were overtaking these companies. They found themselves increasingly challenged in their own markets by foreign, mainly Japanese, competitors and pushed out of many of their overseas markets by Japanese and European manufacturers.

Most of these problems were the result of the failure of the US car manufacturers to foresee the swing away from the big expensive 'gas-guzzlers' to smaller fuel-efficient cars when the price of petrol rose steeply in 1979 as world oil prices increased. The public, fearing the possibility of fuel shortages, suddenly stopped buying big cars, and the economic recession reduced sales even further. Unfortunately the US car manufacturers were caught unawares with no popular small cars in production.

Part of the explanation for this lies in the fact that in 1973, when OPEC greatly increased oil prices (see Energy Crisis), American motorists were protected from the worst effects of the increases by Congress which held down the retail price of petrol to consumers. The car manufacturers, who had tried to introduce smaller models at that time, found that the big cars remained popular and believed that this would always be so.

When in 1979 fuel prices began to rise rapidly, there was a sudden move by US consumers to buy smaller cars. The Japanese, who already manufactured a wide range of such cars, stepped in to fill the gap left by the US manufacturers. By the end of 1980, Hondas, Toyotas, Mazdas and Datsuns were being imported into the USA at a rate of 6000 a day and Japanese cars took 23% of the US market in 1980.

The American car makers have responded to this Japanese 'invasion' by developing and producing their own economy cars. Chrysler's 'K-car', General Motors' 'J-car' and Ford's new 'world car', the Ford Escort, appeared in 1981 in an attempt to win back customers. These new cars are much smaller than the gas-guzzlers, have much more efficient styling designed to cut down wind resistance and save fuel, and have a lot of space inside. In some, micro-computers are used to ensure engine efficiency.

Besides producing new models, design and manufacturing methods have been modernised. Computers have been widely used to help produce more efficient and economic designs. Robots have taken over many jobs previously done by people, and are cheaper, faster and more accurate. Improved industrial relations have been a spin-off benefit as workers, unions and management have realised the need to cooperate to rescue the industry from its problems. Some manufacturers have appealed to the US Government to introduce protection by increasing taxes on foreign cars entering the USA, but so far the Government has resisted this move.

Japanese car sales in the USA

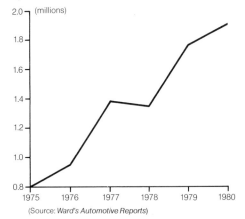

(Source: *Ward's Automotive Reports*)

What is happening of course is the rapid deterioration of a major American industry. Detroit's auto-makers last year lost more than $4 billion, and during the past three years, US annual auto production has slumped by 30% to 6 million vehicles. Today, almost 200 000 American auto-workers are unemployed, and many of them have little hope of ever returning to work in their industry. To them and to most US auto executives, the problem is Japanese imports.

(*Time*, 30 March 1981)

Ford introduces for 1962
two distinguished new series:
Galaxie & Galaxie/500

Enduring elegance...
with the power to please

Only car with 5-billion-mile proof
it's beautifully built to be more service-free!

With Thunderbird styling...
Thunderbird power...
and quality craftsmanship that
sets a new industry standard...
the 1962 Ford Galaxies give
you every essential feature
of far costlier luxury cars

Galaxie by Ford

The Best Selling Car In The World.

The Ford Escort.
Sales estimates based on 1981
calendar year worldwide production figures
establish that Ford Escort is
the best selling car in the world.

There's A Ford In America's Future.

Seat belts save lives: buckle up.

Questions

1. Explain why the US automobile industry is facing major problems in the 1980s.
2. Why do many American drivers prefer foreign cars to those made in the USA?
3. How has the contraction of the US car industry affected autoworkers in cities such as Detroit?
4. Describe how American manufacturers have responded to the 'invasion' of their market by foreign cars.
5. What has the Federal Government done to aid the US car industry?

3. The Political System

Democracy in the USA

THE CONSTITUTION

The political system of the United States is based upon a document written in 1787 called the **Constitution**. The men who drew up the Constitution have become known as the 'Founding Fathers' of the USA. This short document, which consists of seven sections called Articles, lays down the framework of the American system of government. When the Constitution was first drafted the USA was a rural country of 13 States which lay largely on the Atlantic coast. Today the USA is a major world industrial power of 50 States which stretch from the Atlantic in the east to the Pacific in the west. And yet the same Constitution which was drafted in 1787 still applies for the government of the USA today. There have of course been changes and additions to the original document. These are known as Amendments but there have only been 26 of them and of those 26 the first 10 – known as 'The Bill of Rights' – were accepted by 1791.

The Constitution is based upon three important principles:

1. *Federalism.* In 1787 there were only 13 States, and in agreeing to form the United States they agreed to give up some of their independence to create a national government with power over them. The system which was set up is known as a **Federal** form of government in that there are different layers of government: a national layer with responsibility for national affairs and a layer of State governments with responsibility for State and local affairs.

2. *Separation of powers.* The 13 States had in 1776 broken away from the British Empire in what was to become known as the American War of Independence. To the 'Founding Fathers' this marked an opportunity not only to become independent but to draw up a revolutionary form of government which would be the very opposite of the tyranny which existed in most of Europe where monarchs had absolute power. The new system of government would be democratic in that power would come from the people who would elect their rulers. But in addition to this there would be safeguards to prevent the concentration of power in the hands of one person or group of people.

The Constitution, therefore, split government into three parts:

(*a*) those who make the laws: the Legislature,
(*b*) those who enforce the laws: the Executive,
(*c*) those who interpret the laws: the Judiciary.

Each of these three branches of government were to be kept separate.

The Federal Government of the USA

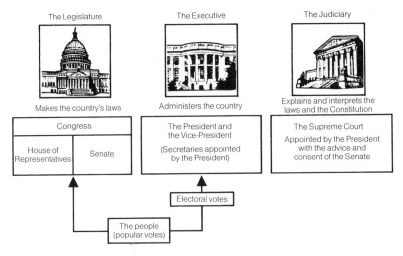

The Legislature
Makes the country's laws

Congress	
House of Representatives	Senate

The Executive
Administers the country

The President and the Vice-President
(Secretaries appointed by the President)

The Judiciary
Explains and interprets the laws and the Constitution

The Supreme Court
Appointed by the President with the advice and consent of the Senate

Electoral votes

The people (popular votes)

3. _Checks and balances._ Finally, to ensure that no branch of government became too powerful, an elaborate system of checks and balances was built into the Constitution so that each branch of government depended on the actions of the other two and in no important area could any one branch act independently.

Questions

1. Briefly explain what the US Constitution is and why it is so important to American politics.
2. Write a short note explaining these features of the Constitution:
   (_a_) Federalism,
   (_b_) separation of powers,
   (_c_) checks and balances.

THE NATIONAL GOVERNMENT

The Legislature

'All legislative powers . . . shall be vested in a Congress of the United States, which shall consist of a Senate and a House of Representatives.'

(_Article 1, Section 1, the Constitution_)

The body which at national level is responsible for passing all the laws affecting the United States is known as **Congress** and is split into two Chambers.

1. The _House of Representatives_ is composed of 435 representatives who are elected from the various States in proportion to their population. A heavily populated State such as California has 43 representatives and a lightly populated State such as neighbouring Nevada is guaranteed at least one representative. Members of the House must be at least 25 years old and have been American citizens for seven years. They must live in the State which they represent and they are elected for a two-year term.

2. The _Senate_ is composed of 100 members who are elected on the formula of two Senators per State, irrespective of size of State. Senators are at least 30 years old and must have been US citizens for nine years. They must also live in the State they represent. Each Senator is elected for six years but these terms of office are staggered

so that one-third of the Senate is re-elected every two years.

The major job of Congress is to pass or reject new legislation. Both Chambers are involved in law making and, in order to become law, a proposal must be passed by both Chambers. Because of the 'separation of powers' principle the Congress has maintained a great deal of power and is regarded as one of the most powerful legislatures in the world. Congress is also very busy but although many proposals are put to Congress only a very few become law. For example in the 92nd Congress (1971–2) over 25 000 legislative proposals were introduced but only 607 (approximately 3%) became law.

In addition to these shared powers over legislation, each of the two Chambers has its own responsibilities over certain other areas:

(_a_) The House of Representatives has the sole power to introduce into Congress legislation dealing with money.
(_b_) The Senate has the sole power to approve of appointments made by the President, for example, ambassadors, and the Senate must approve foreign policy treaties made by the President.

The Senate tends to be the more important of the two Chambers, and Senators are very influential politicians in the USA.

Members of Congress

The average age of members of Congress is about 50, with Senators tending to be older than members of the House. In terms of occupation more than half of the membership of Congress have a legal background, with business executives next. The number of black politicians in Congress is still small: in 1981 only 17 members of the House and none at all in the Senate. There are also very few women. A major contrast with the UK Parliament are the vastly superior facilities which are offered to members of Congress.

As well as a salary of $57 500 (1981 figures), each member of Congress enjoys generous funds to maintain a personal staff who can deal with correspondence, telephone calls, press statements and do research work on matters arising in Congress. Many members of Congress produce their own newsletters informing constituents of what their representative is doing in Washington. In addition to this the Library of Congress provides expert research assistance to allow members to do their work as efficiently as possible.

Questions

1. Briefly describe the composition, membership and main function of the US Congress. You should make sure you distinguish between the House of Representatives and the Senate.
2. Compare the life and work of a US member of Congress with that of a British MP.
3. What special functions does the Senate perform?

The Executive

'The executive power shall be vested in a President of the United States of America ... together with the Vice-President.'

(*Article 11, Section 1,*
the Constitution)

The person entrusted by the Constitution with the responsibility of carrying out the laws which govern the USA is the President. According to the Constitution the President must be at least 35 years old, must have been born in the USA and must have been a resident within the USA for 14 years.

The President and Vice-President are elected for a term of four years and as a result of an Amendment to the Constitution, no person may stand for election as President more than twice. (See later section on 'Elections in the USA' for full details of the election of the President.)

Beyond these Constitutional requirements there are a number of other factors which have influenced what kind of person has generally become President.

(*a*) Presidents have always been white and male.
(*b*) Presidents are usually middle-aged.
(*c*) Until the election of **John Kennedy** in 1960, Presidents were always Protestant.
(*d*) Presidents are usually married with a family.
(*e*) Presidents are usually well-known public figures either in the field of politics as Senators or State Governors or in the military field as famous Generals.

Gerald R. Ford   Richard M. Nixon

Jimmy Carter   Ronald W. Reagan

Powers of the President

Presidential roles

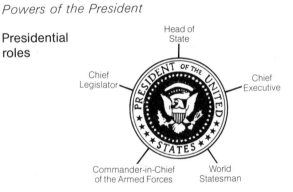

It is said that the US President is one of the most powerful people in the world. Certainly the power enjoyed by Presidents today would have surprised and shocked the 'Founding Fathers', for the Constitution has surprisingly little to say about Presidential powers, and the role of the modern President has to a large extent developed because of the people who have held the post. The powers of the President stem from a number of jobs that the President fulfills.

1. *Head of State.* The President fills the same position in the USA as is carried out by the British monarch. This involves welcoming foreign dignatories, representing the State abroad and attending ceremonial functions.

2. *Chief Executive.* The Constitution lays down that the President 'shall take care the laws be faithfully executed'. The President is therefore responsible for carrying out the laws passed by Congress. Help in carrying out this responsibility is provided by a vast network of civil servants, headed by the President and organised through 12 State departments and many Federal agencies and commissions. The President of course appoints, subject to Senate approval, the members of the Cabinet who form the Government.

3. *Chief Legislator.* Although not part of Congress, the President plays a large role in its legislative programme. The President is expected to have a programme of legislative measures to put before Congress. As well as this role in initiating legislation, the President is also involved at the final stage of passing a bill in that the President must sign all legislation before it becomes law. Unlike the British monarch whose role in signing legislation is a ceremonial one, the President can stop legislation from being passed by refusing to sign it. This is known as the power of veto. Congress can only overcome this veto if they can then find a two-thirds majority for the legislation in both Chambers.

4. *World Statesman.* The President is largely responsible for foreign policy, although Congress is also involved in that Congress declares war and the Senate has to approve foreign treaties. This latter power of the Senate is very important and on occasion the Senate has used this power to major effect. For example, the Senate refused to approve the Treaty of Versailles which ended World War 1, and as a result the USA did not take part in the League of Nations, which later became the United Nations. Despite this, the day-to-day handling of foreign relations is left to the President.

5. *Commander-in-Chief of the Armed Forces.* The President is Commander-in-Chief of all the armed forces and these 'war powers' give the President great power. This is of course especially true in a nuclear age when this gives the President full control over the USA's vast range of nuclear weapons. Some Presidents have used their control of the armed forces to carry out foreign policy without consulting Congress; for example, much of the handling of the Vietnam War was conducted by various Presidents in this way.

The power of the President is therefore very great but there are of course limitations to this power: the approval of Congress is needed for the President's legislative programme; the Senate's approval of Presidential appointments and foreign treaties is required, and the maximum term of office is two four-year periods.

Questions

1. Outline the characteristics of a typical American President.
2. Make use of the main Presidential roles to show why the President is often described as 'one of the most powerful people in the world'.
3. What limitations are there on the President's power?

The Judiciary

'The judicial power of the United States shall be vested in one Supreme Court.'

(Article 111, Section 1, the Constitution)

President Reagan addressing the US Congress

The Constitution set up a **Supreme Court** of nine judges. These judges are appointed by the President with the approval of the Senate. They are appointed for life or until they retire and therefore not every President has the opportunity to influence the composition of the Court.

The Court is independent of Congress and the President, and has the important responsibility of determining whether the actions of Federal and State governments and the legislation passed by these bodies are within the limits of the Constitution. The Court therefore acts as an important check on Federal and State governments, and on occasions has played a very important role in American political history: for example, in 1954 the Court decided that it was unconstitutional for there to be separate schools for white and black children. This decision was to have an important effect on race relations in the USA. The Court also played a major role in the Watergate affair (see page 57) when it ordered President Nixon to release tapes he had made of conversations in the White House.

Questions

1. Briefly explain the composition and role of the US Supreme Court.
2. Illustrate the Court's political importance by reference to its role in race relations and in the Watergate affair.

The Political System in Action

THE POLITICAL PARTIES

Republicans   Democrats

The USA has two major political parties: the **Democrats** and the **Republicans**. Virtually all successful candidates for political office belong to one or other of these two political parties and,

although independent and minor-party candidates do stand in elections, they rarely make a major impact. However, unlike the UK, political parties are not organised on a national basis but on a State or local basis. In fact it is said that national parties only exist every four years at Presidential election time.

A second major difference between political parties in the USA and in the UK is that policy matters play a much less important part in the USA. During elections the political parties make very vague statements of policy, in an attempt to appeal to as wide a section of the voting public as possible. They try to avoid saying anything which is liable to lose voting support. Similarly the parties themselves are wide coalitions containing people of greatly differing political viewpoints.

And yet, although party statements are vague and although the parties contain all shades of opinion, it is possible to distinguish between the two parties. This can be seen most clearly in the categories of voters who support the parties:

The Democrats tend to be supported by the poor, the unemployed, the recent immigrants, the blacks, the inhabitants of big cities, trade unionists, the liberal intellectuals; and, until the 1960s, the south voted solidly for the Democratic Party.

The Republicans tend to be supported by a less widespread group of voters: the skilled workers, the middle classes, the business community, wealthy farmers, rural USA and the WASPs (White Anglo-Saxon Protestants) rather than other racial groups.

The Democrats are identified with 'the ordinary people' and the Republicans with 'the rich and business world'. As a result it is also possible to identify certain policy differences between the parties, which result from these sources of voting support. The Democrats are seen as the party of reform who favour the growth in the power of the Federal Government to help the poor and the ethnic minorities. The Republicans are seen as favouring less Federal Government involvement and are less prepared to use the power of the Government to help the disadvantaged. It would be wrong, however, to think of the Democrats as the American Labour Party and the Republicans as the American Conservative Party, because the parties in the USA are much more coalitions than in the UK. The success of the political parties in the USA can be seen in the following table detailing election results for President and Congress in Presidential election years since 1960.

Year	President	Congress			
		The House		The Senate	
		Democratic	Republican	Democratic	Republican
1960	John F Kennedy (Dem.)	263	174	64	36
1964	Lyndon B Johnson (Dem.)	295	140	67	33
1968	Richard Nixon (Rep.)	243	192	58	42
1972	Richard Nixon (Rep.) (Gerald Ford (Rep.) from 1974)	243	191	57	43
1976	Jimmy Carter (Dem.)	292	143	62	38
1980	Ronald Reagan (Rep.)	244	191	47	53

Although the Democrats and Republicans have alternated for President, the Democrats, with the exception of the Senate in 1980, have controlled Congress.

Questions

1. What are the main differences between political parties in the USA and in the UK?
2. Draw up a table comparing the Democrats and Republicans with regard to support, policies and recent Presidents.

ELECTIONS IN THE USA

Every four years the people of the USA vote for their President, and newspapers and television cameras throughout the world focus on this event. But to the American voter the election of the President is only one election among many, for no country in the world has as many elections as the United States. Every two years (in mid-term Presidential session and in a Presidential election year) voters elect their members of the House of Representatives, a third of the Senate, their State Governors, members of their State

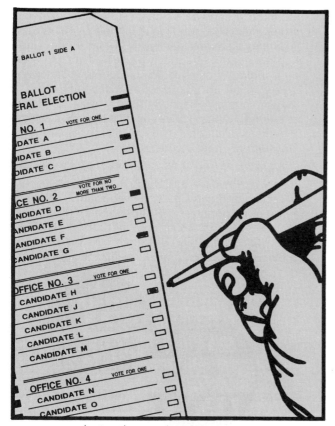

Instructions to American voters

TO VOTE YOUR OFFICIAL BALLOT

Persons voting in the November 1980 General Election in Orange County will each receive two ballot cards identified as Card 1 and Card 2. Card 1 will always have candidates printed on both sides, identified as Side A and Side B. Be sure and vote both sides of Card 1.

Card 2 - Side A will contain all state measures. In some areas Card 2 - Side B will contain local measures or local candidates. In other areas Card 2 - Side B will be blank. If there are local measures or candidates on your ballot Card 2 - Side B, be sure to vote both sides.

To vote your ballot cards, use the special marking pen furnished at the polling place. Make a mark to fill in the red voting box in any office or measure where you wish to vote. On this sample ballot, the voting boxes are printed in black, but on your official ballot the voting boxes will all be printed in red. It is not necessary to fill in the red voting box completely, but make a black mark with the marking pen to fill in most of the voting box. Do not use a ball point pen or any other marking pen except the one furnished at the polling place.

For persons voting in the polling place, do not fold the ballot cards before or after you vote. Leave them flat, place them in the security folder, and return them to the precinct officer at the polling place.

You may use the marking pen to write in the name of any qualified write-in candidate, but you must also mark the voting box following any name written in.

legislatures plus a large number of local officials ranging from city mayors to members of school boards. Altogether there are over a million elected positions in the USA and, in addition to electing politicians, voters in many States are asked to vote on issues which can be inserted on to ballot papers as referenda and propositions. In California's 1974 elections, for example, the voters of Ventura County could elect 35 candidates for office as well as decide on 18 issues.

Since there are so many elective offices, voting can be a complicated affair. First of all a person has to be registered in order to vote. As a result of the 26th Amendment to the Constitution which was approved in 1971 all citizens over the age of 18 are allowed to vote. In many areas, because of the size and complexity of the ballot paper, voting is done by machine. This makes vote-counting accurate and speedy. In some ballots voters have to vote by candidate and in others it is possible to vote by party, where by marking the 'party ticket' it is possible to vote Democrat or Republican (voting for all the candidates of that party). In some States such as California, voters receive 'sample ballot papers' to familiarise themselves with the candidates, procedures and issues. Because of the size of the USA there are different time zones across the country, and the polling booths in New York may be closing just as the booths are opening in California. Since experts can now make fairly accurate computer forecasts from early election returns it is possible for voters to know the probable result of a Presidential election before their polling booths have closed.

Partly because of the number and complexity of elections in the USA, voter turnout is far lower than in many European countries. In the 1976 Presidential election there was a 54.3% turnout and this dropped to 52.0% in 1980. In mid-term elections to vote for Congress, the turnout averages about 35%.

Electing the President

In Presidential election years, in the month of November, the American people vote for their President. But the process of becoming President begins long before November. There are four stages in the campaign for the White House and in order to survive this race a candidate must have great stamina, some luck and probably a lot of money.

Stage 1. This takes place before the election year and may even start a full two years before the election. At this point candidates who are considering running for President sound out opinion, prepare their organisations and begin to plan their campaigns.

Stage 2. This takes place from January to June of election year. It is when the two main parties begin to choose their Presidential candidate from the various politicians who have declared their interest. This is done by each party selecting delegates (representatives) to attend the national conventions at which the candidates are chosen. In many States these delegates are chosen by holding **primary elections** where registered party members can elect delegates who support the Presidential candidate of their choice. A candidate's chances can be boosted or destroyed by a good result in their favour in these primary elections. 'Everyone likes a winner' and a 'bandwagon' effect can be achieved from a run of primary successes. In 1976 Jimmy Carter was very much an unknown outsider until a run of good primary election results brought him to national notice. Those States which do not have primary elections choose delegates under a system of State conventions.

Stage 3. By the time of the party national conventions in July/August it is usually clear which candidates have proved themselves to be the most popular. In 1980 Ronald Reagan had clearly been the most popular of the Republican candidates and was chosen by the delegates for the Republican Convention as their candidate.

Questions

1. Explain why the USA is often called 'the most election-conscious nation in the world'.
2. Make out a table listing the years from 1980 to 1986 and beside each year note which Federal elections, if any, have taken or will be taking place.
3. Describe what voting is like in the USA; you should refer to voting age, the ballot papers and turnout.

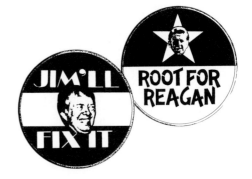

A US political convention

The Democratic Convention was a closer contest and Senator Edward Kennedy ran President Carter a close race for the Democratic nomination. As well as choosing the Presidential candidates the conventions also choose the Vice-Presidential candidates. These two candidates make up what is known as the 'party ticket'. George Bush was chosen in 1980 as the Republican Vice-Presidential candidate and Walter Mondale was chosen by the Democrats. The national conventions are noisy colourful 'jamboree' occasions but beneath the carnival atmosphere a very serious process is taking place.

Stage 4. From August to November the candidates campaign against each other in a long, tiring and expensive campaign. Television plays a very important part in the election and to a large extent the candidates are 'sold' on television, in the same way as advertisers sell soap powder or soft drinks. However, beyond these 'packaged images' voters can occasionally be shown the candidates' views on important issues, and a televised debate between Carter and Reagan had a certain effect on the voting public.

Stage 5. In November the voters of the USA finally vote for their choice for President. But this is not a direct election because in reality the voters are represented by delegates who vote for President in a special **Electoral College** (which never actually meets as a group). Each State is allocated a number of delegates – known as *electoral votes* — · in proportion to their representation in Congress: for example, Alaska has 3 electoral votes while California has 45. Electoral votes are won on a 'winner takes all' system in that the Presidential candidate who in November wins the majority of *popular votes* (votes by the people) in a State is given all the electoral votes of that State. It is therefore important to win the heavily populated States such as New York and California. The candidate who wins the majority of electoral votes (rather than the majority of popular votes) becomes President. It is possible therefore for a candidate to win a majority of popular votes across the whole country but lose the election because he has narrowly lost in the large States. In 1976 Carter beat Ford by 56 electoral votes (297 to 241) but there were less than 2 million popular votes between them. If a mere 9245 voters in Ohio (25 electoral votes) and Hawaii (4 electoral votes) had changed their vote Ford would have won the election, with a total of 270 electoral votes to Carter's 268.

REAGAN

for President

Elections for Congress are separate from the Presidential election and occasionally the President may be of one party while the Congress may be controlled by the other party.

The election of 1980 produced the following results:

President

| Candidates | Party | Popular votes | | Electoral votes |
		Millions	Percentage	
Reagan	Republican	43.07	51	489 (45 States)
Carter	Democratic	34.74	41	49 (6 States)
Anderson	Independent	5.56	7	

Congress

Party	Senate	House of Representatives
Republicans	53	191
Democrats	47	244

Questions

1. Explain the importance of the following in electing the President: primary elections; national conventions; television.
2. Explain fully how the actual election of the President is decided: you will need to explain the role of the Electoral College and you should make use of the 1980 election results as an illustration.
3. Study the following (1968) election result:

   Nixon (Republican): 37 770 237 votes (43.4%); 302 electoral votes
   Humphrey (Democrat): 37 270 533 votes (42.7%); 191 electoral votes
   Wallace (Independent): 9 906 141 votes (13.6%); 45 electoral votes

   The House: 243 Democrats;
                192 Republicans
   The Senate: 58 Democrats;
                 42 Republicans

   Who won the 1968 Presidential election and by how many votes?
   What problem would this President face with his legislative programme and how might he hope to improve this position in 1970?

The Electoral Vote 1980

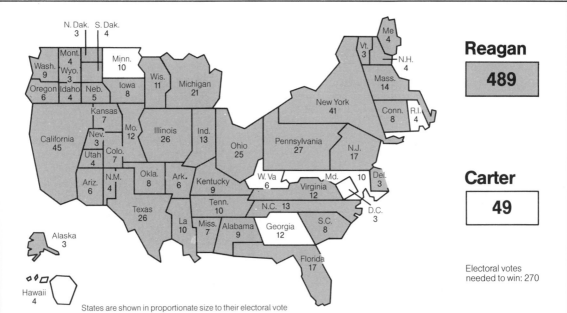

Reagan 489

Carter 49

Electoral votes needed to win: 270

States are shown in proportionate size to their electoral vote

Presidential Power

A major feature of American politics in the period since World War 2 has been the growth in the power of the Presidency. This came about not through any change in the Constitution, but through the actions of various Presidents who made use of their position to build up a vast amount of power. As the USA assumed the role of world Superpower, so the American public expected their Presidents to provide strong and effective leadership both at home and abroad. As the Presidents began to dominate political life, the other organs of government, especially Congress, began to play a secondary role.

There are a number of reasons for this growth in Presidential power. The growth in the amount of Federal Government involvement in the economy and in social problems forced the President to play a larger role. The President's responsibility for foreign policy allowed him to play an ever-increasing role, especially as the USA had become one of the world's two Superpowers. The President's role as Commander-in-Chief of the Armed Forces allowed the President to increase his power in the wars in Korea and then in Vietnam. In neither of these major wars was Congress directly involved, for since there were no official declarations of war the President could commit large number of troops to back up his foreign policy as a result of his control over the armed forces. The President's ultimate control over the decision to launch a nuclear attack has also given him great power. Finally, the press and television have focused on the President as the leader of the USA and have helped to build up his authority.

This growth in Presidential power led to the coining of the term 'the imperial Presidency' to describe the modern President. The imperial Presidency was at its height in the 1960s and early 1970s during the Presidencies of John F. Kennedy, Lyndon Johnson and Richard Nixon and reached its climax just before 1972 when the Watergate scandal brought an end to this growth in Presidential power.

WATERGATE

In 1972 Richard Nixon won a second term of office in a 'landslide' election in which he won every State except Massachusetts and the District of Columbia. Nixon seemed at the height of his power. Yet on 9 August 1974, Nixon

'I cannot tell a lie – I didn't do it!'

became the first US President to resign, and the events which led to his resignation were to cast a great shadow over the prestige of the Presidential office.

The events of the Watergate affair are confused and complicated. These are the major steps in the scandal which led to Nixon's resignation.

Step 1. On 17 June 1972 seven men were caught in the offices of the Democratic Party in Washington, in a building known as the Watergate. They were caught with 'bugging' devices and other spying equipment, and were arrested to await trial.

Because of very busy timetables the court hearings were put back for many months, until after the election.

Step 2. When the case was eventually heard, evidence emerged that showed that the burglars were employed by the Committee to Re-elect the President (commonly known as CREEP).

On 2 March 1973 Nixon announced at a Press conference: 'No one on the White House staff last July and August was involved or had knowledge of the Watergate matter.'

Step 3. The search for the truth was subsequently pursued from three different quarters. Firstly two reporters from the *Washington Post* began to conduct a long enquiry. These two reporters, called Woodward and Bernstein, were later to tell of their investigations in a book called *All the President's Men* which was eventually to be made into a film. Secondly Congress set up a committee of investigation and finally the judiciary set up a

Grand Jury to investigate further charges arising from the Watergate trial.

Nixon continued to deny any White House involvement. In April 1973 he declared: 'There can be no whitewash at the White House.' The various investigations, however, began to reveal a number of disturbing features. The Watergate burglary was only one of a large number of 'dirty tricks' which had been used to disrupt and disorganise the Democratic election campaign. Secondly there had been a plan to cover up the Watergate burglary to hide the involvement of the White House staff.

Step 4. Despite Nixon's denial of White House involvement, subsequent months were to see a string of resignations in connection with Watergate and other scandals. In April 1973 Haldeman and Ehrlichman, Nixon's closest advisers, resigned and in October the Nixon Administration was further rocked when Vice-President Spiro Agnew was forced to resign because of income tax evasion.

Step 5. During the course of the Senate Committee hearings, one of Nixon's aides let it be known that Nixon had tape-recorded all the conversations which took place in the President's Oval Office in the White House. These tapes would prove whether the President had known of the cover-up but Nixon refused to hand over the tapes. The issue went to the Supreme Court who ruled that Nixon must hand them over. The tapes revealed to the American public that Nixon had lied and had tried to deceive the people.

Step 6. The House of Representatives began to prepare charges of impeachment against Nixon and when it became apparent that these would be carried and that the Senate would put the President on trial, Nixon decided to resign. He was succeeded by his new Vice-President Gerald Ford who became the first non-elected President. Ford granted Nixon a full pardon and although this raised a storm of protest, it did help to bury the Watergate affair.

THE PRESIDENCY AFTER WATERGATE

However, the scandal showed the American public the dangers of allowing the President too much power. In particular Congress began to re-assert its authority over the President and the period of the 'imperial Presidency' was over. The Presidencies of the next two office-holders, Ford and Carter, were to show the difficulties which could face Presidents in carrying out strong and effective leadership. An example of this can be seen from the problems which faced Carter in trying to solve the USA's energy problems.

CARTER AND THE ENERGY QUESTION

The energy question was one that President Carter made a major theme in the early period of his Presidency (see Energy Crisis). Carter planned to conserve energy resources within the USA and to cut back on the amount of oil which the USA imported. A large part of Carter's programme was acceptable to Congress, but Carter's proposals on the price of oil and natural gas proved more controversial. Carter proposed to increase petrol prices to the level of world prices by means of taxation. He also planned to discourage large 'gas-guzzling' cars by imposing a sales tax on them.

These aspects of Carter's energy plan met considerable opposition in Congress, especially in the Senate. Despite making this the major element in his domestic programme, Carter finally managed to steer only a compromise package through Congress.

This whole issue underlined the changed Presidential–Congressional relations which had grown out of the Vietnam and Watergate issues. Ex-President Ford wrote in November 1980 that:

'Some people used to complain about what they called an "imperial Presidency", but now the pendulum has swung too far in the opposite direction. We have not an imperial Presidency but an imperilled Presidency. Under today's rules . . . the Presidency does not operate effectively.'

Not everyone would agree with this view, and most Americans still look to their President to provide strong leadership. However, there has certainly been in recent years a restoring of the balance between President and Congress which the Constitution intended.

Questions

1. Explain why the President has become such an important and powerful figure: you should refer to his control of the economy; foreign policy; the war in Vietnam; nuclear weapons and the role of the media.
2. What effect did the growth of Presidential power have on Congress and the doctrine of 'checks and balances'.

3. Explain the term 'imperial Presidency' and to whom it was applied.
4. Briefly describe the main events in the Watergate affair and explain its importance with regard to the idea of the 'imperial Presidency'.
5. What does the cartoon on page 57 suggest about Nixon's guilt?
6. Describe the problems faced by President Carter over his energy programme. How was this connected to the reaction to Watergate?
7. Find out how the present President is managing with his Congress.

Federalism: The State Governments

The USA is a Federal nation and it is important to be aware of the political institutions of the 50 States which make up the Union and of the division of responsibilities between the central Federal Government and the various 50 State governments.

Each State has its own constitution and form of government. In every case the form of government adopted by the States is identical to the Federal one, with a separation of powers and a system of checks and balances:

At the executive level each State has an elected Governor.

At the legislative level each State has an elected Legislature, which in 49 out of the 50 States is composed of two Chambers.

At the judicial level each State has a Judiciary.

Despite these similarities it would be wrong to think of the States as being carbon copies of each other. In size, population, history, climate and economy the States vary enormously. The smallest State is Rhode Island, with 2715 km², the largest is Alaska with 1 466 492 km². California has a population of about 20 million whereas Alaska has just over 300 000. Some States such as California have an income far greater than many independent nations throughout the world. This background knowledge is important in realising the importance of State government in the USA.

Unlike the UK where local authorities have no power to make new legislation, the States in the USA have legislative power over those areas which the Constitution has reserved for them. The division of responsibility between the Federal and State Governments can be seen in the following chart.

Of course problems do emerge from this system. It can lead to confusion to have different laws in different States. People can get married at an earlier age, and can get divorced, in some

Diagram showing the division of responsibility between Federal and State Governments

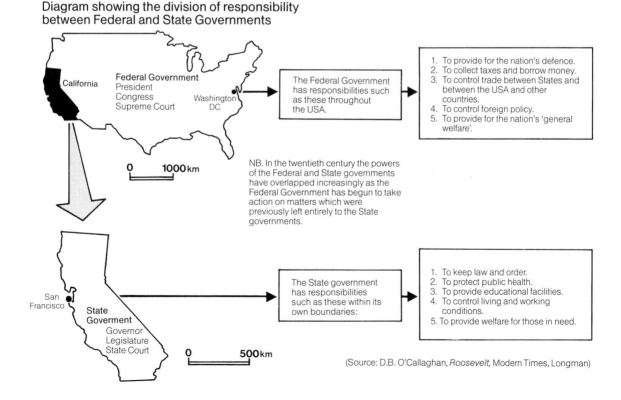

California — Federal Government: President, Congress, Supreme Court — Washington DC

0 1000 km

The Federal Government has responsibilities such as these throughout the USA.

1. To provide for the nation's defence.
2. To collect taxes and borrow money.
3. To control trade between States and between the USA and other countries.
4. To control foreign policy.
5. To provide for the nation's 'general welfare'.

NB. In the twentieth century the powers of the Federal and State governments have overlapped increasingly as the Federal Government has begun to take action on matters which were previously left entirely to the State governments.

San Francisco — State Government: Governor, Legislature, State Court

0 500 km

The State government has responsibilities such as these within its own boundaries:

1. To keep law and order.
2. To protect public health.
3. To provide educational facilities.
4. To control living and working conditions.
5. To provide welfare for those in need.

(Source: D.B. O'Callaghan, *Roosevelt*, Modern Times, Longman)

States but not in others. They can legally drink alcohol at age 18 in some States but not until 21 in others. A more serious aspect of this problem concerns law enforcement. State police operate only within the boundaries of their own States and it is common in American films to see gangsters escaping from police by crossing the State boundary. The FBI (Federal Bureau of Investigation) was set up in 1908 to deal with Federal crimes and to help coordinate the national fight against crime.

Another problem of Federalism stems from disputes over whether issues should be dealt with by the State or the Federal Government. A major feature of American politics in the twentieth century has been the growth of the Federal Government, often at the expense of the State governments. This has been resisted in some areas by those who argue in favour of 'States' rights'. The right to determine education is a State's responsibility but in 1954 the Federal Government intervened in this when it enforced a ruling that all schools should be integrated for both black and white schoolchildren. This was bitterly resisted in many southern States which had separate schools for black and white children. Despite this it would seem inevitable that in a complicated modern industrialised society like the USA, the Federal Government must play a leading part in influencing the national economy and in dealing with major social problems which are to be found in the large American cities.

Questions

1. Describe the form of local government in the States in the USA.
2. Which areas of public life are dealt with by the States?
3. How does the Federal system cause problems for law enforcement in the USA?
4. What is meant by 'States' rights' and how does the example of integrated schools illustrate the difficulties caused by this?

A Day in the Life of the President

'The toughest job in the world.'

'The loneliest job in the world.'

These two statements are frequently used to sum

President Reagan at work in the Oval office

up the job of the President of the USA. They highlight the difficulties and the pressures of the office. Ex-President Gerald Ford has written of the demands of being President: 'It's a hard job being President – but despite all the talk about the heavy burdens, the job is not too big for any one man .... It's job that takes about 12 to 14 hours a day .... Anybody who walks in there thinking he can punch a time clock at 9 in the morning and leave at 5 has got another thought coming.' An insight into these pressures and demands can be gained by looking at a typical day in the life of the President. The following describes a day in President Reagan's period of office, shortly after he had become President.

7.30: Reagan wakens. This is relatively late compared with previous Presidents. Carter, for example, was a 6 a.m. riser.

8.45: After breakfast, Reagan is in the Oval Office for his first business meeting of the day. Along with his personal secretary and chief aides he discusses the coming day's business.

9.15: Reagan meets with Vice-President George Bush and the National Security Adviser to be briefed on foreign policy developments.

9.35: A meeting with Press Secretary and with his adviser responsible for dealing with Congress.

10.07: Reagan chairs a meeting in the Cabinet Room to discuss the various cuts in the Federal Budget which are being planned. A press meeting follows this and then Reagan visits the Lincoln Memorial to lay a wreath and make a short speech to commemorate the anniversary of Lincoln's birth.

13.00: Lunch in the White House 2nd floor dining room. Representatives of various Hispanic organisations have been invited to lunch.

14.15: Back at his desk in the Oval Office, Reagan is making phone calls and signing papers.
During this Reagan meets the Italian Foreign Minister who has been having talks with Secretary of State, Alexander Haig. People from the Press and television are allowed in to photograph the meeting.

16.30: Reagan meets another top aide to discuss new appointments.

17.00: Reagan meets with his personal secretary and chief aides for his 'daily wind-up session'.

19.00: The President and First Lady have dinner at the Vice-President's residence.

21.30: Back to the White House, either to deal with more business or to relax.

Compared with his predecessors, Reagan's pace is more leisurely. This is in keeping with his style and the fact that he is over 70 years of age. But his daily routine is still very demanding, involving many meetings – both business and ceremonial – and many decisions. There is very little time for personal family life and equally little time to stand aside from the daily pressures and reflect on what he is doing. This pattern becomes, of course, even more hectic during a period of crisis.

Questions

1. In what way is the President's job the 'toughest' and 'loneliest' in the world?

4. International Involvement

Strategic Interests

AIMS OF THE USA'S FOREIGN POLICY

'I know of no leader of the Soviet Union since the Revolution who did not pursue the goal of world revolution.'

(*President Reagan, February 1981*)

'International terrorism, trained and equipped by the Soviet Union, will take the place of human rights in our concern because it is the ultimate abuse of human rights.'

(*The USA's Secretary of State, Alexander Haig, February 1981*)

The main aim of the USA's foreign policy since the end of World War 2 has been to try to contain the spread of **communism** in many parts of the world. This confrontation with the USSR reached several crisis points during the 'Cold War' period of the 1950s and again, in the 1980s, USA–USSR relations moved towards serious confrontation, especially over military and defence affairs.

USA: Foreign policy aims

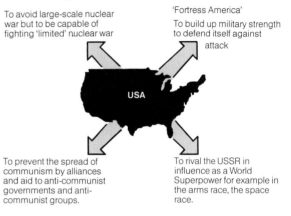

To avoid large-scale nuclear war but to be capable of fighting 'limited' nuclear war

'Fortress America'
To build up military strength to defend itself against attack

To prevent the spread of communism by alliances and aid to anti-communist governments and anti-communist groups.

To rival the USSR in influence as a World Superpower for example in the arms race, the space race.

BACKGROUND

The map below shows the USA's involvement in many different parts of the world in the 1980s. However, it was not always so involved.

The USA's areas of interest in the world.

Between World War 1 and World War 2 the US Government made it clear that they did not wish to be involved in European politics or wars. This period of isolation, when the USA avoided being involved in European affairs, lasted from about 1920 up to World War 2. The Americans did give aid to Britain and the Allies, but it was not until the sudden attack by the Japanese on American ships at Pearl Harbour in 1941 that American troops became involved in World War 2.

This attack persuaded the Government of the USA that it could not avoid being involved in world affairs so it altered its policy to one of *intervention*, which it has followed since then. This policy of intervention became evident after the end of World War 2 when the USA was heavily involved in the peace discussions. The USA disagreed strongly with the USSR over what should happen in Europe after the War, and when a communist government took over in China the USA's foreign policy became one of positive opposition to communism. In the years that followed, the USA intervened in foreign affairs in an effort to stop the spread of communism.

1948–9   *The Berlin Blockade.* US aircraft flew supplies to West Berlin after road and rail links with West Germany had been blocked by Soviet and East German troops.

1950–3   *The Korean War.* US military forces, along with United Nation's forces, fought to prevent South Korea being taken over by communist North Korea and communist China.

1962   *The Cuban Crisis.* US ships prevented Soviet supply ships from reaching Cuba when it was discovered that the USSR had placed nuclear missiles there which threatened the USA.

1965–75   *The Vietnam War.* US military forces became involved in Vietnam helping the South Vietnamese Government to fight against an internal communist rebellion and communist North Vietnam.

In continuing its policy of intervention in world affairs, the USA formed a number of alliances with other countries (see page 67), and also gave military aid to anti-communist governments throughout the world.

PROBLEMS IN RECENT TIMES

The difficulties of trying to prevent the spread of communism, and of trying to extend its own influence to many areas of the world, has caused problems for the USA.

1. *Tension with the USSR.* After several years of **detente** (peaceful co-existence) between the two major Superpowers, the USA adopted a more aggressive approach towards the USSR, following the Soviet occupation of Afghanistan in 1979, by refusing to accept the SALT 2 agreement and by building up the number of nuclear weapons such as **neutron bombs** and **Cruise missiles** that it had.

2. *Costs.* The huge financial cost of military aid and defence weapons, which in the early 1980s was about $200 billion a year, puts a strain on the US economy, which means cuts in money supplied for housing, welfare and schools in the USA.

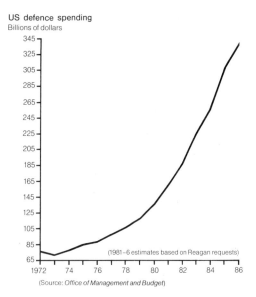

US defence spending
Billions of dollars

(1981–6 estimates based on Reagan requests)

(Source: *Office of Management and Budget*)

3. *Alliances.* The USA complains that some European countries in the **NATO** alliance are not paying enough of the costs of NATO.

4. *Fear of sudden attack.* The fear of a sudden attack on the USA, which might destroy its retaliation missiles, has led to the consideration of huge costly defence systems such as the **M-X missile**, requested by President Reagan in 1982.

5. *Support for anti-communists.* The anti-communist policy has often led the USA to support right-wing military governments such as that of Iran, and therefore indirectly to support

the continuing poverty and lack of human rights which prevail under some of these governments.

6. *'Backyard volcano'*. Increasing unrest in many of the poverty-stricken States in Central America, and the coming to power of communist governments in Cuba and Nicaragua has led to involvement of US 'advisers' and military aid in the Central America, which, because of its poverty and closeness to the USA is sometimes referred to as its 'backyard'. In 1983, US troops invaded Grenada.

7. *Energy supplies*. The supply routes for some of the USA's oil imports from the Middle East have become 'endangered' by the fall of the Shah of Iran, the assassination of Sadat in Egypt, and hostile relations between the USA and Libya.

THE USA'S INFLUENCE THROUGHOUT THE WORLD IN RECENT YEARS

Western Europe

The USA has had close relations with Western Europe since World War 2, when US troops were involved in the fighting and US politicians were involved in the peace treaties afterwards. Also, the USA's aim is to prevent Western Europe becoming communist. The USA and several Western European countries have a military link through the NATO alliance. As part of this alliance there are over 350 000 American troops in Western Europe and also many bases for US ships, submarines, aircraft, and missiles. Although in 1979 Britain and West Germany agreed to accept US Cruise missiles, there has been opposition by the Netherlands and Belgium and in 1981 there were protests by many groups in Western Europe opposed to those missiles.

Eastern Europe

After World War 2 the USA strongly opposed the USSR's decision to keep troops in Eastern European countries. Although the USA made strong protest about the crushing of the anti-government revolts in Hungary and Czechoslovakia, little direct action was taken. Much more serious threats were made later, in 1981, during the Polish 'Solidarity Union' opposition to the Polish Government. The USA warned the USSR of the serious consequences if Soviet troops entered Poland to crush that rebellion.

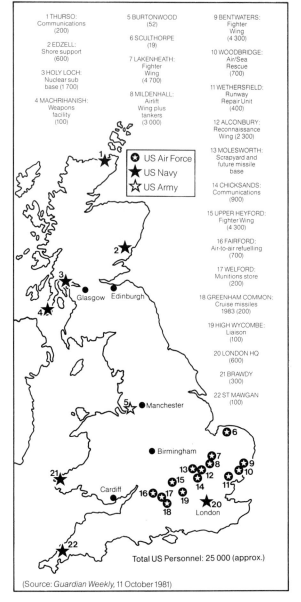

Major United States bases in the United Kingdom

1 THURSO: Communications (200)
2 EDZELL: Shore support (600)
3 HOLY LOCH: Nuclear sub base (1 700)
4 MACHRIHANISH: Weapons facility (100)
5 BURTONWOOD (52)
6 SCULTHORPE (19)
7 LAKENHEATH: Fighter Wing (4 700)
8 MILDENHALL: Airlift Wing plus tankers (3 000)
9 BENTWATERS: Fighter Wing (4 300)
10 WOODBRIDGE: Air/Sea Rescue (700)
11 WETHERSFIELD: Runway Repair Unit (400)
12 ALCONBURY: Reconnaissance Wing (2 300)
13 MOLESWORTH: Scrapyard and future missile base
14 CHICKSANDS: Communications (900)
15 UPPER HEYFORD: Fighter Wing (4 300)
16 FAIRFORD: Air-to-air refuelling (700)
17 WELFORD: Munitions store (200)
18 GREENHAM COMMON: Cruise missiles 1983 (200)
19 HIGH WYCOMBE: Liaison (100)
20 LONDON HQ (600)
21 BRAWDY (300)
22 ST MAWGAN (100)

US Air Force
US Navy
US Army

Glasgow   Edinburgh
Manchester
Birmingham
Cardiff
London

Total US Personnel: 25 000 (approx.)

(Source: *Guardian Weekly*, 11 October 1981)

The USA's Neighbours

Central America. Increasing unrest in Central America has led the USA to fear further communist revolts like the one in Cuba in the 1950s. The Revolution in Cuba brought **Fidel Castro** and a communist government to power only a short distance from the American mainland. By 1979, there was another communist government in Central America when the Sandinistas gained power in Nicaragua. This prompted the USA to send military aid and 'advisers' to help the El Salvador Government against rebels. The USA is afraid of a **'domino'** effect in Central America, with rebellions being supported by Cuba and the USSR.

US aid to support:	USA opposed to:
El Salvador	Cuba
Honduras	Nicaragua
Guatemala	

In this situation, Mexico is important in that it supplies oil to the USA, shares a 4800-kilometre border with it, and thousands of 'chicanos' (Mexican Americans) work in the USA. Mexico has close links with the USA, but also has close links with Cuba and Nicaragua, and has criticised the USA's actions in El Salvador.

Canada. The USA and Canada have close relations, with both being members of NATO and having joint agreement in **NORAD** (North American Air Defence Command). Recently, however, the Canadian Government has been discussing the possibility of limiting the amount of the USA's investment and control of firms in Canada. These firms include some that are part of the USA's $8.6 billion stake in Canada's oil industry.

The Middle East

The main aims of US policy in the Middle East, since the end of World War 2, have been to oppose Soviet influence and to protect the USA's oil supplies from the Persian Gulf. The USA has also given strong military support to Israel to guarantee its security, while attempting in recent years to encourage some form of settlement to the Arab–Israeli dispute.

In the early 1980s, US policy to oppose Soviet influence in the Middle East was given high priority. Military agreements and arms deals were signed with Egypt, Somalia, Oman, and Saudi

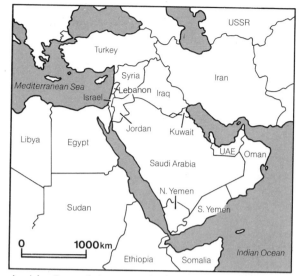

Arabia. Part of the arms deal with Saudi Arabia in 1981 involved the $8.5 billion sale of several US Air Warning and Control (**AWAC**) radar-equipped aircraft. In the same year, a series of joint military exercises, Operation Bright Star, were held in which American forces joined with military units from Egypt and the Sudan. The purpose of this was to show the Soviet Union and its Middle East allies, Syria, Iraq, Libya and South Yemen, that the USA was prepared to give military support to defend its allies and interests in the Middle East.

In carrying out this policy, the USA became involved in a series of disputes with Libya. Tension increased when, in 1981, two Libyan aircraft were shot down by American fighter aircraft over disputed Mediterranean waters near the north coast of Libya. In 1982 the USA stopped importing oil from Libya.

US helicopters flying over the Pyramids in Egypt, 1980

65

Sadat, **Carter** and **Begin** at Camp David after signing the Middle East Peace Treaty, 1979

The USA's support for Israel began in 1948 when Israel was established as a new Middle East State. US financial and military aid was given on a huge scale. Israel's Arab neighbours, however, did not accept the new State. In the Arab–Israeli wars which followed, Israel won and each time gained more land from its Arab neighbours. But the need for Middle East oil in the USA, and fear of increased Soviet friendship with Arab countries, has encouraged the USA to seek some form of settlement of the Arab–Israeli dispute. An agreement between Israel and Egypt was signed at Camp David in the USA in 1979. Israel promised to withdraw its forces and settlers from Egyptian territory by 1982 while Egypt recognised the Egypt–Israel border.

By the 1980s, US policy faced a number of problems. In the late 1970s many Muslim groups in the Middle East wanted a greater part in the government of their countries. In Iran in 1979 this Muslim (Islamic) Revival caused the overthrow of the leader of Iran, the Shah, who had been a close ally of the USA. The new leader, the **Ayatollah Khomeini**, was strongly anti-American. Iran cut off its oil supplies to the USA and over 50 American hostages were held in Iran for six weeks. However, a long border war between Iran and Iraq started in 1980 and this has destroyed much of Iran's oil industry and reduced its anti-American capability.

The USA lost another close ally in 1981 when President **Sadat** of Egypt was assassinated by Muslim extremists. His successor, Mubarak, while accepting the Camp David Agreement, sought a more independent line for Egypt by seeking closer relations with other Arab countries.

Continuing Arab–Israeli hostility poses a major problem for the USA. Although the Camp David Agreement pledged Israel to withdraw from occupied Egyptian territory, Israel still retains control, for military and political reasons, of areas captured from other Arab countries, such as the Golan Heights, the West Bank, and East Jerusalem. In view of this, the USA has found it difficult to persuade Arab countries to seriously consider settlement talks with Israel. In Israel's view the USA's sale of arms to Arab countries seems to threaten Israel and to indicate a swing in US policy towards the Arab countries, especially to oil producer, Saudi Arabia.

A further problem for the USA in its attempts to gain a favourable Middle East settlement is that of the Palestinian Arabs. These people, who live in Israeli territory or in refugee camps in Arab countries, have demanded, through the **PLO** (Palestine Liberation Organisation), that they be given a separate Palestinian area in Israel. The Israeli Government have repeatedly refused to agree. In 1982 Israeli forces entered Lebanon to crush PLO resistence. There was extensive fighting in Beirut until the PLO army agreed to leave. When several hundred Palestinian refugees were massacred by Lebanese forces, the USA sent 800 troops to Lebanon as a 'peace-keeping' force. But these were withdrawn in 1984.

USSR See page 13.

South-east Asia

The success of Chinese communists in gaining control of China in 1949 and the Korean War in 1950–3 caused the USA to become involved in this area to prevent the spread of communism by the 'domino' effect. For this reason the USA still has over 40 000 troops in South Korea. In South Vietnam, however, US involvement became too costly. The USA finally lost the war in Vietnam because, with 57 000 US troops killed, public opinion in the USA turned against helping out and Congress stopped supplying money for the war, which ended in 1975.

The USA's main ally in the area, Taiwan, has expressed concern at the USA's recognition of communist China and at suggestions of US military aid to China.

The USA also has close links with Thailand and Japan, and nuclear submarines of the US fleet have been stationed in Japanese harbours.

Southern Africa

The USA is greatly involved in trade with southern African countries, especially South Africa, and this means it has an interest there. Recent US opposition to the **UNO's** plans for Namibia's (south-west Africa) independence from South Africa, and US refusal to condemn raids by South African troops in black communist Angola, have led some of South Africa's neighbours to criticise the USA's policy for being too favourable to South Africa's white minority government. The view of the US Government is that it is opposing the spread of communism by promising help to right-wing rebels in Angola. The communist Government there is supported by almost 20 000 Cuban troops whom the USA and South Africa want removed.

ALLIANCES

As part of its foreign policy, the USA has formed alliances with a number of countries throughout the world. The main purpose of these alliances was to 'contain communism'. Of the three main alliances listed below, only NATO is still operating.

1. NATO (North Atlantic Treaty Organisation, formed 1949)

A military alliance among the USA, Canada, the UK, France, Iceland, Belgium, the Netherlands, Luxembourg, Denmark, Norway, Portugal, Italy.

Later members: West Germany, Turkey, Greece. In 1966 France withdrew its forces from NATO, although it still shares in research and planning. In 1981 Spain applied to join.

Some of the problems arising in the alliance in the 1980s are given below.

(a) *Finance*. The USA would like greater military expenditure by European partners, but some countries in Europe wish to cut defence spending costs.

(b) *Lack of standardisation*. Many member countries use their own weapons and equipment which cannot easily be used by other NATO troops.

(c) *Internal difficulties*. The new socialist Government in Greece threatens to withdraw Greece from NATO. There is a Greece/Turkey dispute over boundaries. There is increasing protest in Europe over NATO/US plans to site Cruise/Pershing missiles in Europe.

2. CENTO (Central Treaty Organisation, formed 1955)

A military alliance among the UK, Iran, Turkey, Pakistan, the USA. The USA did not officially join CENTO, but signed separate treaties with each of the countries. The alliance was based on the Baghdad Pact of 1953.

Iraq withdrew from CENTO in 1959. Iran, Pakistan and Turkey withdrew in 1979 and CENTO ended.

3. SEATO (South-east Asia Treaty Organisation, formed 1954)

A military alliance among the USA, Australia, New Zealand, the UK, France, Pakistan, the Philippines, Thailand. The alliance was based on the Anzus Pact of 1951.

Pakistan withdrew in 1972. The alliance ended after the USA was defeated in Vietnam in 1975 and withdrew its forces from Indo-China.

Questions

1. State the problems the USA has faced in its foreign policy in recent times.
2. How has US foreign policy changed as regards Israel?
3. Why is the USA anxious about the situation in Central America?
4. What is the policy of the USA towards South Africa?

The Defence of the USA

Defending the USA is one of the most expensive items in the Federal Budget. Between 1981 and 1986 the USA expects to spend $1600 billion on the defence of the nation, rising from $178 billion in 1981 to $367 billion in 1986.

To protect itself against possible attack by the USSR and its Warsaw Pact allies the USA has developed a complex system of computer-controlled radar warning stations. The AWAC system of airborne radar planes has recently extended the range of the USA's radar detection of hostile missiles and plans, and has increased the time available to prepare a defence against them. In addition, the USA has a large number of nuclear weapons which can be fired from a variety of launching systems. All of these systems are on alert 24 hours a day, 365 days a year.

This system of defence is undergoing continuous development and improvement in order to maintain and expand the USA's ability to defend itself in the event of nuclear attack. In recent years the USA's weapon technology experts have produced several very sophisticated and frightening new weapons:

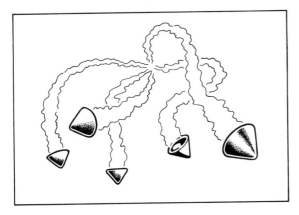

1. MIRV (multiple independently targetable re-entry vehicles)
A MIRVed missile carries more than one warhead, each aimed at a separate target.

3. The neutron bomb
The 'clean' bomb which kills people with the minimum damage to property.

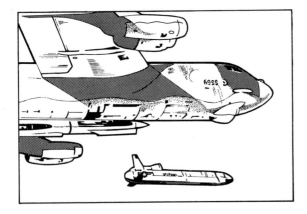

2. The Cruise missile
This is guided to the target by computer and designed to fly at low altitudes, evading radar detection. It can be launched from the ground, aircraft, ships or submarines.

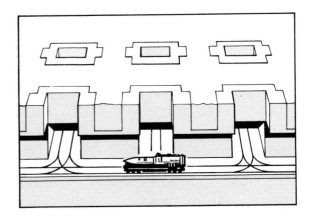

4. M-X (missile experimental) **missile**
This is a powerful missile placed on underground tracks along which it can be moved to one of a number of silos from which it can be launched. Each M-X missile has MIRVed warheads and will be very difficult for the enemy to detect before it is fired.

The USA possesses enough weapons to destroy the USSR several times over. Likewise, the USSR possesses more nuclear weapons than are necessary to destroy the USA. This 'overkill' capacity has developed as a result of the arms race between the two Superpowers to develop more and more advanced and destructive weapons. Both believe in the theory of Mutual Assured Destruction (MAD!), that is, that it would be foolish to start a nuclear war because both sides would be certain to be destroyed. Therefore, nuclear war is unlikely because the possession of such a large number of nuclear weapons acts as a deterrent. However, as the cartoon on the right illustrates, anything is possible . . .

1981

Computer faults led to at least three false alarms indicating that Soviet missiles had been launched and were approaching the USA. B52 bombers were actually at the end of the runway preparing to deliver the US answer by the time the faults were identified.

The defence of the USA

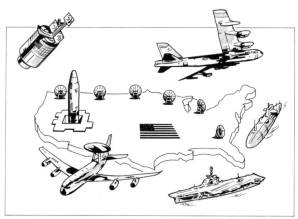

Questions

1. Describe the latest additions to the range of weapons available for the defence of the USA.
2. What is meant by
   (a) 'overkill',
   (b) 'Mutual Assured Destruction'?
3. Explain in your own words the sequence of events illustrated in the cartoon strip.

Military Policy in the 1980s: A New 'Cold War'?

In spite of all the recent advances in American military technology, many people in the USA are worried that the balance of power may be changing noticeably in favour of the USSR. A recent estimate of developments in the race for military superiority between the two Superpowers produced the following figures:

US vs. USSR

A numerical comparison of 1976 and *1981*

		US	USSR
	Strategic nuclear warheads	6,842 *7,192*	2,943 *6,302*
	Strategic nuclear launchers	1,710 *1,628*	2,375 *2,384*
	Submarines	115 *121*	329 *370*
	Large warships	210 *223*	257 *268*
	Tanks	9,181 *11,560*	42,000 *48,000*
	Artillery	4,955 *5,140*	13,900 *19,300*
	Combat aircraft	3,665 *3,988*	4,740 *4,885*
	Manpower in millions	2.13 *2.09*	4.88 *4.84*

These figures relate only to numbers of weapons, but although the USA is generally acknowledged to be ahead in terms of quality many people in the USA are worried by statistics like these. Congress has estimated that the cost of Soviet military activities in 1980 was $175 billion compared with $115 billion in the USA.

As a result, since the beginning of the 1980s, and particularly since the election of Ronald Reagan as President, there has been an increasing importance placed on defence and military spending. In the cuts in **Federal** spending announced in 1981, defence was the area of spending which suffered the least. Cuts of $2 billion in 1982, and $11 billion in 1983 and 1984, are very small in proportion to the total spent on defence, and over the five years 1981–6 spending on defence is expected to increase considerably.

A number of other policy decisions taken in recent years have increased the tension between the USA and the USSR.

Firstly, there was the decision to use Cruise missiles in Western Europe as a first line of defence. By the mid-1980s there are likely to be 464 Tomahawk ground-launched missiles sited in Europe, 160 of them in Britain, each with a 240-kilotonne warhead; 108 Pershing 2 missiles (each with a 400-kilotonne warhead and a range of 740 kilometres) will be sited in West Germany. This decision has met with considerable opposition from anti-nuclear groups in Europe.

An anti-nuclear protest

Secondly, President Reagan announced in 1981 that the United States would build neutron bombs for the first time. This is an indication that the leaders of the USA believe they can fight

70

(and win) a limited tactical nuclear war. Previously they believed that because both they and the USSR had so many destructive nuclear weapons neither would dare to use them because both sides would inevitably suffer great damage. Nuclear war is much more likely when one (or both) of the sides believes it can use nuclear weapons and survive with little damage to itself.

Thirdly, the USA will go ahead with its scheme for the M-X missile, scheduled to be completed by 1990, in spite of a problem about where to site these 96-tonne missiles. The problem arose because a number of Senators did not want the missiles stationed in their States (Utah and Nevada, two of the most suitable sites). The President agreed to go ahead with a scaled-down version of the original plan. At least 100 of the missiles, which can travel 13 000 kilometres and drop their bombs within 90 metres of the target, will be ready by 1986.

The President also announced plans to build 100 new B-1 bombers costing $200 million each as a replacement for the ageing B-52s which are decreasing in their usefulness.

CONCLUSION: ARMS LIMITATION OR ARMS RACE?

The most important conclusion which can be drawn from these recent decisions by the military policy-makers in the USA is that we are entering a new phase of the nuclear 'game' in which the US President may feel that in order to protect his country and his people he may have to allow the launching of nuclear weapons on a limited scale. His military advisers believe that such a war could be fought without it developing into an all-out war of mass destruction. Western Europe is one of the most likely sites for such a war.

But President Reagan is also committed to continuing the arms limitation talks with the USSR, although he is likely to take a much harder line than his predecessor, President Carter. In a speech in September 1981 President Reagan said he wanted 'verifiable arms reductions' or else the Soviets would be 'in an arms race they cannot win'. The talks between the Superpowers resumed in Geneva in November 1981.

Shortly before the disarmament talks resumed, there were several more hopeful signs that the threat of nuclear war might be reduced. President Reagan proposed a new kind of talks on nuclear weapons which he nicknamed START (Strategic Arms Reduction Talks). These would aim to reduce rather than simply limit the amount of nuclear weapons held by the USA and the USSR.

In a major speech made shortly before the re-opening of the talks in Geneva, the President announced that he had written to President **Brezhnev** with proposals for a 'zero option'. This meant that the USA would scrap its plans to install Cruise and Pershing 2 missiles in Europe if the USSR agreed to dismantle its equivalent medium-range missiles which are already in place. President Reagan compared these proposals to 'the first footstep on the moon': it would be 'a giant step for mankind'.

The 'Zero option'

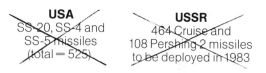

USA	USSR
SS-20, SS-4 and SS-5 missiles (total = 525)	464 Cruise and 108 Pershing 2 missiles to be deployed in 1983

The Soviet news agency Tass dismissed President Reagan's plan as a propaganda action designed to lead the Soviet-US talks on disarmament up a blind alley. The news agency indicated that there was a major flaw in President Reagan's offer: he had produced 'fantastic figures' which failed to mention British and French nuclear missile and bomber forces. The US proposal was described as 'a mere propaganda ploy' designed to cause a stalemate in the Geneva talks and 'to present the American course of escalating the arms race and ensuring military superiority as a "peace initiative"'.

Questions

1. Why might the US Government be concerned about the figures contained in the table on page 70?
2. Describe President Reagan's reaction to such statistics.
3. What recent decisions by the US Government have increased tension between the USA and the USSR?
4. What conclusion can be drawn from these recent decisions?
5. In what way do the START differ from the previous rounds of **SALT**?
6. Explain what you understand by the phrase 'zero option'.
7. Why is the USSR unlikely to accept President Reagan's 'zero option' proposals?

El Salvador

The killings continue in bloody El Salvador

The brutal civil war in El Salvador was between battles last week. In the only major skirmish, Salvadoran soldiers clashed with armed teenagers sympathetic to the rebel cause in the village of San Lorenzo. The toll, according to an army major: 40 guerrillas and one soldier dead. From their hideouts in remote areas near the border with Honduras, leftist guerrillas of the Farabundo Marti National Liberation Front emerged briefly to blockade roads and blow up a number of bridges and power lines. Meanwhile, death squads of both right and left still roamed the land, murdering anyone they suspected of collaborating with the other side.

BACKGROUND

El Salvador is a small country in Central America, with a population of about $4\frac{1}{4}$ million people. For its wealth it relies mainly on the coffee crop, which provides nearly half of its total exports in value.

There has been military rule in the country for over 50 years, although the present Government was elected in 1982. Since the successful communist Revolution in Cuba in 1959, the USA has supplied aid to the Government of El Salvador to help its forces to put down increasing discontent among the poor who have little influence over what happens in the country. Throughout the 1970s the violence of civil war increased, and not long after Ronald Reagan became President of the USA in 1981 he announced that there would be increased aid to the Government forces in El Salvador. In 1984, newly elected President Duarte met rebel leaders in a move for peace.

CAUSES OF THE REVOLUTION

One of the main reasons for the revolt is that the country is in economic difficulties. Many people are poor, and see little hope of improvement. Here are some statistics which show the desperate conditions in which most of the people live.

> 50% of the population are illiterate.
> 40% of the peasants have no land.
> 2% of the population owns 60% of the land.
> On average there are 3 doctors for every 10 000 people.
> 70% of children under 5 are starving.
> 30% of workers are unemployed.
> 50% of population have less than £5 a month.

THE EFFECTS OF THE CIVIL WAR

The violence in El Salvador now causes widespread devastation and death throughout the country. About 10 000 people were killed in 1980 and, by 1984, 50 000 Salvadoreans had been killed.

Death squad victims in El Salvador

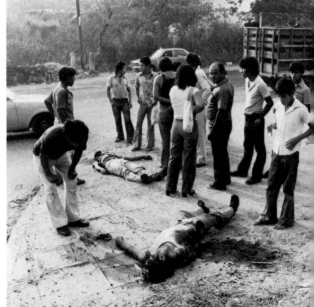

Why is the USA Involved in El Salvador?

1. *America's 'backyard'*. US policy has, for many years, regarded Central America as an area where involvement is important, since it is close to the USA border.

2. *Preventing communism*. By helping the El Salvador Government, the USA is aiming to help stop the rebellion by the left-wing political groups with communist influence.

3. *'Domino theory'*. The USA helps El Salvador to fight against communism because if it does not then El Salvador might 'fall' as did Cuba and Nicaragua. Other countries in the area might then become communist in turn until America itself is threatened.

4. *American companies*. Almost three-quarters of El Salvador's industry is controlled or owned by US firms.

As El Salvador slides ꝺeeper into civil war, its ꝺapital, San Salvador, leads ꝺ macabre … double life.

Most of the time it remains a ꝺusty, down-at-heel tropical ꝺty, its wooden houses and ꝺops interspersed with modꝺrn office blocks … The open ꝺr markets are crammed with ꝺeople and clogged with lorries ꝺ. The taxis and the buses are ꝺll … Bruce Lee is on at the ꝺniversal Cinema, and Jack ꝺemmon and Walter Matthau ꝺre at the Paseo.

Beneath the surface is the ꝺther face of the city, best ꝺxemplified by the conditions ꝺt La Bermeja, poorest of the ꝺty's three cemeteries. Last ꝺeek 24 shallow graves had ꝺeen dug in the paupers' ꝺction where interment is ꝺee. They awaited the daily ꝺtake of corpses, many ꝺnidentified with heads or ꝺmbs missing, or riddled with ꝺun-shot.

Above the city the sound of ꝺe helicopter is becoming ꝺore common as more ꝺachines are brought in from ꝺe United States. Uniformed ꝺatrols of soldiers push along ꝺe crowded pavements.

(Observer, 22 March 1981)

Almost every night an explosion roars across San Salvador just after dark. The 'seven o'clock bomb' usually destroys a bank, an office building or a factory.

Sometimes the blast wrecks a less obvious target, like a cinema or amusement arcade, striking at any element of normal life remaining in a country where the economy is in its death throes.

One citizen in 15 is a refugee, mass murders merit only a few paragraphs in the newspapers, and Government forces cannot move more than a few hundred yards off the highway without risking ambush.

(Observer, 31 May 1981)

Infinitely more frightening are the armed men in civilian clothes riding in trucks. These are either members of Orden, the right-wing terror squad which has kept the peasantry under control for years, or of the Treasury Guard, an autonomous official police force which is held responsible for some of the worst killings.

Who's who in El Salvador's war

Government troops
(16 000 people)
+
US aid (military equipment and advisers)
(1000 people)
versus
Salvadorean Liberation Front
(5000 people)

The USA's Problems in El Salvador

In 1981, announcing more US aid to El Salvador, President Reagan said 'What we are actually doing is, at the request of a Government in one of our neighbouring countries, offering some help against the import, or export into the Western Hemisphere, of terrorism.' This help has included over $100 million of US military and economic aid, as detailed in the following table.

US aid

Military	Economic
14 helicopters 1000 military advisers technicians military equipment riot control equipment	money to help agriculture reform technicians agriculture advisers

Not all Americans, however, support this aid to the El Salvador Government. In May 1981 about 100 000 people marched in Washington in the biggest protest march by Americans against US foreign policy since the time of the Vietnam War. There is a fear that a great deal of US money will simply 'disappear' in the civil war with no success to show for it. There is also concern that the USA is supporting and helping an unpopular Government which has left the majority of its people to live in deprivation. Both France and Mexico have recognised the rebels as a 'representative political force' with whom the USA could, if it wished, negotiate.

Questions

1. Outline the reasons for the civil war in El Salvador.
2. Describe some of the effects of the civil war on El Salvador.
3. Why is the USA involved?
4. What problems does the USA face in giving aid to the Government of El Salvador?

The Role of the CIA

CIA Profile

Name: Central Intelligence Agency
Date of birth: 1947
Background: Developed from World War 2
intelligence services
Duties: Report to the President of the USA
Headquarters: Langley, Virginia
Director: William Casey
Employees: Top secret
Annual expenditure: Classified information

During the 1970s the activities of the Central Intelligence Agency were the subject of several enquiries by Congress and a great deal of discussion and argument among the people of the USA. Many people believe that some of the activities of the CIA in recent years have been illegal and that the organisation has become so powerful that the President and his colleagues in the White House no longer control it effectively.

WHAT DOES THE CIA DO?

Any country which has enemies, either real or potential, needs some kind of organisation responsible for gathering information about that enemy. Because the activities of the CIA are clouded in secrecy, the question of what the CIA actually does is extremely difficult to answer, but the work of an intelligence agency usually falls into three main categories:

1. *Gathering and analysing of information.*
This is the traditional job of intelligence services and has been a feature of military history for centuries. It involves the assessing of an enemy's military strength and whether, or how, the enemy intends using its strength. Much of the work is

routine collection and analysis of vast quantities of information from the media, spy-planes, satellites, and (the more ordinary) human 'spies'. In a world of crises and wars a nation which does not have an efficient intelligence service would be very vulnerable. As far as the CIA is concerned, its job is to find out the facts and lay them before the President, along with advice about how he might use or act upon this information.

2. *Protection of its own secrets.* (counter-intelligence). If a country has an intelligence service collecting information and influencing government policy, inevitably the enemy will try to learn as much as it can about that information and policy. An intelligence service such as the CIA is only useful if the policy makers in the White House trust its honesty and act on the information it provides. But the very fact that it is trusted makes it vulnerable to the planting of false or misleading information by 'the other side'. A vulnerable intelligence service is worse than none at all.

3. *Political activities.* The third, and most controversial, aspect of an intelligence agency's work is intervention in the political affairs of other nations. It is this aspect of the CIA's work, known as 'covert operations' which has led to widespread criticism of the Agency in the USA. In carrying out these operations the CIA is supposed to act as the direct instrument of the President. The US Government defined covert operations in 1948 as activity related to 'propaganda; economic warfare; ... sabotage, anti-sabotage, demolition and evacuation measures; subversion against hostile states, including assistance to underground resistance groups, and support of indigenous anti-communist elements in threatened countries of the free world'. As part of its machinery, therefore, the US Government set up, under control of the CIA, apparatus for the secret

The role of the CIA

transfer of money, the delivery of arms, the distribution of propaganda, the training of friendly intelligence agencies, and other secret methods of putting pressure on some governments and helping others to survive.

CRITICISM OF THE CIA

Since the early 1970s some of the cloud of secrecy surrounding the CIA's activities has been lifted following a number of government investigations and the publication of a number of books by former agents.

There have been three main criticisms:

1. *The cost of CIA operations*. The total cost is disguised by various methods of financial accounting, but it is estimated to be at least twice the figure formally submitted to Congress. A number of Senators and members of Congress are very critical of this secrecy.

2. *Expensive mistakes involving the CIA*. The CIA has been involved in several operations which went very far wrong and were costly in financial and human terms; for example, the Bay of Pigs invasion of Cuba, and the Vietnam War.

3. *Illegal activities going far beyond acceptable covert operations*. During the 1970s, evidence emerged that the CIA was deeply involved in a number of controversial illegal activities inside the USA itself as well as in other countries: for example, the Watergate scandal, plans to kill Fidel Castro, an attempt to overthrow President Allende of Chile, attempts to maintain civil war in Angola.

As a result of these criticisms many ordinary Americans have become suspicious about the activities of the CIA. During the Carter Administration the power and influence of the CIA appeared to be declining, but under President Reagan its power is thought to be increasing once more. The extent of this power is once again shrouded in secrecy.

President relaxes curbs on CIA

Washington, Friday – President Reagan today issued new controversial guidelines allowing the Central Intelligence Agency to operate domestically.

Under the guidelines, which come into force on the President's authority alone, the CIA are forbidden from engaging in electronic surveillance – which would include hidden microphones and other bugging devices – within the United States 'except for the purpose of training, testing or conducting countermeasures to hostile electronic surveillance'.

But the new measures mark a relaxation of the previous tough restrictions on the agency, which followed the scandals of the 1970s when the CIA were discovered to have engaged in domestic spying . . . .

In a statement on the 17-page executive order, President Reagan said: 'These orders are designed to provide America's intelligence community with clear, more positive guidance and to remove the aura of suspicion and mistrust that can hobble our nation's intelligence efforts'.

(*Scotsman*, 5 December 1981)

Questions

1. Describe the main activities of the CIA.
2. For what reasons has the CIA been criticised by many Americans?

PART 3

The USSR Today

1. The People of the USSR

Population Survey

The Union of Soviet Socialist Republics is the largest nation in the world in terms of the land area it occupies. Within its 21 million square kilometres the USSR contains fifteen Republics, occupying 15% of the earth's land surface.

The USSR has a total population of around 262 million people. The table on page 77 lists the major population groups and the areas they live in, but there are many more ethnic groups throughout the Soviet Union. More than 100 of these groups have been identified, descended from ancient tribes such as the Varangians, Turks and Mongols. These groups represent a very wide variety of customs and traditions, language and dress, and ethnic pride.

Yahut women in traditional dress

The Fifteen Republics

1 Russian Soviet Federative Socialist Republic
2 Estonian Soviet Socialist Republic (SSR)
3 Latvian SSR
4 Lithuanian SSR
5 Byelorussian SSR
6 Ukrainian SSR
7 Moldavian SSR
8 Georgian SSR
9 Armenian SSR
10 Azerbaijan SSR
11 Kazakh SSR
12 Turkmen SSR
13 Uzbek SSR
14 Tajik SSR
15 Kirgliz SSR

Wooden spoon carvers at work in the Volga region

Republic (Capital)	Population*	Major Ethnic Composition**
Russian Soviet Federal Socialist Republic (*Moscow*)	139.1 million	82.8% Russians 3.7% Tatars 2.6% Ukrainians
Estonia (*Tallin*)	1.5 million	68.2% Estonians 24.7% Russians
Latvia (*Riga*)	2.5 million	56.8% Latvians 29.8% Russians
Lithuania (*Vilnius*)	3.4 million	80.1% Lithuanians 8.6% Russians 7.7% Poles
Byelorussia (*Minsk*)	9.7 million	81.1% Byelorussians 10.4% Russians 4.3% Poles
Ukraine (*Kiev*)	50.1 million	74.9% Ukrainians 19.4% Russians
Moldavia (*Kishinev*)	4.0 million	63.9% Moldavians 14.2% Ukrainians 12.8% Russians
Georgia (*Tbilisi*)	5.1 million	66.8% Georgians 9.7% Armenians 8.5% Russians
Armenia (*Yerevan*)	3.1 million	88.6% Armenians 5.9% Azerbaijanis 2.7% Russians
Azerbaijan (*Baku*)	6.2 million	73.8% Azerbaijanis 10.0% Russians 10.0% Armenians
Kazakhstan (*Alma-Ata*)	15.0 million	40.8% Russians 36.0% Kazakhs 6.1% Ukrainians
Turkmenistan (*Ashkhabad*)	2.9 million	65.6% Turkmenians 14.5% Russians 8.3% Uzbeks 3.2% Kazakhs
Uzbekistan (*Tashkent*)	16.2 million	65.5% Uzbeks 12.5% Russians 4.9% Tatars 4.0% Kazakhs
Tadzhikistan (*Dushanbe*)	4.0 million	56.2% Tadzhiks 23.0% Uzbeks 11.9% Russians
Kirghizia (*Frunze*)	3.7 million	43.8% Kirghiz 29.2% Russians 10.6% Uzbeks 4.1% Ukrainians

*1981 figures (source: *Central Statistical Board of the USSR*)
**1969 Census figures (source: *The Europa Year Book*)

The Russians, although still the major group in the Soviet population, account for only 52.4% of the people of the USSR. Because of high birth rates in many of the non-Slavic regions of the USSR and their own almost zero population growth, the Russians are likely to be in a minority of the whole population by the end of the twentieth century. The growth of national pride and self-assertion among the non-Russians may present a major problem for the Soviet Government in the future.

In recent years there have been attempts to unite the ethnic minorities and to stress the national greatness and pride of the Soviet Union as a whole (see Issue: Minorities). By stressing the USSR's prestige as a world Superpower the Soviet Government is trying to unite, and thereby reduce the possibility of trouble from, the minorities. Together with this policy of 'Sovietisation' the Government has been pursuing a programme of 'Russification': for example, Russian language is becoming a major component in the education of non-Russian minorities.

In spite of attempts to encourage pride in the

Soviet Union among the minority groups, there have been scattered, but serious, anti-Russian riots in several cities, including Tashkent and Dushanbe. The Government has tried in some cases to 'buy-off' anti-Russian minorities with economic benefits and protection. In others, concessions have been made to minorities linked with the Chinese because of the Soviet Government's fear of China's growing power.

Questions

1. Name four important national minority groups in the USSR.
2. Why are the Russians concerned about high birth rates and the growth of national pride among some of these minorities?
3. What has the Soviet Government done to encourage greater pride in the USSR?

Lifestyles

LIVING STANDARDS

The cost of living chart shows how the average worker's earnings in the USSR compare with those of a worker in the USA. A direct comparison of income is not necessarily a true picture of the differences in lifestyles, however. The purchasing power, i.e. how much that income can buy in terms of goods and services, is also relevant to any realistic comparison. As the chart shows, in the USSR some of the essential goods and services such as housing, heating, bread and dental services are cheaper than in the USA, whereas other items such as good-quality clothes and shoes, and luxury goods such as televisions and motor cars, are more expensive.

On balance, it is probably true to say that the standard of living of the 'average' citizen in the Soviet Union is considerably below that of the 'average' American. 'Averages', however, can be misleading, particularly in countries as vast as the USSR. The items in this unit are therefore designed to give some idea of the varied lifestyles of the people of the Soviet Union.

EMPLOYMENT AND UNEMPLOYMENT

Everyone in the USSR who wants a job has one: there is no unemployment and no 'dole' queue. At first sight this statement may seem surprising. Has the Soviet Union solved one of the most serious problems troubling Western countries in the 1980s? While there is no unemployment, there is under-employment. There is a great

A cost of living comparison (1980)

Cost of living	New York City	Moscow
Manufacturing worker's earnings per week	$265.60	$56.54
Monthly rental 3-room apt.	$1 000	$37
Heat and electricity per month	$82	$4.50
Car	$6 200 (Citation)	$10 000 (Zhiguli)
Vodka (1 litre)	$6	$11
Dental checkup	$32	Free
1 lb chicken	66¢	$2.55
Loaf of bread	62¢	24¢
Jeans	$18.50	$45
Tights	$1.50	$10
Holiday (2 weeks per person)*	$910	$120
Gold wedding ring	$75	$225
Hard-cover novel	$12.95	$3
Colour television	$710	$1 094
Newspaper	25¢ (*Daily News*)	5¢ (*Izvestia*)

*70% of the Moscow figure is paid by the worker's union.

waste of labour resources in the USSR, both in industry and agriculture. Unemployment is often replaced by the inefficient use of manpower and womanpower. Vast numbers of people are employed in industries which could be much more efficient with higher investment in modern technology and methods.

HOUSING

Most of the people of the Soviet Union (80%) live in flats in the cities. These flats are usually small and quite cramped, built in huge blocks up to twenty storeys high. Although they provide adequate living accommodation they provide little in the way of luxury. They are, however, very cheap to rent, and usually the small rental includes the cost of heat and light. The Soviets pride themselves on the fact that rents have remained unchanged for *fifty* years and now take up only a very small proportion of a family's income (less than 2% in 1980). These low rents are made possible by huge Government subsidies, and by themselves would not even cover the cost of maintenance. Eventually, the authorities intend to abolish rents altogether.

Interior view of
Soviet apartment, 1979

Nineteen-storey apartment houses
under construction in Moscow

In the countryside, however, the picture is quite different. There is a considerable gap in standards between the towns and the country, where many people live in old cottages, some without bathrooms, hot water and proper heating.

There is a huge housing shortage in the Soviet Union, in spite of an extensive house-building programme. The Soviet Government calculates that it still needs another 50 million homes to end the shortage. The present target is to build 2.2 million a year in an attempt to solve the problem within the next twenty years. Whether this ambitious target can be achieved, given the USSR's other priorities and problems, remains to be seen. Today, the USSR spends £13 500 million a year on housing: its most expensive social service.

SOVIET SOCIETY

One of the most commonly held, but mistaken, views of people in the West is that the Soviet Union is a classless society. In theory, there are three classes in Soviety society, described in the very first Article of the **Constitution**: the workers, the peasants and the intelligentsia, all of whom cooperate with each other and have common interests. According to Marxist theory the classless society will not be achieved until a state of true **communism** exists.

In fact, the class structure in the Soviet Union is rather different from the Constitution's description. And this class structure has a great bearing on the standards of living of the Soviet people. In spite of the emphasis on equality in the USSR there are wide differences in the amount of power, privilege and living standards of the various groups within Soviet society.

The Soviet Elite

At the 'top' of Soviet society is an elite ruling class of over 1 million people, commonly referred to as the 'nachalstvo', or Establishment. This group includes, at the very top, the most important officials in the Communist Party and the State, together with the highest-ranking military officers. They enjoy special privileges which include exclusive modern flats, chauffeur-driven limousines (which use special centre lanes in city streets, reserved for VIP cars), and access to special shops which do not suffer from shortages and are well stocked with a wide range of goods including meat, fruit and vegetables, good vodka and wine, caviar and foreign goods such as Scotch whisky, French brandy and Japanese radios and stereos. The GUM department store in Moscow has a special section stocked with good-quality clothes available only to members of the elite. In addition to these privileges, which cause much ill-feeling among the ordinary people, the elite also enjoy the use of country dachas (large villas), yachts and reserved holiday resorts on the coast of the Black Sea.

Just below this elite of elites is a larger group which includes top scientists, factory and **State farm** managers, Olympic athletes, cosmonauts, top writers and ballet stars and other important people. They, too, have special privileges, on a less grand scale. They have access to special shops where Soviet money is not accepted, but goods are bought with special certificates. The people in this group also have country dachas, although neither as large nor as secluded as those of the top group. One thing they do not have is political power.

Further down the scale come the journalists, interpreters, Intourist guides and thousands of other Party officials and industrial managers with lesser, but significant, privileges. If a Soviet citizen can get into one of these elite groups he or she can enjoy a standard of living far above that of the ordinary worker or peasant. The elite enjoys great privacy – their homes are guarded against intruders; the exclusive shops, clinics and hospitals they use have no signs up or are hidden from public view – and tries hard to remain inconspicuous.

The descriptions of education, housing and shopping in this unit apply to ordinary Soviet citizens and not to the nachalstvo who enjoy privileges in almost every aspect of their lives.

Shopping

Shopping is a major part of a woman's life in Moscow and she spends several hours every day hunting for groceries. Food shops are open from 8 a.m. to 8 p.m. with just an hour's break for lunch, and they are always busy. If you find shopping a bit of a bore, count your blessings, for Soviet shopping is an art that requires lots of patience and a very good memory.

It seems that simply walking into a shop and asking for your groceries and paying for them is too easy. You must first decide exactly what you want to buy, then memorize from which counter it is sold and how much it costs. Before actually getting anything, you have to queue at the cash desk to pay for your intended purchases – and to complicate matters further there is often a different cashier for different items. In return for your money, the cashier will give you a receipt and you must go and queue at the appropriate counter. If you happen to be buying cheese, for instance, and the shop assistant cuts a piece slightly larger than you have paid for, back you go to the cashier to queue yet again to pay for the difference.

(Tracy Chandler, student of Russian,
Woman's Realm, 31 December 1977)

WOMEN IN THE USSR

'Women and men have equal rights in the USSR. Exercise of these rights is ensured by according women equal access with men to education and vocational and professional training, equal opportunities in employment, remuneration and promotion ... by special labour and health protection measures for women; by providing conditions enabling mothers to work; by legal protection, and material and moral support for mothers and children, including paid leaves and other benefits for expectant mothers and mothers with small children.'

(*Article 35, 1977 Constitution*)

Women at work in Tashkent tractor factory

plus the use of low-priced creches and nurseries. And traditionally the 'babushka' (grandmother) has been very important as babysitter, cook and shopper for the family. But in the USSR today many grandmothers themselves have jobs and are unwilling to give them up, with the result that more and more mothers are either having to give up their job or limit their family to one child.

Abortion is free on demand, but the methods of contraception used are old-fashioned, and the contraceptive pill is still not available. An increasing number of Soviet women today find themselves the 'victims' of divorce. The divorce rate is high and one of the main causes is reported to be heavy drinking among Soviet men. And again, although there is supposed to be equality, divorced women are socially worse off than divorced men in the USSR.

This statement should ensure that there is complete equality of the sexes in the USSR. On the surface this is so – there are many women doctors, teachers and engineers in the Soviet Union, and large numbers are employed in semi-skilled and unskilled jobs in industry – but the equality is more apparent than real. As in the West, the top jobs in almost all industries and professions are held by men. And in addition to having a full or part-time job, Soviet women are expected to do the shopping, which may take several hours a day, and bring up the children.

Women have the right to return to the same job up to twelve months after the birth of a child,

LEISURE AND SPORT

A wide variety of leisure activities is available. Sport is very popular, especially ice-hockey, gymnastics, athletics and soccer. Physical education is taught to all school children from the age of seven onwards and the most promising pupils attend junior sports schools after normal school hours at the age of ten. The very best enter one of the USSR's 600 Olympic reserve schools where the students are coached to the highest standards in their chosen sports, in addition to the usual school subjects. This emphasis on sport from an early age explains the dominant position of the Soviet Union in so many world sports, and the reason why the USSR has collected more Olympic gold medals than any other nation for many years.

USSR's women's national gymnastic team, 1981

1980 Olympic Games

Country	Number of medals won			Total
	Gold	Silver	Bronze	
USSR	80	69	47	196
E. Germany	47	36	43	126
Bulgaria	8	16	16	40
Hungary	7	10	15	32
Poland	2	14	14	30
Romania	6	6	13	25
Britain	5	7	9	21
Cuba	8	7	5	20
Italy	8	3	4	15
France	6	5	3	14

Cultural activities are also popular, particularly classical music concerts, opera and ballet. The Bolshoi Ballet, based in Moscow, is one of the world's leading ballet companies, whose performances draw large audiences. The Moscow State Circus with its unique interchangeable 'sawdust ring cum ice-rink cum swimming pool' is recognised as one of the world's top circuses with many internationally famous acts.

Unfortunately, entry to these shows is not always easily available to the ordinary workers who are often unable to get tickets because they are snapped up on the black market by the nachalstvo. Like workers all over the world, Soviet workers enjoy a summer break from the routine of work. Holidays, which are subsidised by the trade unions or the Communist Party, are available in Soviet and other Eastern European resorts such as those on the Black Sea. Once again, however, the upper groups in Soviet society enjoy special resorts in the best areas, well away from the masses of tourists. Foreign holidays outside the Communist bloc are not available to any but the very highest officials in the USSR.

THE MASS MEDIA

In common with people throughout the world, Soviet citizens rely on newspapers, magazines, radio and television to provide them with information about events in their own country as well as the world beyond. The media in the USSR are, however, closely controlled by the Government and Communist Party. Censorship is accepted; in other words, any news with which the Party disagrees or which it does not wish the people to hear or see is either altered to suit the Party policy or is ignored altogether.

The newspaper with the largest circulation (11 million every day) is *Pravda* which means 'truth'. Compared with Western newspapers, *Pravda* contains very few pages and concentrates on official Party and Government information and announcements, examples of achievements in industry and agriculture, together with scientific, cultural, sports and foreign news. Stories about everyday events such as traffic accidents and crime do not appear, and there are no advertisements. *Pravda* is not censored by the Government because it is published by the Central Committee of the Communist Party and unquestionably follows 'the Party line'.

The other important newspaper, *Izvestia*, with a circulation of about $8\frac{1}{2}$ million, is the Government's own daily paper. Magazines, such as *Krokodil* are also available, but foreign magazines and newspapers are available only to the elite, and even then are censored to remove touchy or critical comments concerning the USSR.

Radio and television broadcasts are also controlled and censored by the Government. Television sets are owned by 80% of Soviet families but only 7% of these are colour sets, which are very expensive. Many of the television programmes are similar to those in the West, with sport, children's programmes, cultural and quiz shows being most popular. The USSR buys programmes and series from the West, and in recent years British programmes such as 'Upstairs, Downstairs' and 'The Forsyte Saga' have been enjoyed by Soviet viewers. By far the largest slice of time, however, is taken up by news and documentary programmes which follow a similar political line to that contained in the newspapers.

SOCIAL PROBLEMS

Not surprisingly, most of the social problems usually found in a modern industrial society – crime, vandalism, divorce, alcoholism and juvenile delinquency – are also to be found in the USSR. Although it is difficult to obtain exact figures to illustrate the extent of these problems it is generally recognised that crime levels are probably lower and alcoholism rates higher than in Western industrialised countries.

In recent years the Soviet authorities have been very concerned about the growing problem of juvenile delinquency. In the USSR the problem is usually referred to as 'hooliganism' and includes mugging, vandalism and other minor juvenile crimes. The causes of this hooliganism are the familiar ones of boredom, overcrowded housing on large estates, split families and alcohol. Alcohol is arguably the biggest problem of all since it is a contributing factor to many of the others. A recent Soviet Government report stated that 84% of young people in the USSR start drinking before they are 16.

Questions

1. Write a short note describing the following aspects of life in the Soviet Union:
   (*a*) employment and unemployment,
   (*b*) housing,
   (*c*) shopping,
   (*d*) leisure and sport.
2. Who are the 'nachalstvo' and what privileges do they enjoy?
3. Which other groups of people in Soviet society enjoy special privileges?
4. What rights does the Constitution guarantee to Soviet women?
5. Do women receive these rights in practice?
6. By what methods does the Soviet Government control the mass media?
7. What social problems is the Government especially concerned about?

ASPECTS OF LIFE IN THE SOVIET UNION (*Soviet Weekly*, 5 December 1981)

THE CENTRAL DAILY PAPERS

	circulation
Pravda	10 700 000
Trud (Labour)	10 500 000
Komsomolskaya Pravda (*youth paper*)	10 100 000
Pionerskaya Pravda (*children's paper*)	8 900 000
Selskaya Zhizn (*farmworkers' paper*)	8 500 000

Papers are cheap! All these, except **Pravda** cost two kopecks, about 1½p. Pravda costs three kopecks, just over 2p.
IN ALL, THE USSR PUBLISHES 8000 NEWSPAPERS AND 5000 MAGAZINES

THE POPULARITY OF SPORT

There are 55 million people in the USSR taking a regular part in physical culture and sport (not counting compulsory P.E. at schools and colleges!). They include:

Track and Field	6 200 000
Volleyball	5 500 000
Ski-ing	4 500 000
Football	4 000 000
Basketball	3 600 000

100 MILLION AT SCHOOL THIS YEAR

General education schools (Up to the age of 17)	44 300 000
Specialised secondary technical schools	4 600 000
Vocational schools (giving professional qualifications as well as general education)	4 000 000
College and Institutes	5 200 000
On special courses to upgrade their working qualifications	42 100 000
TOTAL	100 200 000

ACTIVE GROUPS

	membership
Communist Party	17 500 000
Trade Unions	125 000 000
Young Communist League (age 14–28)	40 000 000
Scientific and technical societies	8 000 000
Red Cross	90 000 000
Society of Inventors and Innovators	10 000 000
Young Pioneers (age 10–15)	25 000 000

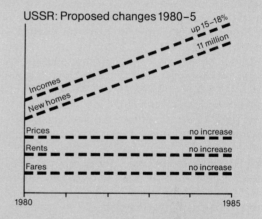

EQUALITY FOR WOMEN

IN THE USSR today, women make up 51.4 per cent of the employed population – and equal pay for equal work is the universal rule. They are found in all sections of industry and all the professions – indeed, heavy engineering employs more women than any other industry. In the local Soviet just on half the members are women and more than two civil servants in three are women. In the Soviet parliament, just on one MP in three is a woman.

The front page banner from the Soviet newspaper, *Pravda*

Minorities

Although the USSR is officially an atheist country there are several different religious groups within its population. These religious groups and the many different national groups (see Population Survey) each make up a small proportion of the total Soviet population, and are referred to as 'minorities'.

NATIONAL MINORITIES

Question: 'When is Russia not Russia?'
Answer: 'When the word Russia is used to refer to the whole of the USSR.'

As we have already seen, within the USSR there are over 100 different national 'minority' groups (USSR Census 1979). The Russians are the largest group (see page 77) and the Yukghirs (about 600 people who live in northern USSR) are the smallest. Each of these varied national groups is allowed to keep its own culture, national costumes, folk customs, and in many cases its own distinctive language. There are over 100 different languages in the Soviet Union.

The various national groups are united by the one-party political system of communism which operates throughout the whole country, run by a government in which the fifteen National Republics are represented. Although many of the national groups have their own language, their own radio and television programmes, and their own newspapers, Russian is taught as a common language in most secondary schools throughout the country, and several newspapers such as *Pravda*, and many television and radio programmes, can be received anywhere in the USSR. Minority groups are also united by a feeling of national pride in the country's social, economic, sporting and space achievement.

Nationalist Problems in the USSR

Although the Government of the USSR has allowed a fair amount of freedom to the various 'nationalities' to develop their cultural identities, there are nevertheless some problems which arise concerning the 'national minorities'.

1. *'Russification'*. There have been protests in some regions that the largest group, the Russians, are taking over in some of the smaller nations. For example, between 1960 and 1980 the number of Russians in the Estonian Republic increased by about 70% because many Russians moved there to take up important jobs. Russians now make up about 25% of the population of Estonia.

2. *Language*. Since most of the books, magazines and papers about new scientific and technological developments are in the Russian language, those written in a 'minority' language tend to have less impact.

3. *Population*. There is some concern within the Russian Republic that although at present it has the largest population, the birth rate has slowed down considerably, while the birth rate of several nationalities in the south, such as the Uzbeks and Kazakhs, has increased.

4. *National identity.* The Soviet Government has strongly resisted demands from national groups for greater political freedom and self-determination beyond the present official representation in the Soviet Government. In 1979–80 nationalist movement leaders in Ukraine and Estonia were tried and imprisoned.

RELIGIOUS MINORITIES

Religious Activity

Easter is Celebrated. The Russian Orthodox Church celebrated Easter on April 26th. Patriarch Pimen performed the service at Moscow Cathedral, calling on all people of good will to oppose the revival of the Cold War.

(*Soviet Weekly*, May 1981)

Tatyana Burdina's father was a priest in Siberia, but she never thought of working in the Church herself. She graduated from a music college and wanted to teach. But now here she was, part of the first group of girls to be accepted into the Leningrad Theological Academy, training to be a choir leader for the Orthodox Church.

(*Guardian*, November 1979)

How is it that in the Soviet Union, a country whose official Government policy is atheism, such religious activities can take place?

There are several reasons for this. Article 52 of the 1977 draft of the Constitution of the USSR states that:

Worshippers in a Russian Orthodox Church in Moscow

'Citizens of the USSR are guaranteed freedom of conscience, that is, the right to profess any religion and perform religious rites or not profess any religion, and to conduct atheistic propaganda, shall be recognised for all citizens of the USSR. Incitement of hostility and hatred on religious grounds shall be prohibited. The church in the USSR shall be separated from the State and the school from the church.'

There have been determined efforts by various religious groups to survive, despite large-scale closure of churches in the 1920s and 1930s and also under **Khrushchev's** Premiership in the late 1950s. There are strong religious traditions in the USSR of the various religious minority groups, the most widespread of which are Russian Orthodox (about 30 million), Islamic (Muslim) (about 40 million) and Catholic (about 4 million).Despite the separation of Church and State in the USSR there are some common aims: for example, the Russian Orthodox Church and **Stalin** were joined in patriotism when German troops invaded the Soviet Union during World War 2. Also, both the Government and Church are concerned at present about certain increasing social problems such as divorce.

Some of the issues concerning Government and religious groups in the USSR are listed below.

1. *Government control.* Although there is not the same widespread persecution of religious

USSR
Churches/Religions

Russian
orthodox

Georgian
orthodox

Armenian
Gregorian

Roman
Catholic

Evangelical
Lutheran

Baptist

Moslem

Jewish

Buddhist

(Full statistics in *USSR in Figures 1977*
Statistika Publishers, Moscow)

groups now that there was in the early days of the new communist rule in the Soviet Union, the Government still keeps a close control on religious activities. A Government body, the Council of Religious Affairs, oversees all religious activity. There is no religious instruction in schools and congregation members have to be officially registered to attend church, while buildings used for religious purposes have to be given official clearance.

2. *Government concern over interest in religion.* Although official Government control is tight, it is, nevertheless, necessary for officials to remind people that 'it can sometimes be observed that there is an intention in some films and television

to give religion an unjustifiably broad showing, which could even be put down to admiration of religious ceremonies and church life'.

(Pravda, March 1979)

Also, 'Religious extremists and fanatics ... Jehovah's Witnesses, Pentecostalists, unregistered Baptists, and some Catholic priests in Lithuania ... are trying to evade civil duties and violate the order of our society.'

(Kommunist, March 1980)

3. *Numbers involved in religion.* Official statistics show that the number of adult people who regularly attend church is only about 10% of the population, and only about 2% of young people under the age of 20 claim religious belief. However, there have been some signs that recently more young people have become interested in religion: for example, the number of students attending colleges which give religious training in the USSR has increased by about 30%.

4. *Islamic 'revival'.* Most of the Soviet Union's 40 million Muslims live in central and southern USSR and have official acceptance of the Islamic faith. Because of their large numbers, and the fact that many of the USSR's southern neighbouring countries are Muslim, the Soviet Government has had to be diplomatic towards its own Muslim population in view of the Islamic 'revival' in Iran, and the movement of Soviet forces into Muslim Afghanistan.

5. *Flight of the Jews.*

'In scarcely any case is the religious problem so closely bound up with the national, as with the Jewish minority in the USSR.'

(Religious Minorities in the Soviet Union, a minority rights group)

The Jews in the Soviet Union have had greater difficulties than most other groups, Because of their identification with Israel, and the strong close religious links of the Jewish faith, the Jewish religion in the Soviet Union is seen as an obstacle to the progress of communism. In the early years of Soviet communism many Jewish schools and synagogues were closed, and many Jewish customs were forbidden. Because of the pressures in the USSR, many Jews apply to leave the country but often visas are refused. These refusals have been strongly condemned as a denial of human rights by successive

governments in the USA, where many Jews live. In 1971, the USA was in a position to bargain with the USSR because the USSR needed to import American grain. To obtain the trade, the Soviet Government agreed to allow over 10 000 Jews to emigrate (previously only a few hundred per year had left). In 1973 this number was increased and over 30 000 Jews left, while in 1979 over 50 000 Jews left. By 1980 about 250 000 Jews (an eighth of the total number of Jews in the USSR) had left, with about 200 000 settling in Israel where they now make up about 5% of the population. The departure of such a large number of people from the country gives the Soviet Government concern because many are skilled people.

Questions

1. How are the different national minority groups brought together in the USSR?
2. Explain what is meant by 'Russification'.
3. What does the Soviet Constitution state about religious freedom?
4. Why might the Soviet Government be concerned about the Islamic 'revival' in Iran?

Problems of Consumers

'The stores are always out of something, low on something else, sometimes rationing flour, meat or butter.'

'The Soviet Union has one of the industrialised world's worst distribution and retail trade systems – shortages of sheets, underwear or children's shirts.'

'We have money but nothing to buy.'

These brief quotations illustrate some of the problems in the State shops which affect ordinary families in the Soviet Union (see also the *Woman's Realm* extract on p. 80). Each large block of flats has its own selection of shops, and large cities also have huge department stores like the famous GUM in Moscow.

Wherever they shop, queuing is part of the daily routine for most Soviet shoppers. Many of them carry a shopping bag or briefcase around with them simply in the hope that something worth buying will appear in the shops. When a shop does have supplies, a queue forms quickly,

Shoppers in the GUM Department Store in Moscow

Another major problem for the Soviet consumer is the poor quality of many of the goods in the shops. Clothes and shoes are poor compared with Western standards and usually leave a lot to be desired in terms of style and colour. Household appliances such as fridges and washing machines are old-fashioned and unsophisticated and Soviet shoppers prefer to buy imported goods when available. As a result, a huge 'black market' dealing in imported products exists in Soviet cities. This black market is illegal but the authorities usually turn a blind eye because it helps to fill the gaps in the Soviet system, reduces the effects of shortages and makes the life of the consumer more bearable. Western tourists to the Soviet Union sometimes experience this black market at first hand when they are approached and asked to sell their clothes, particularly denim jeans which are highly prized in the USSR, for very high prices.

and is usually joined by many who do not even know what is on sale until the information is passed back by word of mouth from those at the front. It is assumed that there must be something worth queuing for so shoppers get in line first and ask questions later.

The shopper in the USSR must also carry cash for shopping at all times because there are no cheque-books or credit cards. Hire-purchase is not available on most items, only on poorer-quality goods such as radios and televisions which are old-fashioned and do not sell well.

The list of scarce items is practically endless. They are not permanently out of stock, but their appearance is unpredictable – toothpaste, towels, axes, locks, vacuum cleaners, kitchen china, irons, rugs, spare parts for any gadget from a toaster or a camera to a car, stylish clothes or decent footwear, to mention only a few listed in the Soviet press. Travelling in the provinces I have also noticed the lack of such basic food items as meat. In cities like Nizhnevartovsk and Bratsk during winter, people had become so accustomed to that fact that the meat departments of food stores had simply shut down.

(Hedrick Smith, *The Russians*, Sphere Books 1976, p. 83)

'A trifle large, but still a brand name!'

WHY DO THESE PROBLEMS EXIST?

Most of the problems are the result of the emphasis, in the long-term economic development of the USSR, on the expansion of heavy industries such as steel and shipbuilding which are vital to the security of the Soviet Union. This emphasis, begun by Stalin in the

1930s, continues today. In spite of improvements in the quality and supply of consumer goods in recent years, military spending still dominates the Soviet economy and interferes with plans to raise the standards for consumers.

Much more investment is needed in industries which make consumer goods. For this, greater priority needs to be given to civilian spending; at present the armed forces have first call on money and workforce. Also, the USSR needs increased access to Western technology. But the signs are that the Government is reluctant to move very far from its militarist outlook which is to give overwhelming priority to protecting the security of the USSR from outside attack. The system of centralised planning, which leads to over-production of some items and under-production of others is yet another cause of the problems, in spite of recent attempts at improvement. And the inefficiencies in the distribution and retail system (mainly due to transport difficulties) magnify the problems.

Questions

1. What are the main problems facing consumers wishing to buy goods in Soviet shops?
2. Why is there a 'black market' in many Soviet cities?
3. Explain the causes of the problems facing consumers.
4. Use the extract from the *Observer* Magazine to compare shopping in the USSR with shopping in your own area.

When you first walk out (from your hotel), you'll be overwhelmed by the numbers of people walking around: even early on a Monday morning, when British cities would be half dead, the Moscow shops are crowded with people. Inside GUM, which stands alongside Red Square opposite the Kremlin and is usually described as a department store but is in fact a three-tiered covered bazaar containing dozens of different little shops, it looks every day like Christmas Eve in the West. People were actually queueing to buy shoes at 9.30 a.m.

The queue is almost as noticeable a feature of Moscow as the Kremlin (it has been estimated that the average housewife queues for two hours a day). This is partly because of the system: one must queue once to select one's goods, a second time to pay for them and a third time to collect them. But mainly also because of the shortages.

You'll know when a sudden supply of sought-after goods has become available by spotting that half the people in sight are carrying a supply of them. I was surprised to find at 11 p.m. one night that every second woman on the Metro was carrying either a large carton of washing powder or a big box of soap. One Sunday afternoon person after person had a string bag full of lemons. Many men carry large, plastic briefcases, which give them an earnest, professional air, but these are most likely to be carried for shopping.

(*Observer* Magazine, July 1980)

2. The Economy

The Planned Economy: State Control

THE SYSTEM IN THEORY

'The foundation of the economic system of the USSR is socialist ownership of the means of production in the form of State property (belonging to all the people), and collective farm and cooperative property.'

(Article 10, 1977 Constitution)

'The land, its minerals, waters and forests are the exclusive property of the State. The State owns the basic means of production in industry, construction and agriculture; means of transport and communication; the banks; the property of State-run trade organisations and public utilities, and other State-run undertakings; most urban housing; and other property necessary for State purposes.'

(Article 11, 1977 Constitution)

The 1977 **Constitution** of the USSR gives a clear indication of the importance of State control of the whole economy of the Soviet Union. The State (on behalf of the people) owns the nation's factories, farms, shops and transport systems and has complete control over them.

The Soviet economic system differs from that of Western countries in several other ways. There is no need for high spending on advertising because of the State's control of all aspects of the economy. Competition between different firms producing similar products does not exist, again because the State is the only producer. Special offers, reduced prices and seasonal sales are not necessary because of the lack of competition. There is no emphasis on the selling of consumer goods the way there is in the West. This aspect of the economy is given low priority. The State tries to produce good-quality goods to sell at the lowest possible prices to the people.

All the most important decisions on the economy are taken centrally in Moscow by the Council of Ministers (see page 106) and the **Politburo**. The State Planning Commission (**GOSPLAN**) has overall responsibility and, in theory, has the job of arranging for the production, distribution and selling of every single item from matches to machinery. It is also responsible for ensuring a regular supply of all the raw materials needed by industry. The diagram below shows how GOSPLAN controls all aspects of the Soviet economy.

The State lays down targets of production for every industrial and agricultural unit in the country. A **five-year plan** outlines the progress

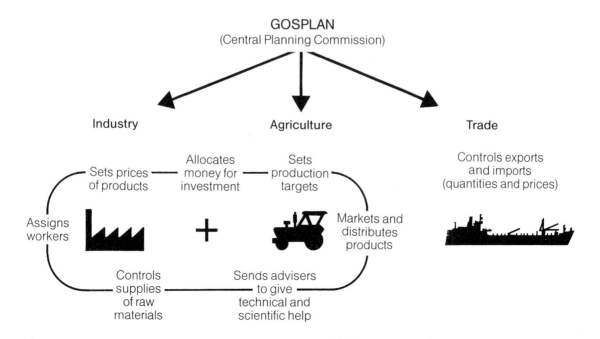

GOSPLAN
(Central Planning Commission)

Industry   Agriculture   Trade

Sets prices of products — Allocates money for investment — Sets production targets

Controls exports and imports (quantities and prices)

Assigns workers

Markets and distributes products

Controls supplies of raw materials — Sends advisers to give technical and scientific help

being aimed at over that period of time, and each five-year plan is sub-divided into annual plans setting targets for factories and farms.

HOW THE SYSTEM DEVELOPED

The modern system of Soviet centralised State planning based on the five-year plans was first introduced by **Joseph Stalin** in 1928. At that time the Soviet economy was weak and was based on agriculture rather than industrial strength. Stalin introduced the new system of central control in order to produce an economic revolution which would modernise the USSR and strengthen it against possible attack from the capitalist West. The State would direct the whole economy as if the Soviet Union was one gigantic firm producing many different products.

Stalin pushed through his plans ruthlessly, and a great deal, including the lives of millions of people, was sacrificed to the aim of strengthening the USSR. The five-year plans concentrated on the development of heavy industry and energy supplies, including coal, oil, and electricity. Materials for construction, such as steel, cement and timber, and the production of machinery were also given high priority in an attempt to catch up with the advanced industrial countries. The production of consumer goods which would improve the standard of living of the Soviet people was considered less important. In spite of this, and the human cost of Stalin's policies, there can be little doubt that, after the temporary interruption of World War 2, these policies laid a firm foundation for tremendous industrial development in the Soviet Union.

THE SYSTEM IN PRACTICE: ACHIEVEMENTS AND PROBLEMS

The figures in the table show that although there have been variations in the success rates of different parts of the economy, the general picture is one of tremendous progress and

The Soviet achievement, 1928–80

	1928	1940	1950	1960	1970	1980
Electricity (*billion kW h*)	5.0	48.3	91.2	292.3	740	1295
Steel (*million tonnes*)	4.3	18.3	27.3	65.3	116	148
Oil (*million tonnes*)	11.6	31.1	37.9	147.9	353	603
Gas (*million cubic metres*)	0.3	3.4	6.2	47.2	200	435
Coal (*million tonnes*)	35.5	116.0	261.1	509.6	624	716
Cement (*million tonnes*)	1.8	5.7	10.2	45.5	95.2	125
Motor vehicles (*thousands*)	0.8	145.4	362.9	523.6	916	1327
Tractors (*thousands*)	1.3	31.6	116.7	238.5	459	not known
Leather footwear (*million pairs*)	58.0	211.0	203.0	419.0	676	744
Television sets (*thousands*)	–	0.3	11.9	1726.0	6 700	7500
Domestic refrigerators (*thousands*)	–	3.5	1.5	529.0	4 100	5900
Grain (*million tonnes*)	73.3	95.6	81.2	125.5	186.6	189
Vegetables (*million tonnes*)	10.5	13.7	9.3	16.6	21.2	25.9
Meat (*million tonnes*)	4.9	5.0	4.9	8.7	12.3	15.1
Milk (*million tonnes*)	31.0	29.4	35.3	61.7	83.0	90.7
Eggs (*billions*)	10.8	12.2	11.7	27.4	40.7	67.7

development. The table clearly illustrates the concentration of effort on the heavy industries and energy supplies, the late development in industries producing consumer goods, and the continuing weakness of the agricultural sector of the ecnomy.

The economic revolution begun by Stalin and continued, with modifications, by his successors has brought about the transformation of the USSR from an economy based almost entirely on agriculture to that of a modern industrial nation with many successes in technological and scientific progress. Examples of Soviet economic and industrial achievement abound. But the picture is not entirely rosy: the Soviet economy suffers from several major difficulties, the solutions to which will not be easily found.

1. The system of centralised planning which dominates the economy ensures that little or no initiative is left to individual managers and industrialists. This system favours cautious methods and approaches, and means that industry prefers to follow the older, well-tried methods rather than experiment with new ideas. As a result, the economy suffers from inflexibility: it is not able to respond to changes in consumer demand when they occur. Over-production of other items for which there is growing demand, is a regular feature in the economy, even today.

Attempts to decentralise economic control by means of Regional Economic Councils (introduced in 1957 by **Khrushchev**) and other reforms have resulted in some increased flexibility, but the major decisions are still made in Moscow.

2. The difficulty of improving the standard of living of the Soviet people by increasing the production of consumer goods remains. After a period of rapid growth in the 1960s and early 1970s the slowing of economic growth has led to a slowing down of improvements in standards of living for the people. Soviet consumers, who are increasingly demanding a greater variety and a regular supply of well-designed good-quality goods in the shops seem likely to be disappointed for some time to come, particularly if the greater priority given to military spending continues.

3. The greatest weakness in the overall economic performance – the wide and unpredictable variations in agricultural production – remains. Apart from meaning that the USSR is unable to produce enough food to feed the people and livestock, the weaknesses in agriculture also affect other areas of the economy and have meant that targets of production have had to be revised downwards several times in recent years.

4. The Soviet economy uses up huge quantities of raw materials every year. Supplies of coal, iron ore and oil have been readily available, but in the near future these supplies will be exhausted, so new sources of raw materials are having to be developed and exploited. These new sources are available within the USSR, notably in Siberia, but only at great cost and with great difficulty because of the remoteness and hazardous weather conditions.

Questions

1. Explain the importance of GOSPLAN in the Soviet economy.
2. Why did the earlier five-year plans concentrate on the development of heavy industry and energy supplies?
3. Using the information in the table 'The Soviet achievement, 1928–80' describe the main achievements in the Soviet economy.
4. What are the four main problems in the Soviet economy today?

The Economy in Action

We can get an insight into the Soviet economy by examining how two large industrial plants are organised and how they operate.

Case Study: The Belarus Tractor Factory in Minsk

This factory located in Minsk is one of the largest producers of agricultural machinery in the Soviet Union. It employs about 25 000 people and produces 90 000 tractors every year. The factory's output is determined according to a five-year plan agreed to by the factory and the Government. This fixes the monthly and yearly work schedules. The Deputy Director of the factory described his production targets to an American journalist as follows:

'We have a five-year plan, a yearly plan and a monthly plan. If we set the goal of 90 000 tractors in a year, that works out to roughly 330 a day. We have to work rhythmically, turning out the prescribed number every day. If we only make 100 today, we simply can't make 560 tomorrow.'

Minsk Tractor Works, Byelorussia

The workers work a two-shift system from 7.40 in the morning till midnight and are paid on average 205 roubles a month for a 41-hour week. The wages are fixed according to a 'piecework' rate, which depends upon the quality of work and the number of pieces produced. Those workers who exceed their production targets receive a bonus at the end of the year. This is called the 'thirteenth pay'.

If a worker has a grievance he or she can complain to their trade union but these unions are organised and controlled by the State and, as a result, serious disagreements between management and workers are very rare. Almost every aspect of an employee's life centres on the factory. The factory provides nurseries and summer camps for workers' children. Holidays to Black Sea and Baltic holiday resorts are organised by the factory. There is a factory 'palace of culture' with theatrical facilities and a large sports stadium. Factory canteens sell very cheap meals and a factory apartment, including heating, electricity and telephone, costs only 12–15 roubles a month.

Case Study: The Lenin Komsomol Car Factory in Moscow

Like the tractor factory in Minsk this is another huge industrial plant. Its main product is the 'Moskvich', a popular Soviet family car. The production targets for this are of course fixed by a five-year plan. Workers are paid according to work done and receive on average about 190 roubles a month. They are encouraged to work harder by posters and slogans on the factory walls.

Again like the tractor factory and many other large Soviet factories this is more like a 'company town' than an ordinary factory. It has its own construction department to build flats for its workers. It has nurseries and creches for workers' children and holiday homes on the Black Sea and in the countryside near Moscow. It has an ice-rink, dance-hall, theatre-concert hall, swimming pool, games hall and sports stadium.

There are special grocery shops on the factory premises so that workers can avoid some of the queues which are so common for Moscow's shoppers. Also workers can get priority in buying a car from their own factory: instead of the usual waiting time of over a year, employees can buy a car after only six months waiting.

Questions

1. Explain the importance of Government planning for the tractor factory.
2. Make use of the case studies of the tractor and car factory to write a note describing how workers' wages are assessed in the USSR.
3. 'Almost every aspect of an employee's life centres on the factory'. Use the two case studies to explain this statement.

AGRICULTURE: LIFE IN THE COUNTRYSIDE

Before the Russian Revolution in 1917 most of the land in the USSR belonged to a small number of landowners. After the Revolution these large estates were taken from the landowners and the land was distributed among the peasants. For a period of about ten years the land was left in peasant hands. From 1928 onwards the peasants were encouraged – in many instances this had to be done by means of force and a great deal of suffering – to give up their private plots of land and join together in large farms owned by the State. This was known as **collectivisation** since the peasants had grouped their small farms into large collective units.

The form of agricultural organisation set up during the 1930s is still basically the pattern of organisation in the countryside today. There are two types of farm in the USSR: the **collective farm** (kolkhoz) and the **State farm** (sovkhoz).

The Collective Farm

There are about 30 000 collective farms in the USSR. Although these vary in size, they are much bigger than farms in most of Europe, being on average about 6000 hectares (15 000 acres) in size. Usually each farm will cater for two or three villages. The land in the collective, like all land in the USSR, belongs to the State and is leased to the farmers. The collective is run by a committee which is elected by all the members of the farm. All the equipment, farm buildings and most of the livestock are owned and operated jointly by the collective. Farmers are allowed to keep a small private plot of land and a few animals for their own use.

The produce of the collective is disposed of in a number of ways:

1. a portion of the produce is allocated to the State as a form of taxation,
2. some of it is used to buy new machinery, livestock and seed and to pay for the running costs of the farm,
3. the remainder of the produce may then either be sold to the State or in the local market or else distributed among the members of the collective.

The money obtained from the sale of the remainder of the produce or the produce itself forms the income for the collective and therefore each farmer is either paid in the form of cash or produce.

The amount 'paid' to each farmer depends upon the amount and type of work done. This is calculated according to what are called 'work-day units'. The number of units allocated depends upon the amount of work done and the skill involved in doing that work. At the end of the year each farmer's work-day units are added up and divided according to the total income of the farm. During the 1960s a new system of payment began to be used in the collective farms. Farmers began to receive monthly money payments which were in the form of advances against their annual income. In addition the farmers were guaranteed that these payments would conform to a minimum wage so that each farmer would be sure of a certain level of income.

Of course, the farmers are also entitled to the income from their private plots. Although these private plots only account for a small percentage of the agricultural land in the USSR they account for a large proportion of the country's produce. During the 1970s the private plots provided about 17% of the Soviet Union's total agricultural produce. In particular, they provide a large share of the country's potatoes and vegetable produce and of the dairy cattle, pigs and sheep.

The State Farm

There are about 17 000 State farms in the USSR. These tend to be larger than the collective farms. They are owned and operated by the State and the workers are paid employees just as in large industrial plants. Because of this the State farms are sometimes called 'agricultural factories'. They are run by managers who are appointed by the Ministry of Agriculture, not elected as in the collective, and all the produce is taken by the State.

The number of State farms in the USSR has been increasing and the number of collectives has been declining. The number of collective farms reached a peak in 1940 when there were 235 000 and this has fallen to about 30 000 today. In 1950 there were only about 5000 State farms but this has now reached 17 000. The reduction in the number of collectives has resulted from a policy of amalgamating them into larger farms. The increase in the number of State farms is mainly due to this being the form of organisation that has been used when new land

A Soviet State Farm

was opened up for farming, as in the Virgin Lands scheme (see page 96).

In addition to the collective and State farms there are still some individual peasant farms but these are usually in remote areas where the population is too widely scattered to allow for collectivisation.

Living Conditions

Living conditions vary considerably throughout the Soviet countryside but, with few exceptions, standards of living are distinctly poorer in the countryside than they are in the towns and cities. Despite attempts since the 1960s to improve conditions in the villages, there are still many examples of considerable rural poverty. A study published in the Soviet Union in 1979 revealed that in the area of Novosibirsk only 9% of the families in the country areas had piped water in their homes and only 4% had drains. Partly because of this poverty many people, especially the young, are leaving the countryside to find work in the towns and cities. The latest census of the Soviet Union showed a flow of 15.6 million people from the countryside in a period of nine years.

Case Study: Life in the Soviet Countryside

Sergei and Matryona Plakhov work on a large State farm outside Moscow. Sergei is responsible for the up-keep and maintenance of the fleet of tractors on the farm and at busy times he helps out as an extra tractor driver. His wife, Matryona, works with a team of other women doing various jobs on the farm, the type of work depending on the time of year. They are paid a wage by the State, like factory workers.

The Plakhov family live in a new block of flats in a small town. Because the town has been built to house and serve the workers on the State farm, it is known as an 'agro-town'. Here the Plakhovs can enjoy most of the modern amenities to be found in the cities: shops, schools, kindergartens, clinics, laundries and even a small cafe-type restaurant.

Sergei and Matryona used to live and work in a more remote collective farm, in the district where they were both born and brought up. Sergei's parents still live and work there, Matryona's parents were, however, both killed by the Germans during the 'Great Patriotic War'. Sergei's parents live in a traditional village wooden house, although it has recently been modernised when the village was supplied with piped running water and electricity.

It was the poor standard of living on the collective farm that made Sergei decide to leave to work on a State farm. Sergei and Matryona grimly remember what conditions were like in the countryside when they grew up during the 1950s and 1960s. Peasants on collective farms were given poor prices for their produce. They were not given State pensions and a guaranteed minimum wage until the 1960s and they were even forbidden to have an internal Soviet passport, which is needed to move around the country. By the mid-1970s, when Sergei and Matryona decided to move to the State farm, conditions had begun to improve, but not enough to keep many younger people on the land.

The Plakhovs still feel that life in their 'agro-town' is below city standards and younger people still leave to work in the city. The eldest of the Plakhov children has recently left home to live in Moscow where he has a job in a car factory. However, his younger brother hopes to go to agricultural college and become a farm administrator and possibly even manager of a State farm. The Plakhovs feel that their move has been worthwhile. They have a better income, a

— Помогла бы, внучка, репку вытянуть...
— Так у вас же мышка есть!

Рисунок Г. АНДРИАНОВА

The Soviet magazine, *Krokodil*, satirises the generation gap between an old peasant woman and her idle granddaughter who is dreaming of the bright lights. The girl refuses to help gather in the crop of turnips.

94

more modern house, their children have a better education. But, like their fellow residents in the flats, they miss their private plots. Flats don't have vegetable gardens far less room for a cow and two pigs. However, land is being set aside on the outskirts of the town for allotments and the Plakhovs hope to benefit from this. The Plakhovs like working on the land. It is what they have always done. But along with their fellow workers they sometimes feel that if they and their farm manager were left to get on with farming, without outside advice from party officials and others, they would be able to produce more and get better bonuses.

Questions

1. What is meant by 'collectivisation'?
2. Explain the main differences between collective and State farms: refer to size, management and methods of paying farmers.
3. What is the importance of the private plot in Soviet agriculture?
4. Explain the point of the Soviet cartoon on page 94.

ECONOMIC DEVELOPMENT

What is BAM?

The Baikal–Amur Mainline railway (BAM) is one of the biggest industrial and engineering developments ever to take place in the USSR. Begun in 1975, and completed in October 1984, the railway line runs eastwards from Lake Baikal, through eastern Siberia for a distance of about 3000 kilometres to Komsomolsk-on-Amur, near the Pacific Ocean. It is the second trans-Siberian railway to be built.

Constructing the BAM railway line, 1981

Construction Problems

The railway line is being built through some very difficult countryside where the engineering problems include laying the track through thick forest ('taiga'), across marshland, and over many rivers. As the weather can be extremely cold and unpleasant, and the construction work is very far from main population areas, it is difficult to get workers to come to this area. Much of the basic construction work is done by groups of **Komsomols** (Communist Youth Party members) who volunteer to work on the project for several months at a time. The cost of the whole project will be thousands of millions of roubles.

Why is this Railway Line Important to the USSR?

There are several reasons why the Soviet Government has supported this very expensive development:

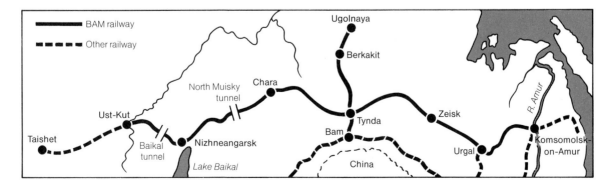

1. It will allow the Soviet Union to open up vast mineral wealth (oil, coal, copper, iron ore and tin) in eastern Siberia.

2. Much timber from the huge forests of Siberia will be transported along this line.

3. Planners have laid out schemes for several new industrial centres along the route.

4. An area of about 600 kilometres wide on each side of the line has been zoned for economic development.

5. New towns and communities are planned for the area.

6. This second trans-Siberian railway will help to increase imports and exports through the Soviet Union's Pacific coast seaports.

7. The new railway line runs parallel to, but further north than, the present trans-Siberian railway line. This takes it further away from the Soviet–Chinese border and therefore further away from possible Chinese attack.

Questions

1. What problems have had to be overcome to build the BAM railway line?
2. In what ways should BAM help Soviet trade?
3. What military advantage is there in building the railway line further north than the present line?
4. In what ways should BAM help in the development of Siberia?

Soviet Agriculture: The Eternal Problem?

One of the most serious problems facing the USSR for many years has been its inability to produce enough food to feed its people. For a Superpower like the Soviet Union which prides itself on its economic achievements, failures in agriculture have been a great embarassment and a continuous problem. The most serious difficulty is in grain production, although the performance has also sometimes been poor in vegetable and dairy production. Shortages of grain in one year lead to shortage in livestock, meat and eggs the next. For the Soviet people the main effect is shortages of essential foodstuffs in the shops, and long queues to snap up supplies when they do become available. The USSR often has to import huge quantities of grain to compensate for unreliable production.

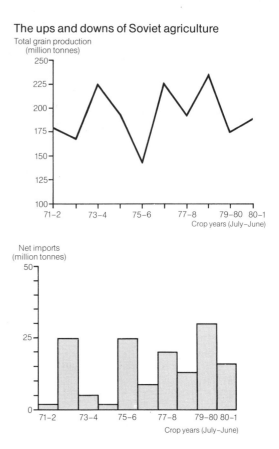

The ups and downs of Soviet agriculture

CAUSES OF THE PROBLEM

Production problems resulting from the climate are an obvious cause of the USSR's poor agricultural performances. Much of the country's arable land lies in the far north where huge variations in seasonal temperatures and erratic rainfall result in fluctuations of as much as 40% in harvest yields from one year to the next. Farmers in other areas such as Kazakhstan have to battle against the extreme conditions of temperatures of $-40°C$ and severe snowstorms in winter, and long dry spells and high winds which produce regular duststorms in summer.

In 1954 Premier Khrushchev introduced a scheme to cultivate an area of approximately 36 million hectares of previously undeveloped steppe in Kazakhstan and Siberia. He regarded cultivation of these 'virgin lands' as being very important in the effort to produce more food for the Soviet people. In spite of the extremes of weather conditions in these areas the scheme had some success in the 1950s, but by 1962 the failure of the Virgin Lands scheme to live up to earlier expectations was one of the reasons for Khrushchev's downfall.

Investment in the area has continued,

Transport problems in Siberia

however, and as a result of this, coupled with great human effort and the use of advanced technology to minimise soil erosion and climatic problems, the Virgin Lands are still of great importance to Soviet agriculture. Today, the farms of the Virgin Lands supply about one-third of the Soviet Union's grain. Output still fluctuates widely, however, and failures of the grain harvest in Kazakhstan have been one of the reasons for the Soviet Government's need to buy grain from abroad in recent years.

The climate is a factor which is obviously beyond the control of any government, but other problems make the situation worse.

President **Brezhnev** ordered that investment in agriculture should be a major priority (as did Khrushchev before him). During 1980, agriculture received 27% of all new capital invested in the Soviet Union, yet the grain harvest of 181 million tonnes was 54 million tonnes short of the target. Unfortunately, the problems have their origins in Stalin's policies which saw the destruction of the most experienced farmers (the kulaks) and the slaughtering of huge numbers of livestock. Fifty years later the USSR has still not managed to recover from the damage done to its agriculture during the rush to 'collectivise'. By the time of Stalin's death in 1953 the USSR's grain production averaged only 88 million tonnes, and food production per head of population was no higher than it had been in 1928.

Soviet agriculture also suffers from lack of investment: not enough money has been invested in tractors, machinery and modern scientific aids, with the result that farming methods in many cases are old-fashioned and inefficient. More than 25% of the Soviet workforce is employed in agriculture, compared with 4% in the USA where farms are highly mechanised. Soviet farms also suffer from the fact that the people working on the land are not always the most suitable for increasing production. In recent years young able-bodied workers have taken their skills to urban areas where they can find greater opportunities and escape the hardships of the countryside. Those who remain behind are predominantly old, female and lacking in necessary skills such as tractor driving and knowledge of the best use of fertilisers and pesticides.

The problems are made even worse by the shortage of spare parts for tractors, combine harvesters and other machinery. Although the USSR is the world's largest producer of tractors, the tractors are not very reliable and are liable to break down when they are most needed: for example, during the sowing, reaping, ploughing and harvesting times when they should be working hardest.

Rural land-use in the Soviet Union

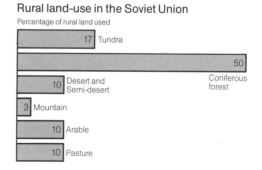

Percentage of rural land used

17	Tundra
50	Coniferous forest
10	Desert and Semi-desert
3	Mountain
10	Arable
10	Pasture

Even when things go right and the grain yield meets the target set, there are problems of transport and distribution. Much of the Soviet Union's grain comes from the distant areas of south-east Russia, Western Siberia and Kazakhstan, and this means long and expensive rail journeys to markets. The long distances involved, coupled with poor weather and inefficient transport, mean that much-needed food often gets held up on farms or in railway yards where it rots or is destroyed by vermin. The poor standard of rural roads, which are often dirt tracks that turn to mud during autumn rains, is a further drawback for Soviet agriculture.

The result of all these problems is that in the poor years the Soviet Government has to buy grain on the world market. In effect this usually means that they have to buy from the USA, with obvious implications for Soviet prestige. This also makes them very vulnerable: for example, in 1980 President **Carter** stopped shipments of US grain to the USSR following the invasion of Afghanistan.

PRIVATE PLOTS

The picture of weaknesses in agricultural production and supply would be even worse without the important contribution of the peasants' private plots. Article 13 of the 1977 Constitution states that 'Citizens may be granted the use of plots of land, in the manner prescribed by law, for a subsidiary small-holding (including the keeping of livestock and poultry), for fruit and vegetable growing or for building an individual dwelling.' The Government encourages the peasants to develop their plots, and productivity is much higher than on the State or collective farms. It is estimated that these plots, which account for about 3% of the total cultivated land in the USSR, produce nearly one-third of the country's milk and meat, one-third of vegetables, more than one-third of eggs and almost one-fifth of wool, and are also the main suppliers of potatoes. But private plots make no real contribution to solving the grain shortages, as they account for only 1% of the total grain production.

Some Soviet farmers spend more time looking after their private plots than working on State or collective farms, and earn large sums of money by selling their produce in local markets.

SOLUTIONS?

'Collective farms and State farm workers! Increase the efficiency of production! Make better use of land, machinery and fertilisers! Maximum care and attention to the future harvests!'

(*Communist Party slogan, November 1980*)

The difficulties facing Soviet agriculture are so great that this appeal to the peasants by the Communist Party is unlikely to have any major impact until the Government itself solves the many problems undermining the Soviet agricultural effort. Until then, it seems likely that in order to feed the people, the Government will have to accept the vital role of the peasants' plots and, in the worst years, the need to buy supplies from a rival Superpower.

The Soviet leadership recognises the problem. President Brezhnev has invested huge amounts of money and effort in an attempt to increase production. And in 1980 he promised rural workers more and better housing, better amenities, more shops and recreation facilities in an attempt to persuade them to work harder on the land. But recognising the problems is only a start to finding solutions, and agriculture will probably remain a painful thorn in the flesh of the Soviet Government for the forseeable future.

Questions

1. Why is there concern in the USSR about the level of agricultural output?
2. Which products are in short supply?
3. Describe the main problems which affect the USSR's agricultural performance.
4. Explain the importance of 'private plots'.
5. What solutions to the country's agricultural problems have been proposed by the Soviet Government?

Developments in Siberia

INTRODUCTION: THE IMPORTANCE OF SIBERIA

The development and exploitation of the huge mineral wealth of the Siberian wastelands is likely to be of crucial importance to the USSR for many years to come.

The Soviet Union is by far the world's largest individual oil-producing country, but it faces serious energy problems in the 1980s. It has enormous known oil reserves but there are great difficulties in finding the oil, getting it out of the ground and transporting it to where it is needed. Rising petrol prices (doubled between 1978 and 1980), the shelving of plans to increase car and truck production, and lengthy appeals in *Pravda* to save energy indicate that the Soviet Union needs to locate and develop new energy resources quickly.

The main reason for this energy problem is geographical. Most of the USSR's population and industry are in the western (European) half of the country. The major oil reserves and the areas most likely to yield new supplies in the future lie thousands of miles away in Siberia. Transporting the oil from its source to where it is needed requires more railways and pipelines than the Soviet Union has or will be able to build in the near future. Reserves of natural gas and coal (the USSR is estimated to have reserves capable of lasting 350 years) are also located in Siberia, where distance and climate combine to make exploitation difficult.

The reasons for the USSR's need to develop its Siberian resources are obvious. But the methods being used are under criticism from conservationists and others both within and outside the Soviet Union. The official view is that the Siberian developments represent a tremendous achievement by Soviet technology in the battle against the wilderness. This view is presented in Government reports and publicised in official publications and newspapers. The extracts given below are from the magazine *Soviet Union*, printed in Moscow and delivered to over 100 countries throughout the world. They outline the official view of the Soviet Government.

The opposing view – that the Siberian developments mean destruction and pollution of the environment – is presented in extracts from a recent book, *The Destruction of Nature in the Soviet Union* by Boris Komarov. The author is a Soviet ministry official in close touch with scientific and political affairs, who has therefore used a pseudonym. His manuscript, smuggled out of Moscow, stresses the destructive nature of the Siberian developments.

THE OFFICIAL VIEW

'The tundra is desolate and forbidding. Yet today the preparatory work for a massive offensive against Siberia's natural riches is being carried out. Builders are erecting modern blocks of flats in Nadym, a city where an industrial supply centre for the Siberian gas deposits is arising. Electricians are stringing high-voltage power lines. A railway line leading to Urengoi is under construction. Pipes for the big gas pipelines that are being laid are delivered here from Siberian rail junctions.'

(*Soviet Union*, No. 3 1977)

'Urengoi, where development of a large natural gas deposit has begun, is situated in one of the harshest, most forbidding places in the world. So far, this is a roadless area that can be reached only by air – and the 'air-lift' is operating at full capacity. Medvezhye, a town standing in what was a desolate waste only a short time ago, is slightly west of Urengoi. Nadym, further west, has 20 000 inhabitants. This area is now at the centre of big economic projects. Nadym, situated near the Arctic Circle, is a modern town of builders, transport workers and gasfield workers. Factories which make structural elements and industrial equipment have been built.'

(*Soviet Union*, No. 3 1977)

'The State allocates large sums for the Siberian development programme. Construction work is much more expensive than the average in the Soviet Union because the builders usually have to begin from scratch. In many places the rail and motor road network is only being developed – yet building materials, equipment, manufactures and foodstuffs have to be delivered.

The town of Cheryomushki cost 40 million rubles to build. It costs the State between 25% and 30% more to build 1 square metre of housing here than it does in Leningrad. It costs 5 times as much to build 1 km of surfaced motor road in Siberia than in the central areas of the European part of the Soviet Union.'

(*Soviet Union*, No. 6 1978)

'Today West Siberia is the country's largest construction site. It is no exaggeration to say that mankind is following developments there with special attention. it is now generally recognised that Siberia can supply much not only to the Soviet Union but to the world. The American magazine 'Newsweek' said not long ago that "The Russians have tamed Tyumen after eighteen years of superhuman effort that brought concrete roads, oil rigs and pipelines, boom towns and traffic jams to a silent wilderness three times the size of Texas."'

(*Soviet Union*, No. 8 1978)

'In winter there are the severe frosts. In summer the swamps are a source of countless midges. A successful battle against the midges is waged in the towns but they continue to be a problem at the extraction fields and pipeline projects. In Siberia, tens of thousands of eyes are focussed on the state of the winter roads across snow and ice, on the cloud cover (work is inconceivable without help from aircraft) and on the dates when the rivers become free from ice.

The Urengoi–Chelyabinsk gas pipeline route crosses 123 rivers and streams and runs through swampland and water-logged countryside for nearly 1000 kilometres.'

(*Soviet Union*, No. 8 1978)

THE COST

'Siberia and the North include boundless plains, remote taiga, mountain ranges, and gigantic rivers and lakes. Here are found all our country's fabulous natural riches, about which every Soviet citizen hears from childhood onward. Much of this is true. Siberia is a unique chance for the Soviet system, a land where new relationships with nature could be built without repeating the gross errors of the past.'

(Komarov, *The Destruction of Nature in the Soviet Union*, Pluto Press, p. 112)

'Rivers large and small in Siberia and the North are being mercilessly mutilated by gold dredges. Picturesque and fertile valleys are being turned into dumps of gravel and shingle, and for hundreds of kilometres along their course the water is white or brown with roiled sand and silt. Even the simplest species of fish cannot survive in such water.' (p. 116)

'On the one hand, along the path of the Baikal-Amur-Mainline (BAM) can be found more examples of intelligent, sensitive treatment of the forest and the landscape as a whole than on any other building site of former times. Yet the scale of the destruction of nature around the railway exceeds anything previously known.' (p. 116)

'In Tynda heavy "smog" frequently descends in the winter . . . Since it is impossible to start their motors in the mornings, the drivers frequently let the vehicles run all night in neutral, and, of course, air pollution increases.' (p. 117)

'Mountain ranges large and small occupy a large part of the BAM region; but after clearing, the mountain forests hardly ever regenerate. The thin soil layer is easily eroded from the slopes after felling; the permafrost reaches the surface, and trees can hardly take root. Studies by botanists and forestry experts in Siberia have shown that barely 20% of all cleared forests have been restored throughout the whole north-east of Siberia.' (p. 118)

'Untouched Siberia is an illusion . . . industry is devouring the "green, fragile bosom of Siberia" from all sides, like sulphuric acid, and has already reached its radiant orb – Baikal . . . current methods for exploiting Siberia are ways to destroy it.' (p. 127)

Workers' temporary accommodation in Siberia

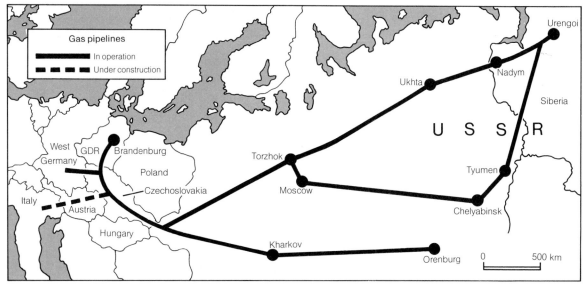

The gas pipeline from Siberia to Europe

Working Conditions in Siberia

Two bulldozers, one driven by Anatoly Tunguskov and the other by myself, set out from Nadym to accompany a column of 10 trucks, three tractors and two heavy-duty tractors. We were delivering four trailers, building material and fuel for the first group of settlers. We covered about 40 kilometres the first day. There were many lakes on the way. The first two days went without a hitch. On the third day Anatoly's bulldozer went through the ice. We had a tough time dragging it out. When we finally pulled it out it was all covered with ice. We had to change the oil and grease, and that took a long time. We started out again in the morning, but as luck would have it Anatoly went through the ice again. This time it was in a shallow place and we soon dragged his bulldozer out .... We reached the site of the future town on the evening of the seventh day. We cleared an area for the trailers and a landing place for helicopters. When the unloading was finished the trucks and tractors set out on the return trip. Fifteen of us remained there.

(Extract from the diary of bulldozer operator
Nikolai Kravchenko)

From the mid-1980s Western Europe will benefit from the enormous supplies of natural gas discovered in Siberia. West Germany (1981) and France (1982) have already signed agreements to import the gas by way of a huge new pipeline which is under construction.

Work starts on pipeline to bring Siberian gas to Western Europe

THE SOVIET Soyuzintergazstroi association has started construction of the Urengoi-Uzhgorod pipeline over 2900 miles long, which will deliver West Siberian gas to the Soviet border, ready for export.

An agreement on the basic terms of Soviet natural gas deliveries to the West German firm Ruhrgas was signed in Essen last week.

The 25-year agreement envisages the deliveries of 10 500 million cubic metres of gas a year, starting from 1984.

The agreement follows long-term mutually beneficial economic co-operation between the two countries.

(*Soviet Union*, 28 November 1981)

Questions

1. Why is the development of the Siberian resources vital to the USSR?
2. What arguments might someone speaking for the Soviet Government use to support the view that developments in Siberia are a great achievement?
3. Describe the main criticisms put forward by those opposed to the Government's methods of developing the area.

The Salyut 6: Soyuz space complex

On Board Space Station Salyut 6
Among its technological features were two docking ports (to receive visiting spacecraft, including a new class of fully automated, unmanned supply ship) and large, winglike solar panels (to convert sunlight into electricity). Salyut carried myriad scientific and observational gear, notably a multi-spectral camera, telescopes for scanning the heavens, kilns for processing materials in zero-g atmosphere, even a small garden for growing plants in orbit.

The space station had plenty of amenities for its occupants: 20 viewports, exercise machines for physical fitness and, for the first time in orbit, an on-board television receiver to help relieve the long hours of isolation. The monotony was also broken by the visits of other cosmonauts, who arrived in Soyuz ferry craft, the workhorses of the Soviet manned space effort. In addition to regular supplies, they carried mail, such special snacks as fresh borsch, strawberries and quail pâté, not to mention a guitar. Though Salyut was designed to last 18 months, it continues to function thanks to on-board repairs by the cosmonauts plus periodic shipments of fuel, food, water, air and equipment.

The achievements of the Soviet Union in space technology have been outstanding. In 1957 the first *Sputnik* was launched into space, and Yuri Gagarin completed the first manned flight into space in 1961. By mid 1981 the 20-tonne *Salyut 6*, launched in 1977, was still in orbit and had set a space endurance record for cosmonauts of 185 days on board. The Soviet Union had also launched *Cosmos Number 1277* as part of its continuing space research programme which costs about £10 billion per year.

In some other areas of transport, there have also been technological advances. *Comet* hydrofoils have been used in the USSR for over 20 years. Now an ocean-going hydrofoil is being developed which can withstand force 6 storms. A new type of nuclear powered ice-breaker is being developed for the Soviet Arctic fleet. The new ship will be 40 000 horse power and will be a combined ice-breaker and cargo ship.

There have also been achievements in other areas of industrial technology:

1. The USSR is a world leader in power engineering and has built up a wide-ranging electricity supply industry.

2. The steel industry produces huge volumes of various types of steel, while a special material, titanium armour, has been developed for tanks and other military vehicles.

3. Development of Siberian oil and natural gas is taking place in spite of problems with climate, transport and remoteness (see previous unit).

PROBLEMS OF SOVIET TECHNOLOGY

'The USSR is still short of energy, rail transport is chaotic, and not enough metal is being produced. Meat and milk are scarce while common consumer items such as toothpaste, washing powder, needles and thread and babies' nappies are hard to find.'

(*President Brezhnev, speech to Supreme Soviet 1979*)

President Brezhnev added that these 'bottlenecks and shortages', despite large investments, caused imbalances in the economy.

In 1980 Mr Kirilenko, a senior member of the Politburo, criticised the Soviet machine tool industry, which is the biggest in the world. 'It uses too much steel, is not sufficiently automated, and fails to produce what the customers need.'

Some of the problems facing Soviet technology can be seen by looking at the pattern of the country's trade. The USSR imports many items such as computers, automation products, food technology, electronics and chemical equipment, while it exports mainly raw materials. In 1980 almost half of the Soviet imports from West Germany were machinery and transport equipment, while three-quarters of Soviet exports to West Germany were raw materials such as oil and natural gas.

In vehicle production, although Soviet cars such as the Volga are produced, these do not have the refinements of Western cars and are not modern enough to sell abroad. In 1971 the Italian company Fiat was called in to set up a huge car factory at Togliatti to produce Lada cars which could compete in foreign markets because they were up to date in design. By 1980, 750 000 Lada cars were being built of which about 10 000 were sold abroad where their relatively inexpensive price is attractive to buyers. In the same year, a deal was signed with West Germany's Porsche car company to improve the Lada, with the aim of producing a new model by 1984. One problem of importing technology on a big scale is that often foreign firms will be required to do repairs and supply spare parts for several years.

Why are there Problems in Soviet Technology?

Despite large-scale investment and some notable achievements, particularly in space technology, there are still problems with Soviet technology. The main reasons for this are listed below.

1. Much of the money for research and development is directed to special areas such as space, heavy industry, military.

2. Changes in consumer demand are not always recognised quickly enough to alter the production.

3. Some planning for consumer goods aims at quantity targets rather than quality.

4. Poor transport systems such as railways can mean hold-ups in delivery of raw materials and finished products.

5. 'New technology and new ideas are being introduced far too slowly.' (Yuri Andropov, 1982)

Questions

1. Give four examples which show that some technology in the USSR is very advanced.
2. What problems concerning technology have been mentioned by Soviet leaders?
3. In what ways do Soviet imports reflect the problems of industrial technology?
4. State the main reasons for the problems facing Soviet technology.

3. The Political System

The Soviet Constitution and the CPSU

THE CONSTITUTION

At a special session of the **Supreme Soviet** of the USSR on 7 October 1977 President Leonid Brezhnev announced that after widespread discussion throughout the USSR a new **Constitution** was about to be adopted, on the sixtieth anniversary of the Great October Socialist Revolution.

Like the USA, the Soviet Union has had a written Constitution since its foundation. The first Soviet Constitution of 1918 was rewritten in 1924 and again in 1936 to take account of developments in the USSR. The latest Constitution follows the general ideas and principles of the previous Constitutions. It sets out the principles and aims of the organisation of the socialist State, and defines the rights, freedoms and obligations of its citizens.

The document emphasises the leading and guiding role of the Communist Party of the Soviet Union (**CPSU**) which is presented as the nucleus of the political system. The 174 Articles of the 1977 Constitution cover almost every aspect of life in the USSR and are much too long to print here. A selection of the most important Articles is given below and should be referred to in conjunction with other chapters and units on the Soviet Union.

Introduction

'The supreme goal of the Soviet State is the building of a classless communist society in which there will be public, communist self-government. The main aims of the people's socialist State are:

to lay the material and technical foundation of communism,

to perfect socialist social relations and transform them into communist relations,

to mould the citizens of communist society,

to raise the people's living and cultural standards,

to safeguard the country's security, and

to further the consolidation of peace and development of international cooperation.'

The Political System

'The USSR is a socialist State of the whole people, expressing the will and interests of the workers, peasants and intelligentsia, the working people of all the nations and nationalities of the country.' *(Article 1)*

'All power in the USSR belongs to the people...' *(Article 2)*

The Economic System

'The foundation of the economic system of the USSR is socialist ownership of the means of production in the form of State property (belonging to all the people), and collective farm and cooperative property.' *(Article 10)*

'The land, its minerals, waters and forests are the exclusive property of the State...' *(Article 11)*

'Earned income forms the basis of the personal property of Soviet citizens. The personal property of citizens of the USSR may include articles of everyday use, personal consumption and convenience, the implements and other objects of a small-holding, a house, and earned savings...' *(Article 13)*

Soviet Society

'The social basis of the USSR is the unbreakable alliance of the workers, peasants and intelligentsia.' *(Article 19)*

'In the USSR, State systems of health protection, social security, trade and public catering, communal services and amenities, and public utilities, operate and are being extended.' *(Article 24)*

'In the USSR there is a uniform system of public education, which is being constantly improved, that provides general education and vocational training for citizens, serves the communist education and intellectual and physical development of the youth, and trains them for work and social activity.' *(Article 25)*

Foreign Policy

'The USSR steadfastly pursues a Leninist policy of peace and stands for strengthening of the security of nations and broad international cooperation.' *(Article 28)*

'The USSR's relations with other States are based on observance of the following principles:

sovereign equality;
mutual renunciation of the use or threat of force;
inviolability of frontiers;
territorial integrity of states;
peaceful settlement of disputes;
non-intervention in internal affairs;
respect for human rights and fundamental freedoms;
the equal rights of peoples and their right to decide their own destiny . . .'   (*Article 29*)

Equality of Citizen's Rights

'Citizens of the USSR are equal before the law, without distinction of origin, social or property status, race or nationality, sex, education, language, attitude to religion, type and nature of occupation, domicile, or other status.'
(*Article 34*)
'Women and men have equal rights in the USSR.'   (*Article 35*)
'Citizens of the USSR of different races and nationalities have equal rights.'   (*Article 36*)

Basic Rights of Citizens

'Citizens of the USSR have the right to work (that is, to guaranteed employment and pay . . .).'   (*Article 40*)
'Citizens of the USSR have the right to health protection.'   (*Article 42*)
'Citizens of the USSR have the right to maintenance in old age, in sickness, and in the event of the complete or partial disability or loss of the breadwinner.'   (*Article 43*)
'Citizens of the USSR have the right to housing.'
(*Article 44*)
'Citizens of the USSR have the right to education.'   (*Article 45*)
'Citizens of the USSR have the right to enjoy cultural benefits.'   (*Article 46*)

Structure of the USSR

'The USSR is an integral, federal, multinational State formed on the principle of socialist federalism as a result of the free self-determination of nations and the voluntary association of equal Soviet Socialist Republics.'
(*Article 70*)
'Each Union Republic shall retain the right freely to secede from the USSR.'   (*Article 72*)

The Electoral System

'Deputies to all Soviets shall be elected on the basis of universal, equal and direct suffrage by secret ballot.'   (*Article 95*)
'Elections shall be universal: all citizens of the USSR who have reached the age of 18 shall have the right to vote and to be elected, with the exception of persons who have been legally certified insane.'   (*Article 96*)

The State Emblem of the USSR is a hammer and sickle on a globe depicted in the rays of the sun and framed by ears of wheat, with the inscription 'Workers of All Countries, Unite!' in the languages of the Union Republics. At the top of the Emblem is a five-pointed star.   (*Article 169*)
The State Flag of the USSR is a rectangle of red cloth with a hammer and sickle depicted in gold in the upper corner next to the staff and with a five-pointed red star edged in gold above them.
(*Article 170*)

THE COMMUNIST PARTY OF THE SOVIET UNION (CPSU)

'The leading and guiding force of Soviet society and the nucleus of its political system, of all State organisations and public organisations, is the Communist Party of the Soviet Union. The CPSU exists for the people and serves the people . . .'

(*Article 6, 1977 Constitution*)

In spite of the highly developed system of councils and committees which are a feature of the Soviet political system, real power lies with the CPSU. Members of the Party occupy the most important posts and have great influence throughout the political system. There are 17.5 million members of the Communist Party and 40 million Young Communist League members (aged 14–28). The Young Pioneers organisation caters for 25 million younger children aged 10–15. The Pioneers wear red scarves and have as their motto *Vsegda Gotov*: Always Ready.

Members of the CPSU are mostly young and male. To be accepted as a full member of the Party is a great honour and is only achieved after a period of one year's probation. Members must accept every decision and carry out every policy of the Party; if they fail to do so they may be disciplined or even expelled.

The CPSU has three main functions.

1. It decides the home and foreign policies of the Soviet Union. It is responsible for the targets set out in the five-year plans and also for the detailed policies of how these targets are to be achieved. It also makes decisions about the USSR's relations with other nations.

2. It is responsible for appointments to all the important jobs in politics, industry and agriculture. No one can reach a position of real responsibility and power without the approval of the Party.

3. It carries out the campaign of political education designed to foster the growth of 'unanimous opinion' throughout the Soviet Union. In doing so, its aim is to ensure that the opinions of the people reflect the wishes of the Soviet leaders in order to bring about the transition from a socialist to a communist society in the USSR.

The All-Union Party Congress (for representatives from all States of the Soviet Union) is the supreme organ of the CPSU. It meets every five years to hear reports from the Central Committee (the group of Party members who carry out its work between Congresses), to elect the Party Leader and the members of the **Politburo** (the small group of Party Leaders who control the work of the CPSU when the Central Committee is not in session). It is the Politburo which makes the most important political decisions and has the greatest political power in the Soviet Union.

Questions

1. Briefly describe the general contents of the 1977 Constitution.
2. Explain in your own words what the Constitution says about:
   (a) the economic system,
   (b) Soviet foreign policy,
   (c) equality of citizens' rights.
3. What are the main functions and responsibilities of the CPSU?

The Political System in Action
FEDERALISM

The USSR is a **Federal** system consisting of fifteen Union Republics. Each Republic has in theory a great deal of devolved power to carry out decisions and policies at local or Republican level. In practice, however, most of the important decisions are made in Moscow and government, therefore, tends to be very centralised.

Each Republic is divided into regions which are in turn divided into districts, towns, settlements and villages. At local levels citizens elect Soviets (councils) for two-year periods and these provide the means by which local government is carried out. At national level citizens of the USSR elect the Supreme Soviet of the USSR to provide national government.

THE STRUCTURE OF POWER

Although in theory the organisation of the Communist Party and of the Government is separate, in reality it is sensible to think of one overall structure in which the CPSU dominates or in Soviet terminology 'leads' and 'directs' the other.

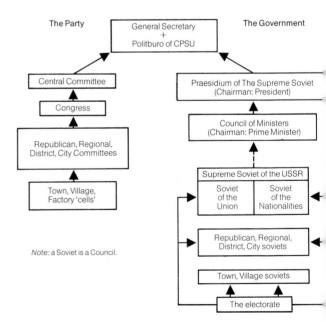

Note: a Soviet is a Council.

THE SUPREME SOVIET

According to the Constitution of the USSR the **Supreme Soviet** is 'the highest organ of State power' and has sole 'legislative power' in

The Supreme Soviet in session

government. In other words only the Supreme Soviet can in theory pass new laws and is equivalent to **Congress** in the USA, or to Parliament in the UK.

The Supreme Soviet is composed of two Chambers:

1. *The Supreme Soviet of the Union*. This body is elected on the basis of one 'deputy' per 350 000 of the population. There are 750 members of this Chamber. In as much as it represents the population of the USSR it is similar to the House of Representatives in the USA.

2. *The Supreme Soviet of Nationalities*. This body represents the Federal system of the USSR by giving equal representation to each of the fifteen Republics which make up the USSR. There are 750 members in this Chamber which includes 32 from each of the fifteen Republics. In as much as it represents the regions of the USSR it is similar to the Senate in the USA.

The Supreme Soviet is elected for a fixed term of four years. Of the 1500 deputies elected in March 1979, 34.8% were industrial workers, 16.3% came from collective and State farms and the rest came from higher occupational categories or were full-time Party officials. Not all deputies are members of the Party: in 1979 71.7% were CPSU members. Also in 1979, 67.5% of the deputies were male, 32.5% female and just over 20% were under 30 years old.

The Supreme Soviet meets in the Kremlin only twice a year for a few days at a time. As a result it has very little time for debating legislative proposals and although in theory it is the supreme legislative organ in practice it merely 'rubber-stamps' laws presented to it. However, the deputies are more involved in the work of the sixteen standing commissions attached to each Chamber and in recent years they have begun to discuss Government policies and performance more critically. In addition, like MPs in the UK, deputies are involved in constituency work helping the people they represent in dealings with officialdom. At its first meeting the Supreme Soviet elects a new Soviet government. This is called the Council of Ministers and the Chairman is the Soviet Prime Minister.

The Supreme Soviet also elects a Praesidium of 39 members which is responsible for acting when the Supreme Soviet is not in session. The head of the Praesidium is President of the USSR.

Questions

1. Describe the function and composition of the Supreme Soviet of the Soviet Union.
2. In what ways is the Supreme Soviet of less importance than the UK Parliament or the US Congress?
3. What kind of people become deputies to the Supreme Soviet?

ELECTIONS IN THE USSR

All candidates for election to the Supreme Soviet must be nominated by a representative group such as a trade union, factory, youth club or by the Party. In the 1979 election the candidates in each constituency were all unopposed but in theory there is no reason why more than one candidate should not be adopted. Not all candidates are members of the Party but no candidate who opposed or criticised the Party would be allowed to stand. A number of dissidents tried to be nominated in 1979 but without any success.

All citizens over the age of 18 have the right to vote and voting is by secret ballot. The turnout at elections is always high but in 1979 it was the highest ever with 99.99% of the electorate voting: only 24 000 voters did not vote. The vote in favour of the official list of candidates was almost as high as the turnout, with 99.8% and 99.91% vote for each of the two Chambers, the Soviet of the Union and the Soviet of Nationalities.

Elections: Two Different Views

The importance of the elections in the USSR is a subject of dispute. Here are two contrasting views: one from the Soviet Union and one from the West.

The Soviet View

'The principle of equality in voting is strictly observed. Each voter has only one vote.

Secrecy of voting is guaranteed to every elector. Only the voter himself is present in the booth or room where the ballot is filled in, and all ballots are dropped into a sealed ballot-box.

A candidate who has received more than half the votes is considered elected, provided that at least half the voters participated in the elections. Should no candidate receive a majority vote, fresh elections are conducted within a fortnight.

Elections to the Supreme Soviet of the USSR are always marked by a high degree of response from the population.'

(*USSR: Questions and Answers*, Novosti Press Agency)

'By their unanimous voting for the candidates, the Soviet People expressed complete support for the domestic and foreign policies of the Communist Party and the Soviet State.'

(The Soviet news agency TASS, on the 1979 election results)

'Soviet electoral law does not limit the number of candidates standing for election in one constituency. However, out of all the candidates proposed by the various organisations and groups of working people as possible nominees, as a rule only one runs for election in the given constituency.

Why is this so?

The reason for this is that in the USSR there are no rival social forces or Parties with opposing interests, who would advance different programmes and struggle for control of representative bodies. There is only one Party in the Soviet Union – the Communist Party. The people – workers, peasants and intellectuals – have entrusted this Party to represent their interests and aspirations. That is why candidates for the post of deputy in the USSR are people's candidates and are nominated on behalf of a single bloc of Communists and non-Party people. In these conditions there would be no sense in artificially splitting the vote among several candidates with a single platform and it has become traditional to run only one candidate.'

(*USSR: Questions and Answers*, Novosti Press Agency, 1967)

The View of a Western Critic

'In each polling station private voting cabins or rooms must be provided "for the filling up of their voting bulletins by the voters", to quote the election law. No one other than the voter is allowed in the voting room or cabin – exception only being made for the illiterate or physically handicapped who require assistance. These provisions are the essentials of any fair system of voting. But it is here that the importance of the single candidate becomes apparent. The voter is officially instructed to cross out the names of all candidates except the name of the one for whom he or she wishes to vote, and then to drop the ballot paper into the ballot box. But with one single name invariably on the ballot paper there is in fact nothing for the voter to cross out. All that the voter who is prepared to vote for the official candidate has to do is to drop the paper into the ballot box unmarked in any way whatever. It follows from this that people who in fact retire to the private cabin immediately draw attention to themselves since they can only wish to do so in order to cross out the single name on the paper or to write something on the ballot paper which will in some other way indicate dissent. Such an open indication of dissent, in a small district voting office, in the presence of the local party officials, or at least of the electoral commission officers, is an act of defiance which naturally enough few Soviet voters are anxious to commit.'

(Adapted from L. Schapiro, *The Government and Politics of the Soviet Union*, Hutchinson University Library)

Questions

1. Briefly describe voting in the USSR: refer to voting age, turnout, nomination of candidates and voting procedure.
2. Describe and comment on the main differences between the Soviet accounts of elections and that of the Western critic.

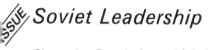

Soviet Leadership

Since the Revolution which brought the communists to power in 1917 the Soviet Union has had six leaders: **Lenin**, **Joseph Stalin**, **Nikita Khrushchev**, **Leonid Brezhnev**, **Yuri Andropov** and **Konstantin Chernenko**, the present leader. With the exception of Lenin, these men became leaders not because they were the heads of Government but because they were in control of

the Communist Party. Chernenko, as General Secretary of the CPSU, heads the Politburo, the most important and powerful group of politicians in the Soviet Union.

However, although the CPSU has been in power for over 60 years it has still not developed a tradition or procedure to provide for the succession from one leader to another. There are no formal elections; leaders 'emerge' because of support they have among different factions in the Politburo. The periods of strong leadership have been punctuated by periods of power struggle or periods of collective leadership. After Lenin's death in 1924 a power struggle took place between Stalin and Trotsky which eventually ended in Trotsky's expulsion from the Soviet Union in 1929 and assassination in Mexico in 1940. Stalin's death in 1953 was followed by a period of collective leadership from which Khrushchev emerged as leader. After a number of policy errors in foreign affairs and the economy, Khrushchev was forced to retire and once again a period of collective leadership led to the emergence of one strong leader: Brezhnev. When Brezhnev died in November 1982, he was quickly and smoothly succeeded by Yuri Andropov. However, within fifteen months Andropov had died, to be succeeded in February 1984 by Konstantin Chernenko. This showed that changes have taken place since Stalin succeeded

The Politburo 1980. Front row, left to right: Andrei Kirilenko, Mikhail Suslov, Leonid Brezhnev. Second row: Victor Grishin, Arvid Pelshe, Nikolai Tikhonov. Third row: Dmitry Ustinov, Yuri Andropov, Andrei Gromyko.

In February 1980 the Politburo of the CPSU consisted of:

L. I. Brezhnev	(*born 1906*)	General Secretary of the Central Committee of the CPSU
	(*died November 1982*)	and Chairman of the Praesidium of the Supreme Soviet,
		i.e. President of the USSR
A. N. Kosygin	(*born 1904*)	Chairman of the Council of Ministers, i.e. Prime Minister
	(*died December 1980*)	
A. A. Gromyko	(*born 1909*)	Foreign Minister
D. F. Ustinov	(*born 1908*)	Minister of Defence
Yu. V. Andropov	(*born 1914*)	Chairman of the Committee of State Security (KGB)
N. A. Tikhnov	(*born 1905*)	Deputy Chairman of the Council of Ministers
K. U. Chernenko	(*born 1911*)	
V. V. Grishin	(*born 1914*)	
A. P. Kirilenko	(*born 1906*)	
D. A. Kunaev	(*born 1912*)	
A. Ya Pelshe	(*born 1899*)	
G. V. Romanov	(*born 1923*)	
M. A. Suslov	(*born 1902*)	
	(*died January 1982*)	
V. V. Shcherbitsky	(*born 1918*)	

Lenin. No longer are there violent struggles for power as with Stalin and Trotsky. However the uncertainty about Brezhnev's and Andropov's successor emphasised that the CPSU still has no constitutional method of choosing a Party leader.

A brief study of the list of the Soviet Union's most powerful politicians in 1980 shows another problem about Soviet leadership today. The Politburo is made up of old or relatively old men: by 1980 the average age was 70. When Andropov succeeded Brezhnev he was 68, ten years older than Brezhnev was when he became Party leader. When Chernenko became Party leader he was 72, making him the oldest person ever to be selected for the country's most important position. These changes in the Soviet leadership do not overcome the problem that sooner or later a whole new generation of political leaders will assume power in the Soviet Union.

A VIEW OF THE KREMLIN

While Adam Munro was changing trains at Revolution Square before 11 a.m. that morning of 10th June, a convoy of a dozen sleek, black, Zil limousines was sweeping through the Borovitsky Gate in the Kremlin wall . . . . The Soviet Politburo was about to begin a meeting that would change history.

The Kremlin is a triangular compound with its apex, dominated by the Sobakin Tower, pointing due north. On all sides it is protected by a fifty-foot wall studded by eighteen towers and penetrated by four gates.

The southern two-thirds of this triangle is the tourist area where docile parties troop along to admire the cathedrals, halls and palaces of the long-dead tsars. At the mid-section is a cleared swathe of tarmacadam, patrolled by guards, an invisible dividing line across which tourists may not step. But the cavalcade of hand-built limousines that morning purred across this open space towards the three buildings in the northern part of the Kremlin.

The smallest of these is the Kremlin Theatre to the east. Half exposed and half hidden behind the theatre stands the building of the Council of Ministers, seemingly the home of the government, in as much as the ministers meet here. But the real government of the USSR lies not in the Cabinet of Ministers, but in the Politburo, the tiny, exclusive group who constitute the pinnacle of the Central Committee of the Communist Party of the Soviet Union, or CPSU.

The third building is the biggest. It lies along the western facade, just behind the wall's crenellations, overlooking the Alexandrovsky Gardens down below. In shape it is a long, slim rectangle running north. The southern end is the old Arsenal, a museum for antique weaponry. But just behind the Arsenal the interior walls are blocked off. To reach the upper section, one must arrive from outside and penetrate a high, wrought-iron barrier that spans the

The Kremlin

- Square of the 50th Anniversary of the October Revolution
- Sobakin Tower
- Revolution Square
- State department store GUM
- Lenin Mausoleum
- Red Square
- Alexandrovsky Gardens
- Old Arsenal
- Palace of Congresses
- Kremlin Theatre
- Kremlin Palace
- Borovitsky Gate
- Kremlin Embankment
- Moskva River

N / W—E / S

ISSUE

gap between the ministers' building and the Arsenal. The limousines that morning swept through the wrought-iron gates and came to rest beside the upper entrance to the secret building.

In shape the upper Arsenal is a hollow rectangle; inside is a narrow courtyard running north/south and dividing the complex into two even narrower blocks of apartments and offices. There are four storeys including the attics. Halfway up the inner, eastern office block, on the third floor, overlooking the courtyard only and screened from prying eyes, is the room where the Politburo meets every Thursday morning to hold sway over 250 million Soviet citizens and scores of millions more who like to think they dwell outside the boundaries of the Russian empire ....

The room in which the Politburo meets in the Arsenal of the Kremlin is about fifty feet long and twenty-five feet wide, not enormous for the power enclosed in it. It is decorated in the heavy, marbled decor favoured by the Party bosses, but dominated by a long, T-shaped table topped in green baize.

(Frederick Forsyth, *The Devil's Alternative*, Hutchinson 1979, pages 46–7)

Questions

1. What is the importance of the Politburo and General Secretary of the CPSU?
2. 'The CPSU has still not developed a procedure to provide for the succession from one leader to another.' Comment on this statement with reference to the history of Soviet leadership.
3. What is the main problem about the top Soviet leadership at present?

Protest in the USSR

FREEDOM TO PROTEST

'Citizens of the USSR enjoy full social, economic, and personal rights and freedoms, proclaimed and guaranteed by the Constitution of the USSR and by Soviet laws.'

(*Article 39, 1977 Constitution*)

'"the rich could afford what the poor could not." It is precisely this injustice we strove to abolish . . . to secure every person's right to work, health care, material provision in old age, and housing . . . and to put the political rights of citizens on a material foundation.'

(Leonid Brezhnev, *Socialism, Democracy and Human Rights*, Pergamon Press 1981)

In the USSR, as in many other countries, people are free to complain and protest about many topics. Indeed *Pravda* receives hundreds of letters a day, many complaining about problems such as long queues, shortages of certain goods, housing defects. Despite this official toleration of protest, the Government does not allow certain types of protest or dissent.

WHAT IS DISSENT?

Dissent is protest against the basic political and moral beliefs of a country. The person who dissents, the **dissident**, not only disagrees with the Government about its beliefs, but also writes articles in newspapers and magazines to publicise these views. In the USSR these unofficial writings, *samizdat*, are published secretly and passed round by 'underground' methods since such writings are banned by Government officials who see them as attacking the State and betraying the Soviet Union.

111

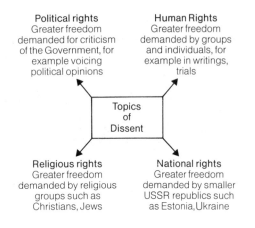

Political rights
Greater freedom demanded for criticism of the Government, for example voicing political opinions

Human Rights
Greater freedom demanded by groups and individuals, for example in writings, trials

Topics of Dissent

Religious rights
Greater freedom demanded by religious groups such as Christians, Jews

National rights
Greater freedom demanded by smaller USSR republics such as Estonia, Ukraine

THE PROGRESS OF DISSENT

The dissident groups and their support in the USSR increased in the 1960s after Premier Khrushchev criticised the policies of the former leader Joseph Stalin. When two dissident writers, Andrei Sinyavsky and Yuli Daniel, were put on trial in 1966, several thousand people in the USSR signed petitions supporting them. When, in 1975, the USSR signed the Helsinki Agreement, which included Soviet guarantees of human rights, the dissident movement seemed safer. Indeed, a small unofficial group led by Dr Yuri Orlov was set up to check that the Soviet Union was keeping its promise on human rights. Even at that time, however, the dissident movement was mainly made up of writers, scientists, and university teachers and there was not widespread support from large numbers of ordinary Soviet citizens.

By the late 1970s, President Brezhnev and the Soviet Government began to put stricter controls on dissidents and their writings, which were often smuggled out of the Soviet Union. Prominent dissidents such as Alexander Ginzburg, Yuri Orlov, and Anatoly Scharansky were arrested. The Soviet branch of Amnesty International was closed, and in 1980, before the Olympic Games in Moscow, a number of dissidents, including scientist Andrei Sakharov, were forcibly moved from Moscow. Only a few people signed forms protesting about Sakharov's move to 'internal exile'. Despite this, dissent continues and recent *samizdat* writings have included items on greater freedom for trade unions in the USSR and greater independence for the Republic of Estonia.

TREATMENT OF DISSIDENTS

The Soviet Government view of protest is that it should be made through official means such as Communist Party meetings, and therefore 'unofficial' protest is banned. Those who make such protest are often treated severely. In some cases, dissidents have been removed from their jobs or have been moved ('internal exile') to other areas of the Soviet Union. These areas are usually 'closed' to foreign visitors, and visas to visit them are almost impossible to obtain. In other cases, such as that of writer Alexander Solzhenitsyn, the dissidents may be officially exiled from the USSR altogether. Some dissidents are arrested and put on trial, accused of 'anti-Soviet propaganda'. They may be imprisoned or sent to labour camps, or even to psychiatric hospitals on the grounds that they are mentally ill. The harshness of the treatment of some dissidents has often led to criticism of the USSR, especially by the people in the USA.

'We believe that with each country, concern for human rights should begin at home. There should be an end to privilege and exploitation. The establishment of socialist public ownership is the main guarantee of not only the political, but also the social and economic rights of man in the USSR.'

(President Brezhnev, *Socialism, Democracy, and Human Rights*, Pergamon Press 1981)

'I'm for human rights. That is an American position and I do not think we will ever retreat from it or ever should. There are no human rights under the Soviet Union, as we see them. What I believe is we do our utmost to bring about improvement in human rights in those countries that are aligned with us.'

(President Reagan, *Time*, 5 January 1981)

Internal Exile

The following description of 'internal exile' in the 'closed' city of Gorky was written by Andrei Sakharov in 1980.

The city of Gorky

'I live in an apartment guarded day and night by a policeman at the entrance. He allows no one to enter, but family members, with a few exceptions .... There is no telephone in the apartment. A radio-jamming facility has been set up in the apartment just for me. In terms of everyday life, my situation is much better than that of my friends sent into exile or, particularly, sentenced to labour camp or prison. I still do not know which branch of Government or who personally made the decision to have me exiled. Every time my wife leaves, I do not know whether she will be allowed to travel without hindrance, although she is not formally under detention.'

SOME DISSIDENT VOICES

Political

Alexander Solzhenitsyn

A Soviet writer and novelist who spent some years after the end of World War 2 in forced labour camps. His book *A Day in the Life of Ivan Denisovich* described conditions in one of these camps. Freed in 1956. Other novels banned in the USSR are *Cancer Ward* and *Gulag Archipelago*. Also wrote unofficial articles criticising the USSR over censorship. Awarded the Nobel Prize for Literature in 1970. Expelled from Soviet Union in 1974.

Alexander Solzhenitsyn

Statements

'The West is powerless, deprived of will and reason, practically on its knees, before the Soviet Juggernaut.'

'Western intellectuals are blind to the evils of Communism.'

'The Union of Soviet Socialist Republics should be dismantled and the Republic of Russia should go back to Orthodox Christian religion.'

'Fixed trials and fixed judges, who get instructions from political leaders, make a sham of Soviet justice.'

Human Rights

Andrei Sakharov

A Soviet nuclear scientist, 'father' of the Soviet Hydrogen bomb. Member of the Soviet Academy of Sciences. He was awarded the Nobel Prize for Physics in 1975. Supporter of human rights in the Soviet Union. Removed from his job as a nuclear physicist. Arrested in 1980, before Olympic Games, and 'resettled' in the city of Gorky, 400 kilometres east of Moscow.

Andrei Sakharov

Statements

'There are few people in the USSR who react seriously any more to slogans about building Communism.'

'All my activities stem from a desire for a free and worthy destiny for our country and our people. I consider the United States the leader of the movement toward a free society.'

'I don't find that socialism has brought a better social order.'

'The action against me is part of a widespread campaign against dissidents. Its specific cause was probably my statement about events in Afghanistan.'

Human Rights

Andrei Amalrik

Founder of one of the first underground dissident publications in the Soviet Union. Expelled from university in 1963. Arrested and sent into exile in Siberia. Went into voluntary exile in 1976. Killed in a car crash in Spain, in 1980, on his way to a meeting in Madrid to publicise how the Soviet Union had broken the 1975 Helsinki Agreement on human rights.

Andrei Amalrik

Statements

Became known world-wide with the publication, in 1970, of an essay 'Will the Soviet Union survive until 1984?'

'I have been against the Soviet system since I was a child.'

'The Soviet empire will collapse when the Kremlin is forced to withdraw its military divisions from the Warsaw Pact to fight a war with China.'

Nationalism

Mart Niklus

A language teacher from the Soviet Republic of Estonia, by the Baltic Sea. Imprisoned from 1958 to 1966. A leading Estonian dissident. Signed a 'Baltic Appeal' in 1979. Sentenced in Tallin, capital of Estonia, to fifteen years imprisonment for anti-Soviet propaganda.

Statements

The 'Baltic Appeal' demanded 'independence for the Baltic republics of Lithuania, Latvia and Estonia'.

Protested 'against the Soviet invasion of Afghanistan and the holding of the Olympic Games in Moscow.'

'I have been put in a cell with thieves, hooligans and other human outcasts.'

Religion

Gleb Yakunin

Set up a group called the Christian Committee for the Defence of Believers Rights in USSR in 1976. Not supprted by the official Orthodox Church. Arrested in 1980 for 'anti-Soviet propaganda' and sentenced to six years in a labour camp and five years in internal exile.

Statements

'The Christian Committee is to check and report on any abuses of believers' rights in the Soviet Union, and to advise believers of their legal rights. Our survey covers Russian Orthodox Christians, Roman Catholics in Lithuania, Seventh Day Adventists and other groups.'

Questions

1. Explain the terms 'dissent' and *samizdat*.
2. In what ways were tighter controls put on dissidents in the Soviet Union in the 1970s?
3. What types of treatment are given to dissidents who are found guilty of anti-Soviet propaganda?
4. Describe the restrictions placed on Andrei Sakharov during 'internal exile' in the city of Gorky.

4. International Involvement

Strategic Interests

AIMS OF THE SOVIET UNION'S FOREIGN POLICY

'Not war preparations that doom the peoples to senseless squandering of their material and spiritual wealth, but consolidation of peace – that is the clue to the future. The main line in the foreign policy of our party and government, is centred as it always has been on reducing the danger of war, and on controlling the arms race.'

(President Brezhnev, *Congress*, 26 February 1981)

The main aims of the Soviet Union's foreign policy, as put forward by recent Soviet leaders, differ from those of Lenin in the early days of the communist Government in the Soviet Union, when world war in support of the spread of world **communism** was put forward as a possibility. Recent leaders have adopted more peaceful aims.

USSR: Foreign policy aims

To avoid large-scale nuclear war which could destroy the USSR itself: 'peaceful co-existence'.

To build up military strength to defend itself against attack by, for example, increasing missiles, building up sea power.

To support socialist/communist revolutionary movements in various parts of the world such as Cuba, Vietnam, Mozambique.

To rival the USA in influence as a World Superpower, for example in the space race.

BACKGROUND

Even before the Revolution in 1917, the then leaders of Russia, the Tsars, were concerned about the possibility of attacks from the East and West. When the Bolsheviks gained power in 1917, their long-term aim of world revolution was held back by the immediate need to do something about the desperate poverty and weakness of the new communist State. They were also concerned about the protection of the Soviet Union from countries who were hostile to communism and were therefore possible enemies. For several years after the Revolution, the Soviet Union had very few allies. At the outbreak of World War 2, the Soviet leader Stalin signed a non-aggression treaty with Hitler's Germany in the hope that peace could be kept between the two powers. However, in 1941, German troops invaded the USSR and remained there until their defeat in 1945. The loss of some 20 million Soviet people during the German invasion left a lasting memory in the Soviet Union. After World War 2 the USSR gained control of several East European countries which became 'buffer' States between the USSR and the capitalist West. **COMECON** and the **Warsaw Pact** were set up to strengthen links between these countries and the Soviet Union. Despite the tensions of the period of the Berlin Blockade 1948–9 and the Cuban Crisis 1962 the Soviet Union has managed to achieve at least some of its four main foreign policy aims up to the present time.

PROBLEMS IN RECENT TIMES

Although the Soviet Union has succeeded in building up its power and avoiding major war, it nevertheless faces difficult problems in its foreign policy in the 1980s.

1. *Fear of encirclement.* An alliance of major military powers, such as the USA, Western Europe and China would mean that the USSR would have a potential ring of 'hostile' forces around it.

2. *Fear of isolation.* Large majorities in the UN General Assembly have twice recently criticised the USSR for sending troops into Afghanistan. Many of those voting against the USSR, were 'non-aligned' countries, who do not support either the USSR or the USA.

3. *Increasing border problems.* The dispute with China (see page 125) continues while the Muslim revival in Iran has not been in favour of the USSR. The presence of some 80 000 troops in neighbouring Afghanistan has not solved the rebel problem there, and there is continuing unrest in Poland (see page 123).

The USSR's fear of encirclement

Lined up against the USSR

4. *Detente in ruins?* In recent years the Soviet Union's relations with the USA have deteriorated with the USA's boycott of the Moscow Olympic Games in 1980 and a refusal to sign **SALT** 2. Also, a military build-up is proposed by the Government of the USA under President Reagan who has accused the USSR of building up its military power.

5. *Increasing costs.* The support and aid given to countries such as Cuba and Vietnam is a continuous strain on the Soviet economy. These costs are increased by the need to build up military forces to cover several frontiers at once. For example, the USSR has large numbers of troops and weapons on its Chinese and European borders. Also, the expense of military technological developments is increasing.

SOVIET INFLUENCE THROUGHOUT THE WORLD IN RECENT YEARS

Since the early 1970s the USSR has pursued its general foreign policy aims in many parts of the world, with varying success.

Eastern Europe

Although the East European countries are closely linked to the USSR through the Warsaw Pact and COMECON there have been strains and tensions among the members. In 1948 Yugoslavia, under President Tito, took an independent line from the rest of the East European countries. Romania has taken some independent initiative such as receiving a visit from China's Chairman **Hua** in 1978, and voicing criticism of Soviet actions in Afghanistan in 1980. The most serious strains occurred during 1956 when Warsaw Pact forces had to crush a revolt in Hungary, and again in Czechoslovakia

The USSR's areas of interest in the world

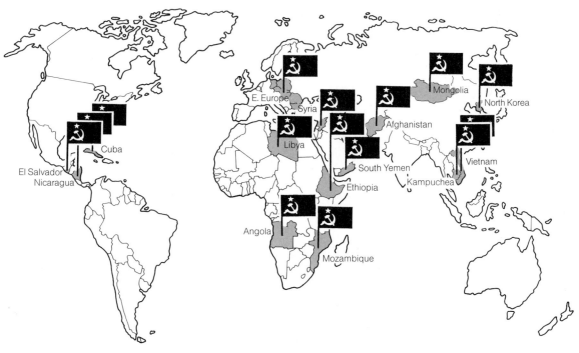

in 1968 (see page 123). In the early 1980s the unrest in Poland (strikes organised by the **Solidarity** trade union, and demands for reforms) led to fears by the leaders of the Soviet Union that the unrest might spread to other Warsaw Pact countries. Trade unionists and other groups in these countries might demand similar freedoms to those gained for a time in Poland (see page 124) before martial law was declared in 1981.

Western Europe

Relations between the USSR and Western European countries have often been dominated by the **Cold War** and the establishment of the 'iron curtain' between Eastern and Western Europe. Soviet foreign policy is aimed at preserving the present situation in Europe, with Germany remaining permanently divided into East Germany and West Germany. Although Warsaw Pact forces outnumber **NATO** forces, the Soviet Union has in recent years strongly condemned the possibility of neutron bombs being sited in Western Europe. The Soviet Union has suggested that there should be a freeze in the siting of medium-range nuclear missiles by both sides. The USSR would not place more SS-20 missiles or Backfire bombers (see page 121) in Eastern Europe if NATO agreed not to set up **Cruise missiles** and Pershing rockets in Western Europe.

Despite the military tensions between East and West Europe, there has been cooperation in terms of trade. West Germany is the Soviet Union's most important trading partner in Western Europe, and West German firms were involved in building the Siberia–Europe gas pipeline. Daimler Benz, the West German car company have been working with the Soviet motor industry since 1976 and in 1981 set up a permanent office in Moscow. In 1979 French-Soviet trade increased by 30%. France sells machine tools, compressors and electronic equipment to the USSR, and imports Soviet gas, oil and timber. Italy's Fiat car company built the Togliatti factory in the Soviet Union. This factory now produces Lada cars which sell all over Europe. Britain is about seventh in the list of importance of USSR trade with Western European countries. In 1980 British exports to the Soviet Union increased by 8% to £450 million while British imports from the Soviet Union fell by 5% to £786 million. In 1979, the British ICI company sold more than £20 million worth of items to the USSR.

The USA See page 13.

Central America

In 1959 **Fidel Castro** came to power in Cuba by overthrowing the Government of Cuba with the help of communist forces. After two years however, an invasion at the Bay of Pigs by

The nuclear balance in Europe 1981

USSR (Warsaw Pact)		Number of warheads	NATO		Number of warheads
All systems					
Missiles*	1277	1597	Missiles*	382	742
Europe-based nuclear-capable aircraft including:	4018	5031	Europe-based nuclear-capable aircraft including:	1170	1515
Long-range aircraft	913	1926	Long-range aircraft	246	459
Most deadly systems			Poseidon (*USA*)	40	400**
SS-20	160	480	SSBS 2 and 3 (*France*)	18	18
Backfire	100	400	Polaris (*Britain*)	64	64
Fencer	370	370	MSBS (*France*)	80	80
			F-111 (*USA*)	156	312
Total	630	1250	A-6E (*USA*)	20	40
			Total	378	914

*Excluding artillery and very short-range missiles.
**The USA has committed 400 Poseidon warheads to Saceur for European targeting. These are also counted against the American SALT 1.

(Adapted from the *Economist*, 16 May 1981)

opponents of Castro's communist Government was defeated and the Cuban leader appealed to the Soviet Union for aid. Soviet supply ships carried equipment and missiles to Cuba, and in 1962 President **Kennedy** ordered US Navy ships to blockade the route to Cuba to prevent Soviet ship reaching the island. This 'Cuban crisis' was very close to being a real war between the USA and the USSR.

Cuba is still given aid by the USSR and Cuban troops and technicians have helped support communist revolutions in various countries in Africa, such as Angola. The USSR supports Cuba by supplying materials, especially oil, at below world prices, and buying Cuba's sugar exports in return, and this is a heavy expense. In 1978 Soviet aid to Cuba was about $3 billion, a quarter of Cuba's total production.

In Nicaragua the Sandanista revolutionaries gained power and appealed to the USSR for aid, although, as with the socialist rebels in El Salvador, the Soviet Union has given little direct aid in this case.

Africa

In Africa the policy of the Soviet Union is to give aid indirectly, for example by economic cooperation with African governments through COMECON, or military and technical aid in the form of Cuban forces. Angola, Mozambique,

Algeria, Ethiopia and Libya all have close economic or military links with COMECON countries. In some cases the Soviet Union gives aid directly to African governments, for example military equipment to Angola and Mozambique to oppose South Africa.

In 1981 the Soviet Union issued a direct warning to South Africa to stop border raids on Mozambique and backed this up by sending Soviet ships into the Indian Ocean near South Africa.

South-east Asia

By far the most serious problem confronting the USSR in its foreign policy in South-east Asia is the continuing hostility of China to the Soviet Union (see page 125). Not only is China itself hostile to the USSR but, by signing a friendship treaty with Japan in 1978, it has caused the USSR to fear the build-up of an alliance between China, Japan and the ASEAN (Association of South-east Asian Nations: Thailand, Indonesia, Malaysia, Singapore and the Philippines). The USSR's own relations with Japan have declined in recent years owing to a dispute over the ownership of the Kurile Islands, north of Japan. Soviet influence is strong in the area, however, because of the USSR's alliance with Vietnam. There are now several thousand Soviet advisers

President Brezhnev (3rd left) and President Samora Michel of Mozambique meet in Moscow, 1980

in Vietnam, and Soviet ships use the Vietnamese ports of Danang and Cam-Ranh Bay. Several thousand Vietnamese troops are permanently based in Laos and Kampuchea.

Middle East

Soviet interest in the Middle East arises from several factors:

1. The Soviet Black Sea Fleet requires sea routes through the Mediterranean sea to reach the Atlantic and Indian Oceans, because many seaports in the Baltic Sea and further north are frozen during winter.

2. 60% of the West's oil is carried through the Gulf area from six Middle East countries, and this oil is vital to the economies of Western countries. In the event of any future East–West military confrontation, therefore, Soviet influence in the Middle East would enable the USSR to disrupt the passage of oil to the West.

3. After the Islamic Revolution in Iran there has been increasing Muslim influence in the Middle East. This could spread to the Soviet Union's large Muslim population.

4. The USSR supports Syria in its opposition to Israel although attempts to gain Arab friendship have proved difficult. For example, Egypt, once supported by the USSR, is now supported by the USA.

In pursuit of the aim of stability in the Middle East, President **Brezhnev** in 1981 offered to sign a treaty with the USA and China to respect the Gulf States' non-alignment with any major Power. The treaty aimed to prevent the setting up of foreign military bases in Gulf States, and to keep the use of sea bases in the Gulf area open to all. This suggestion was not agreed to by the other major Powers.

ALLIANCES

As part of its foreign policy, the USSR has formed alliances with a number of countries, mainly close to its borders.

1. Warsaw Pact (Warsaw Treaty Organisation, formed 1955)
A military alliance among the USSR, Poland, East Germany, Czechoslovakia, Hungary, Romania, Bulgaria, Albania. Albania withdrew in 1961.
Some of the problems arising in the alliance in the 1980s are as follows.

(a) *Finance*. The high costs of military expenditure are partly responsible for economic difficulties in some of the member countries such as Poland and the USSR.

(b) *Internal difficulties*. Problems arise when there are adverse reactions of member countries to invasions of each other's territory. This happened with the Hungarian uprising in 1956, and Czechoslovakian uprising in 1968. Similarly, differing attitudes among members towards Polish unrest in 1981 caused tension.

2. COMECON (Council of Mutual Economic Assistance, formed 1949)
An economic/trading alliance among the USSR, Czechoslovakia, Poland, Hungary, Bulgaria, Romania.
In 1950, East Germany joined, in 1962 Mongolia joined, in 1972 Cuba joined and in 1978 Vietnam joined. Albania joined in 1949, but left in 1961. There are also close links with Angola, Ethiopia, Laos and North Korea.

Questions

1. Describe the five main problems facing the Soviet Union in its foreign policy in the 1980s.
2. What trade links does the USSR have with Western Europe?
3. In what ways does the USSR give aid to African countries?
4. Why does the Soviet Union have a special interest in Middle East affairs?

Military Strength

'For the past two decades, the Kremlin leaders have been amassing arms in all categories – conventional and nuclear, short-range and intercontinental, undersea and airborne. They have built up the capability of waging everything from counterinsurgency warfare and paramilitary operations to blitzkriegs and nuclear Armageddons. The arsenal is out of all proportion to the Soviets' legitimate needs of self-defense.'

(*Time*, 23 February 1981)

This quotation sums up the American view of Soviet military strength and shows a fear that the USA has been falling behind in the arms race. How powerful is the Soviet military machine?

The USSR has certainly become a rival to the USA in terms of conventional armed forces and of nuclear weapons. It has also shown an ability to use this power throughout the world as indicated by the following two examples.

1. From 1977 to 1978 the USSR, in a massive movement by air and sea, supplied Ethiopia with about $2000 million worth of military equipment including aircraft, tanks and artillery.

2. In December 1979 the USSR launched a major military airlift into Afghanistan which was to deliver an estimated 85000 troops and equipment.

These two instances illustrate the ability of the USSR to transport huge quantities of troops and supplies, coordinate air and ground attacks and control military action on a distant battlefield via satellite communications systems.

The Soviet military machine

Strategic nuclear warheads	6 302
Strategic nuclear missiles	2 384
Submarines	370
Large warships	268
Tanks	48 000
Artillery	19 300
Combat aircraft	4 885
Manpower in millions	4.84

The Soviet Union has concentrated on Intercontinental Ballistic Missiles (ICBMs) and Submarine-Launched Ballistic Missiles (SLBMs). Soviet missiles tend to be less sophisticated than those of the USA but they are larger and heavier. Their warheads are up to three times the size of the Americans but they are less accurate.

The main ICBMs are the SS-17, the SS-18 and the SS-19. The SS-17 has a range of 10 000 kilometres and most have a MIRVed warhead (see page 68). The SS-18 is the largest Soviet ICBM at present. The SS-19 is the replacement for the older SS-11 which still forms a large part of the Soviet ICBM arsenal.

The USSR has more SLBMs than ICBMs. There are three types of SLBMs: the SS-N-6, the SS-N-8 and the SS-N-18.

The USSR has far fewer Strategic bombers than the USA. The two long-range bombers

The Soviet nuclear force

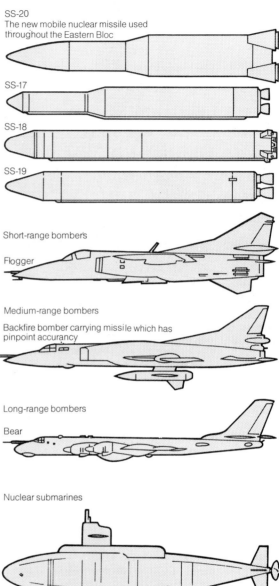

Missiles

SS-20
The new mobile nuclear missile used throughout the Eastern Bloc

SS-17

SS-18

SS-19

Short-range bombers

Flogger

Medium-range bombers

Backfire bomber carrying missile which has pinpoint accurancy

Long-range bombers

Bear

Nuclear submarines

used by the USSR are the Tupolev Tu-95 (Bear) and the Myasishchev M-4 (Bison). In addition to these the USSR has the highly accurate medium-range 'Backfire' bomber.

The USSR also has missiles with ranges of 3000 to 5000 kilometres. These 'theatre' weapons are intended for targets in China and Western Europe. The most important of them is the SS-20, which is a mobile missile carried on a tracked launch vehicle with a range of 5500 kilometres.

The Soviet battle cruiser, *Kirov*, in the Baltic

In addition to this nuclear arsenal the USSR also possesses, with her Warsaw Pact allies, a vast array of conventional forces and weapons. The USSR and the Warsaw pact greatly outnumber NATO in tanks, and since the 1970s the Soviet navy has been greatly strengthened.

A DIFFERENT VIEWPOINT

The Soviet armed forces are not without problems, however. The equipment has a number of faults. Tanks are liable to break down and their inside space is so cramped that their crew have difficulty if they are over 5 ft 5 in (1.63 m) tall. Members of the crew can only load the gun with their left hand.

An insight into Soviet military life was revealed in a book called *The Liberators* (Hamish Hamilton) written by a former officer of the Red Army who uses the code name of Victor Suvorov. Suvorov was a tank commander and in his book he tells of poor morale, defective equipment and major language difficulties among the different nationalities which make up the Red Army. The following extract comes from a review of his book in *The Observer*, October 1981.

His best story centres on a massive exercise, rehearsed for the General Staff and members of the Politburo to watch, in which a heavily reinforced army was to cross the Dnieper.

... The scheme for the Dnieper exercise was that the T-64s (tanks) of Suvorov's battalion would cross the river submerged, the tanks taking air through a snorkel device. But as all troops know, crossing a wide river under water requires luck and great care .... It is possible for an inexpert crew to drive them round helplessly in circles.

To make sure that this part went well thousands of troops were employed to pave the river bed with steel matting and build concrete furrows to keep the tanks running in a straight line: an operation that would be out of the question in war.

... A motor battalion was to move up to the river, covered by artillery and air bombardment. It would then secure a bridgehead into which Suvorov's tank battalion would be the first to cross .... According to the operation plan, when the infantry were halfway across, the guns should have switched to firing in depth. But the artillery showed no sign of letting up ... it was impossible for the armoured carriers to continue, and they started to circle in the water, crashing into one another in the current ....

When eventually the artillery, slowly and reluctantly, started to fire in depth, the battalion moved towards the bank. But not one carrier managed to get out of the water, because the guns had cut the opposite bank to pieces. Eventually the battalion commander did the only thing he could: he ordered the crews to get out and wade or swim ashore.

Later, says Suvorov, the exercise was shown on television: but with cuts by the censor to cover up the confusion.

Questions

1. Why has the USA become particularly concerned about the development of Soviet military forces and how they are used?
2. Briefly outline the main areas of Soviet military strength.

Poland

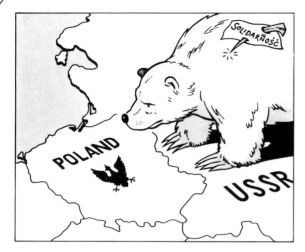

BACKGROUND

Since the end of World War 2 the countries of Eastern Europe have been under the control of the USSR. East Germany, Czechoslovakia, Hungary, Bulgaria, Romania and Poland have all had communist governments. These governments rule with the support of the Soviet Union, although over the years they have been given more and more independence. The East European countries are also bound economically to the Soviet Union through membership of COMECON, and militarily through membership of the Warsaw Pact. These countries, which are part of the Soviet bloc, are known as 'satellite' countries.

The USSR regards control of Eastern Europe as necessary for its own security. In the years after World War 2 it took control of this area, because the Soviet leaders were very conscious of how Hitler had invaded their country through Eastern Europe and of how this had led to the death of 20 million Soviet people. As the Cold War developed in Europe, so the USSR came to feel more and more the need to keep Eastern Europe for security. Soviet control of Eastern Europe has not gone unchallenged. On two occasions the USSR has had to use armed force to prevent one of its satellites from breaking away. The first occasion came in 1956 when an uprising in Hungary was suppressed by the Soviet Army. The second occasion was in 1968 when a reforming government in Czechoslovakia was removed after intervention by Warsaw Pact forces. These two events have underlined how important the Soviet Union regards its control over Eastern Europe to be. Shortly after the intervention in Czechoslovakia, the Soviet leader Brezhnev pronounced that if there were a threat to socialism in Eastern Europe then it was the duty of other socialist countries to stop that threat. This became known as the 'Brezhnev

Eastern Europe

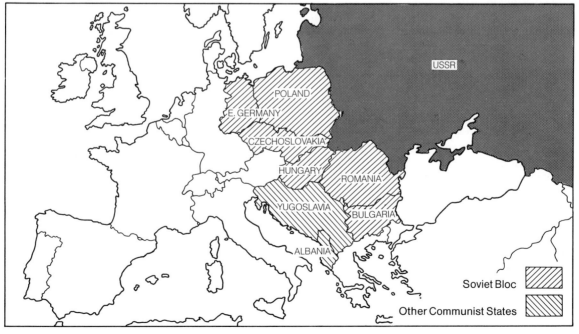

Doctrine' and highlighted the fact that Eastern Europe was a Soviet sphere of influence in which the Soviet Union ultimately decided how far reform could proceed.

Of all the East European countries, Poland has perhaps been the one to emphasise most often and most clearly its wish to be independent. Poland is the largest of the satellite countries and has often gone its own way. Polish agriculture is still largely in private hands and the Roman Catholic Church has survived early persecution to become a major force in Polish affairs.

On several occasions disturbances in Poland have led to changes of government. In 1956 a near-revolt led to a change of leadership when Gomulka became party leader; in 1970 riots led to Gomulka's dismissal and replacement by Edward Gierek. Gierek was faced with a recurrence of popular unrest in 1976. Usually the trigger for these disturbances was government pressure to increase food prices. But they revealed a deep-seated hostility to the political system in existence in Poland.

THE EVENTS OF 1980/1981

During 1980–1 events in Poland were to become of major importance to the USSR and its Warsaw Pact allies. In July 1981, Gierek announced that food prices were to be increased. This led to a series of strikes throughout Poland which were to culminate in August in a virtual general strike centred on the Lenin shipyard in Gdansk, the scene of industrial trouble in 1970. The leader of the striking shipyard workers, **Lech Walesa**, was to become a national leader of the Polish workers.

As a result of the August strikes a number of very important events occurred in Poland.

1. Gierek was replaced as Party Secretary by Stanislaw Kania.

2. The Polish Government agreed to the formation of 'free trade unions' which were independent of the Communist Party. This soon came to be known as 'Solidarity' and quickly grew to over 10 million members.

3. The Polish economy, which was already in a weak state, became weaker still. This meant that it became very difficult to pay back the $27 million owed by Poland to Western banks. It also resulted in serious food shortages in Poland, which became worse as the crisis deepened.

These events had major significance for the communist leadership of Poland. The recognition of Solidarity and of the right to strike was a major victory for the Polish workers. No other communist government in Eastern Europe recognised trade unions which were not controlled by the Party. Even more important were the developments which took place after the recognition of Solidarity. As Solidarity made more and more demands, it began to be clear that the Communist Party could only govern Poland with the approval of the trade unions and many people wondered if Poland was moving to a new type of Communist State in which the Party shared power with other groups in society.

CONSEQUENCES FOR THE USSR

Of course these developments were of crucial importance for the Soviet Union and her allies in the Warsaw Pact. The USSR viewed the events in Poland with alarm and warned against the reduction in the leading role of the Communist Party. East Germany and Czechoslovakia were also highly critical of Solidarity and feared the spread of the 'Polish contagion' into their own countries. On several occasions Soviet and Warsaw Pact manoeuvres seemed to indicate that the events of 1968 in Czechoslovakia would be repeated and that outside armed force would bring to a halt the reforms in Poland. However, the USSR made it clear that it would leave the Polish Government to solve its own problems, but warned that intervention might be necessary if Poland were to collapse into chaos or if the Polish Communist Party lost its leading role.

MILITARY RULE

During 1981 the crisis in Poland continued to deepen. Food shortages became worse. The Government accused Solidarity of seeking political power. Solidarity accused the

Lech Walesa   General Jaruzelski

Tanks in the streets of Gdansk, 1981

Government of not fulfilling promises made in 1980. In October 1981 Kania was replaced by General Jaruzelski as Party Secretary.

On 13 December the crisis came to a climax when the authorities used the Polish army to impose a state of martial law. Strict regulations were brought into effect, Solidarity was 'suspended', its leaders, including Lech Walesa, were detained. Also detained were other leading Polish dissidents, including members of the Polish Communist Party which was purged of its reformist element.

Jaruzelski announced that these measures were essential to prevent Poland sliding into chaos; he accused Solidarity leaders of plotting to seize power and promised that martial law would be lifted once stability returned and that the reform movement would continue. The imposition of military rule was opposed in Poland by the Church and the remnants of Solidarity. Strikes took place and at least seven miners were killed in disturbances. Later in October 1982 Solidarity was finally banned. This was followed in November by the release of Lech Walesa and, in December, General Jaruzelski announced that martial law was to be suspended.

There was some controversy over the extent of actual Soviet involvement in the imposition of martial law. The USSR did appear reluctant to be seen openly intervening, but the suppression of Solidarity by the Polish authorities themselves would have been a satisfactory solution for the USSR. Many doubt whether the Polish crisis has been solved, but martial law has contained the problem and shown that once again an 'errant' East European country has been brought back into line.

Questions

1. Why has the USSR regarded control over Eastern Europe as essential?

2. How has it maintained this control?
3. In what ways has Poland in the years up to 1980 shown its wish for more independence from Soviet influence?
4. Briefly describe the main events, and their importance in Poland, of the period July 1980 to the end of November 1981.
5. Outline what happened in December 1981.
6. Explain why the USSR was so concerned about these events in Poland and comment on their actions during the crisis.

The Sino-Soviet Dispute

One of the most serious issues facing the USSR in its foreign affairs is the split with its large communist neighbour, China. This worsening of relations with China is all the more disturbing for the USSR since previously the two countries had been on friendly terms.

FRIENDSHIP

After the Revolution in China ended in 1949, the new communist Government of China relied on the USSR for help and guidance in building itself into a powerful communist State. An Aid Treaty was signed between the two countries, under which Soviet aid was given to build up China's economy. Much of China's agriculture and industry had been destroyed during the Revolution, and there was widespread poverty. The Soviet aid helped China in its first **five-year plan** developments. Soviet advisers also helped in the build-up of the Chinese army.

BEGINNINGS OF THE DISPUTE

After a number of years of friendship between the two countries, some disagreements began to arise. By the 1960s China was criticising Soviet advisers, while the USSR refused to extend its military cooperation by giving atomic secrets to China. A few years later, the USSR withdrew its advisers from China altogether. Why did the dispute arise between the two large communist neighbours? The main reason was that China had a different view of the meaning of communism from that of the Soviet Union. It felt the USSR had strayed from true communism, and China should be regarded as the leader of world communism. This difference of views was increased because the two leaders, Mao Zedong of China and Khrushchev of the Soviet Union, did not agree on many other items either. Also, the Soviet Union had criticised China's attempt to improve rapidly its output in industry and agriculture during the 'Great Leap Forward'.

By the late 1960s, the dispute had reached more serious proportions when China claimed part of the USSR, and in a clash at the Assuri River in 1969 some Soviet border guards were killed by Chinese troops. After Mao died in 1976, new Chinese leaders Hua Guofeng and Deng Xiaoping took over, and the Soviet Union hoped that there would be a change in the strong anti-Soviet attitude in China's foreign policy. But the new leaders carried on the criticisms of the Soviet Union, and the hostility between the two large communist powers continued.

FUTURE RELATIONS?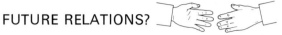

Despite the tensions in the relations between the USSR and China, there is less direct confrontation between them than before. The new Chinese leaders are aware that time is needed for China to build up its economy and army before it can effectively challenge the Soviet Union as the leader of world communism. The Soviet leaders, for their part, have little desire to have a hostile China as a neighbour. Indeed, President Brezhnev, in a major speech at the Congress of the Soviet Communist Party in February 1981, said 'Special mention must be made of China. At present changes are under way in China's internal policy. Time will show what they actually mean. If Soviet-Chinese relations are still frozen, the reason for this has nothing to do with our position. The Soviet Union has never wanted, nor does it now want, any confrontation with the People's Republic of China.' In 1982 President Brezhnev offered to discuss Sino-Soviet border problems but there was little response from China.

USSR

1. The visit of Chairman Hua, the new Chinese leader, to Yugoslavia and Romania in 1978 was seen by the USSR as an attempt by China to gain influence with Soviet allies.

2. China signed a treaty with the USA in 1979 and increased links with Western Europe and Japan. Also, in 1979 China ended the 30-year-old Sino-Soviet Friendship Treaty.

3. China's activities in South-east Asia brought strong criticism from the USSR when China invaded Vietnam (the Soviet Union's ally) for two weeks in 1979.

4. There is Soviet concern over China's determination to modernise rapidly the Chinese army and its military equipment on a large scale.

5. The new Chinese leadership continue to be hostile to the Soviet Union. 'Chinese policy is aimed at wrecking detente and whipping up militarism and political groups against the Soviet Union.'   (Soviet Magazine *New Times*, 1981)

China

1. The Soviet Union's movement of troops into Afghanistan in 1979–80 was criticised by China. As a result, China refused to attend the Olympic Games in Moscow in 1980.

2. The attempts by the Soviet Union to encourage 'detente' between the USA and the USSR were seen by China as lulling the USA into a false sense of security.

3. The Soviet Union's activities in South-east Asia: for example, the Friendship Agreement in 1978 between the USSR and Vietnam indicate further Soviet expansion in this area.

4. China is concerned about the massive superiority of Soviet military equipment, the number of Soviet troops on China's northern border and the great strength of the Soviet navy in the Pacific Ocean.

5. The Soviet leadership's aim in foreign policy. 'The Soviet Union is aiming for world domination. The "new Tsars" activities in South-east Asia showed Moscow's long-term programme to encircle China.'
(*Chinese Deputy Premier, Deng Xiaoping, 1978*)

The Soviet View of Detente

'Throughout the 60 years of the existence of the Soviet state our foreign policy has been directed at guaranteeing peace and security for our country and for all nations. To avert the threat of war, to contain the arms race and to develop and expand cooperation which would benefit all states are what the Soviet Union's initiatives in the international arena are aimed at today as they were previously. We intend to continue to conduct a policy of detente.'

(*President Brezhnev, 1978*)

From shortly after the Cuban missile crisis in 1962 until the Soviet invasion of Afghanistan in 1979, the most publicised aim of Soviet foreign policy was the pursuit of **detente** in order to achieve peaceful cooperation with the West. During this period millions of words were spoken and written by Soviet leaders emphasising the importance of detente. There were also many signs that the Soviet leaders meant what they said: the USSR accepted the idea of 'spheres of influence' and, for example, stopped trying to force the Western powers out of West Berlin; there was more economic, cultural and sporting cooperation; treaties and talks on arms limitation and human rights multiplied.

Why has the Soviet Union pursued this policy of detente in recent years? Since the mid-1920s Soviet leaders have abandoned the early Bolshevik hopes of revolution on a world scale. The main aim now is to build a strong nation, safe from attack and invasion, in which the people can enjoy a high standard of living. Many of the Soviet leaders' speeches have concentrated on the need to reduce the arms race in order to ensure the survival of the human race, a sentiment echoed in the West.

But, apart from this genuine humane desire for fewer weapons of mass destruction worldwide, the Soviet Union pursued the path of detente for other, more practical, reasons:

1. The Soviet Union wanted much-needed breathing space to concentrate on improving the standards of living of the Soviet people. This was necessary in order to devote more effort to consumer goods production to satisfy the rising expectations of the people, without completely abandoning its high military spending.

2. The developing Sino-Soviet dispute in the 1960s and 1970s led to increased tension between the USSR and China. This new development in international relations meant that there was a possibility that the USSR might find itself increasingly isolated and threatened by the USA and China. A limited amount of cooperation with the USA was a sensible practical move towards preventing any possible encirclement by a Sino-Western alliance.

3. By the 1960s the Soviet Union had made many notable advances, political and economic, which it now wanted to consolidate. The policy of detente in Europe enabled the USSR to tighten its grip on the satellite States in Eastern Europe without fear of intervention by the West (for example, in Czechoslovakia). Trade links and important markets for Soviet industry were established and expanded in Eastern Europe and further afield.

This devotion to the policy of detente does not, however, mean that the Soviet Union has abandoned all of its long-term international objectives. The expansion of the conventional weapons of war, research and development of more sophisticated and destructive nuclear weapons, and the readiness to protect its interests on foreign soil (for example, in Afghanistan) are signs that the Soviet Union is determined to maintain its position of strength in the modern world.

Questions

1. What signs of detente were there in the 1960s and 1970s?
2. Why have the Soviet leaders followed a policy of detente in recent years?
3. It would be a mistake to assume that the USSR has abandoned its long-term objectives. Why?

PART 4

China Today

1. The People of China

Population Survey

POPULATION SIZE

'Almost a quarter of the world's children are now growing up in the People's Republic of China.'
'By the year A.D. 2080 China's total population could equal the total world population in 1980.'
'In 1980, China's total population was about 1000 million people.'

Until recently there were no exact statistics of China's huge population. An official population census was held in 1982 and China was found to have a total population of 1008.

FUTURE POPULATION

The continuing increase in China's population brings a number of problems.

1. Although there are improvements in food production on communes the effect of these is

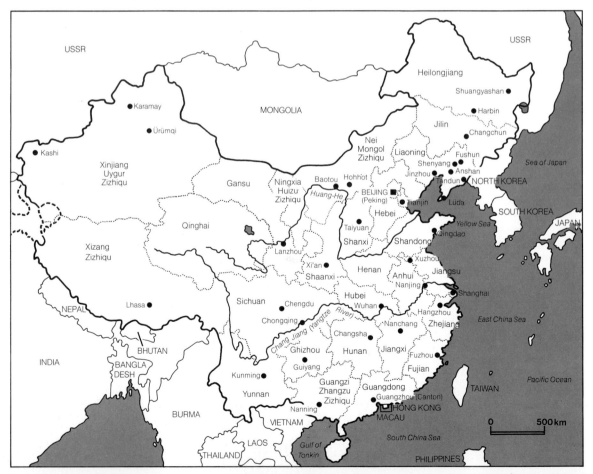

cancelled out by the growing numbers of people to feed.

2. As the population increases and as continued modernisation in industry and agriculture means that more machinery is used, it is becoming difficult to provide jobs for everyone.

3. China might have to export valuable raw materials such as oil to pay for imported food to feed the growing population.

LIMITING THE POPULATION: TOO MANY PEOPLE?

During most of **Mao Zedong's** time as leader of China, people were encouraged to have large families. The reason for this was that people were needed on the land to increase food production, and in the army to build up the troop strength.

By the end of Mao's rule, however, it was recognised that some limits on population size were necessary if China was to 'modernise'. Since then a birth control programme has been introduced to encourage women to have fewer children (see Issue: Birth Control).

WHERE THE CHINESE LIVE

Most people in China live in the east of the country in the agriculturally productive regions near the Huang He (Hwang-ho) River. Although there are a number of cities with populations of over 1 million people, most Chinese (about 85%) live in the countryside. This means there is an imbalance in the number of workers in the

countryside compared with the number of workers in city areas.

The city of Shanghai has over 10 million people, making it one of the largest cities in the world, along with London, New York and Tokyo.

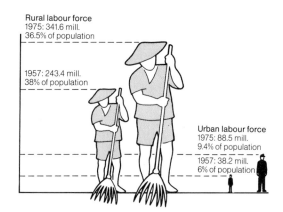

Rural labour force
1975: 341.6 mill.
36.5% of population

1957: 243.4 mill.
38% of population

Urban labour force
1975: 88.5 mill.
9.4% of population

1957: 38.2 mill.
6% of population

MINORITY GROUPS IN CHINA

Over 90% of the people in China are Han Chinese. As well as the Han Chinese, there are over 50 national minority groups totalling about 50 million people. These minority groups live mostly in the more barren mountainous areas of western China.

The minority groups are encouraged to retain and develop their own customs and habits, and have representatives on the National Peoples' Congress (the most important group of elected representatives in the Government). Some groups also have their own local governments to run their affairs. However, Chinese Central Government insists that 'unity of nationalities' is most important in building a strong communist society, and this pressure for unity creates problems for minority groups. Also, because there are so many Han Chinese, the national minority groups feel they are in danger of losing their identity.

China's national minorities (*main groups*)

Nationality	Population	Area of residence (see map on page 128)
Zhuang	12 million	Guangxi, Yunnan
Hui	6 million	Ningxi, Henan
Uygur	5 million	Xinjiang
Yi	5 million	Sichuan, Yunnan
Miao	4 million	Guizhou, Hunan
Tibetan	$3\frac{1}{2}$ million	Tibet, Quinghai
Mongolian	3 million	Inner Mongolia, Xinjiang
Manchu	$2\frac{1}{2}$ million	Liaoning, Jilin

(Source: *China Pictorial*, 1981)

Density of population in China

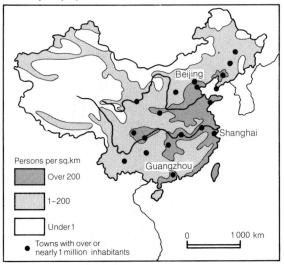

Persons per sq.km

- Over 200
- 1–200
- Under 1

• Towns with over or nearly 1 million inhabitants

0   1 000 km

Beijing

Shanghai

Guangzhou

1. State three facts which indicate how enormous China's population is.
2. What problems will be caused in the future by such a large population?
3. Why did Mao Zedong encourage the Chinese people to have large families?
4. What problems are faced by minority groups in China?

Lifestyles

STANDARD OF LIVING

Compared with the standard of living of people in the United States or the Soviet Union, the people of China are poor. Even in comparison with some middle-income countries, China could be termed a 'poor' country in that few families own 'luxury' consumer goods such as television sets, refrigerators or cars. Large-scale private ownership has not been an aim of Chinese Government policy. Many Chinese families would consider themselves wealthy if they owned a bicycle, a radio, a watch, and a sewing machine.

> The bicycle is king in China. It is a status symbol, commuter transport, and beast of burden. Forty-gallon oil drums, stacks of bricks and packing cases all move inexorably across the early morning Canton. The wheels begin to turn at dawn producing a thin string at the side of the roads. By six-thirty the file is coagulating at the junctions, and by seven o'clock the cycles are six deep and there is mayhem at every cross-roads. All cars, buses and lorries are reduced to a plaintively honking ribbon at the road's centre.

(*Guardian*, 1 June 1978)

Nevertheless, China is not a poverty-stricken country compared with its near neighbour, India, since China has less malnutrition, better education, and free health services. In China, the poor are better cared for than in most poor countries.

> We saw much to admire in China in addition to the magic of its landscape and the cohesion of its society. Nowhere did we see starving people or people in rags although where drought or flood has struck they exist. Everywhere the children looked well fed and well cared for; clinics, dispensing Chinese herbal remedies, functioned in the streets of the cities; public health standards are good and life expectancy is 67 for men and 70 for women. The condition of the Chinese cities in no way resembled those of India. Nor is China, visibly, an oppressive totalitarian society. The army is not greatly in evidence, the loudspeakers no longer blare propaganda, portraits of Mao no longer abound. The visitor has mixed feelings returning to the capitalist jungle of Hong Kong and even in Canton, where both spivs and beggars are rapidly making their appearance; he can see why the Chinese rulers fear the contagion of the west.

(Peter Jenkins, *The Guardian*, 9 May 1981)

COMPARING THE LIFESTYLES OF THREE CHINESE FAMILIES LIVING IN THE TOWN

The following information compares the living standards of three families living in the city of Tianjin, near the capital, Beijing (Peking).

1. *Well-off family.* Wang Shufang is a department store clerk. Her husband also works at the store. Her mother and father, also working, live with them in the same house. The house is on the first floor of a two-storey building and has two rooms.

Some of Beijing's two million cyclists

Income and expenditure of three representative families for 1980

	Well-off family Wang Shufang's (4 working members)		Middle-income family Wang Xiujun's (2 working members)		Low-income family Jin Wenjiang's (1 working member)	
	Yuan	£	Yuan	£	Yuan	£
Total net family income*	3 252.00	899	1 609.00	445	1 093.50	302
Monthly per-capita	67.75	18.80	44.69	12.30	22.78	6.30
Total expenditures	3 317.00	917	1 560.50	431	1 082.50	300
Total food expenses	1 750.00	484	831.00	230	722.00	200
Total clothing	946.00	261	282.00	78	184.00	51
Books and entertainment	157.00	43	26.00	7	39.00	10.50
Fuel and other articles	119.00	33	69.00	19	65.00	18.00
Rent	67.00	18	32.00	8.80	(private house)	
Water and electricity	34.00	9	24.00	6.50	10.00	2.75
Transportation	6.00	1.50	36.00	10.00	26.00	7.00
Repairs	12.00	3.50	13.00	3.50	7.00	1.90
Living space	23 m²		14.5 m²		11 m²	

*Includes wages, supplementary wages, subsidies and bonuses, after payments for support of old people living outside the household and money spent on gifts.

(Adapted from *China Reconstructs*, July 1981)

2. *Middle-income family.* Wang Xiujun is a technician in a synthetic fibre factory. Her husband works in the city's Number 4 radio factory. They have a six year old daughter. The family of three live in a one-room flat on the top floor of a six-storey apartment.

3. *Low-income family.* Jin Wenjiang is a bench worker at the Number 4 building construction works. His wife does temporary work. There are two children who both attend school. The family live in one room and cannot afford money for repairs.

(Adapted from *China Reconstructs*, July 1981)

CHANGES IN RURAL LIFESTYLES

Most people in China live on large **communes** in the countryside. Each commune includes some towns and several villages and has its own hospitals, schools, theatres, libraries, and workshops. The commune is run by an elected committee who make decisions about how the commune work is organised. The workers are grouped into teams (see page 147). The land, except for a few small private plots, is owned by the commune. Workers are paid for their work with produce and some money.

Since the late 1970s the Chinese Government has encouraged some changes in that people may sell food from their private plots to make extra money. Workers may also now earn small bonuses if they exceed the commune target and some small private businesses and street markets are encouraged (see page 145).

Durable consumer goods owned by the three famiies

Item	Wang Shufang	Wang Xiujun	Jin Wenjiang
Bicycles	4	0	1 (home-made)
Sewing machines	1	1	0
Wrist watches	2	3	1
Radios	2	1	1 (home-made)
TV sets	1	1	0
Phonographs	1	0	0
Tape recorders	1	0	0
Electric fans	1	0	0
Easy chairs (pairs)	1	1	0

(*China Reconstructs*, July 1981)

Chinese peasant

Our revolution brought about a redistribution of wealth to the people. Then we decided to go for economic growth–to raise everyone's low standard of living. But we found that population growth was eating into the fruits of our economic growth–we had to produce more just to stand still. So we introduced policies that would show people the advantages of smaller families. We raised the marriage age and adopted a really vigorous family planning programme. The result is that we–the most populous nation on earth–have succeeded in controlling population growth. But none of this would have worked if it was not for our all-round community development programme. Old people here no longer need have sons as an insurance against destitution in old age, because the community takes good care of its aged and health care for all has meant that there is no need to have lots of children to make sure that some survive.

(Source: *New Internationalist* June 1977)

LIVING IN CHINA

As in most countries, the standard of living in China is better in the cities than in the countryside. Indeed, in China, the city dwellers are about twice as well off as the rural Chinese.

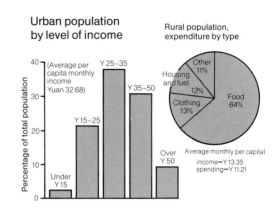

Urban population by level of income

Rural population, expenditure by type

City Life

Huang Yeh-kian, an English-speaking interpreter assigned to the Foreign Affairs office of the Shanghai Revolutionary Committee, considers himself a 'middle-income Chinese', a strange admission in a supposedly classless society. He earns $40 a month – $15 more than the national everage – and his wife, a teacher, brings home $38 a month. Together they have acquired bicycles, watches, a sewing machine and even a TV set. 'We have everything we need, except a bigger apartment,' Huang says.

The Huangs have two children, thus qualifying for 215 square feet of living space, but there is a critical housing shortage in Shanghai, and the family is crammed into one tiny room, about 130 square feet. They share a kitchen and toilet with two other families in what was once a three-room apartment. Laundry hangs from every window, from the branches of plane trees lining the city streets, from telephone wires and power lines.

To an American, it would be slum living at its worst. But the rent is only $1.81 a month, the gas bill $1.61, electricity less than 60 cents and water 40 cents. Medical care is free. Huang and his wife manage to save about $20 a month. Their children are well dressed. They can afford to go out for a $3 restaurant meal, to take in a 20-cent movie or to spend an evening at Shanghai's puppet theatre. And Huang is confident life will get better. 'My name is on the list for a new apartment,' he confides. 'Construction has started again. It will take a long time, but I will eventually get it.'

Countryside life

On the Feng Peng commune 12 miles outside Shanghai, Li Yung-hsin proudly shows off the wealth accumulated by his family of eight – three bicycles, six watches, one sewing machine and two radios. Li works as the grain keeper in charge of a storage silo; his wife makes bricks, and his 65-year-old mother does stoop labour in the rice fields. The Lis supplement their wages by raising four pigs every year, which they sell to the state, and they grow vegetables for their own use on a small private plot.

Li is satisfied with his life, which he says has improved markedly in the past two years because of good harvests – and the first wage increases on the commune in fifteen years. 'Before, we were very miserable,' he said. 'We didn't have enough to eat, and we wore homemade clothes. Now we have enough of everything. We are simple people and we don't need much.' Indeed, the Li household has almost no furniture, no running water – the toilet is an outhouse with a bucket of water from a nearby canal – and no electricity. But Li recently added a second storey to his cement house, which means his family now sleeps only two to a room. He is well off by village standards and reckons that he will have enough saved in the next five years to marry off a sister, two daughters and a son. 'Weddings are expensive,' he explains. 'The television will have to wait.'

THE MASS MEDIA

Television is still fairly new in China and although in 1981 about 7 million sets were owned, most Chinese can not yet afford television. The sets themselves are mainly small-screen black and white sets, often owned communally by a factory or commune work groups. Over half of the programmes are for entertainment, often films, while about one quarter of the time is for news, and the remainder is for sport, science, and education programmes.

Most families in China possess a radio set, and throughout the day can listen to programmes of music, commune news, local news, and national news. The national news programme is produced by the Government Central Broadcasting Organisation, and is broadcast to the whole of China about three times per day. Radio Beijing broadcasts overseas in 40 different languages. It is now possible to listen to BBC and Voice of America broadcasts.

The main newspaper in China is the official Chinese Communist Party *People's Daily*. It has a circulation of 10 million. In 1981, this newspaper also produced an English language paper, the *China Daily* for visitors. The *Red Flag* magazine is published monthly, and contains many official Party statements. There are also local papers in most regions and major cities.

At one time advertising was not allowed in China but some is now permitted in newspapers and on billboards, after a change in Government policy.

LANGUAGE

The Chinese mainly speak Mandarin. It is not an alphabetical language but depends on tones and sounds for its meaning. Recently, the method of translating these Chinese sounds into written English has been changed to a Chinese system called *Pinyin*. From 1979 the Pinyin system has been used in translation. This has meant that many Chinese names have changed their spelling in English. For example,

Peking becomes Beijing
Hong Kong becomes Xianggang
Yangtze River becomes Chang Jiang
Mao Tse-Tung becomes Mao Zedong
Teng Hsiao-Ping becomes Deng Xiaoping.

THE VERY YOUNG AND OLD

Nurseries for very young children, under three years old, are run by local factory or village groups with the help of government subsidies. Children can go to nursery each day and go home at night, or they can stay for the whole week and go home at weekends. A small fee is paid by parents to keep their children at a nursery, where the children are looked after by 'child-care' workers. Many children attend nurseries since often both parents will be working, and there may not be aged relatives to look after children at home.

In China, retired workers (men at 60, women at 50) receive a pension of about three quarters

Advertisement for an arts and crafts factory in Zhengzhou, Jenan Province

Retired commune workers at the Home of Respect For the Aged, Zhejiang Province

West Bromwich Albion toured China in 1978 and shortly afterwards a Chinese international team played Celtic in Glasgow. In 1982, the Chinese football team narrowly missed qualifying for the World Cup Finals in Spain. The Chinese are also interested in developing sports such as tennis. In 1981 Jimmy Connors of the USA won the Canton Tennis Championship which was the first professional tennis tournament to be held in China.

TOURISM

During the era of Mao Zedong, foreign tourists were not encouraged to visit China and few visas were issued. The new Government's policy of closer links with foreign countries, however, has resulted in a huge increase in the numbers of tourists since 1978. In 1979 there were about 500 000 tourists mainly from the USA, Western Europe, Japan. By 1981 there were about 100 000 tourists from the USA alone. Most tourists are in groups organised by travel agencies and their tour may include not only the tourist 'sights' such as the Great Wall of China and the Forbidden City in Beijing but also visits to communes, schools, and children's nurseries.

of their former wage. Old people are well respected and looked after. Many live with their families and look after the young children while both parents are at work.

SPORT

Partly because of lack of facilities, China does not have a wide range of international sporting achievements. Where basic facilities can be used, however, for example in table-tennis, the Chinese have become world champions, and have produced many players of a very high standard. Performances in swimming, gymnastics, and athletics are also reaching a high grade in international terms. A clearer indication of the standard in athletics, for example, was given when China entered the 1984 Olympic Games in Los Angeles in the USA.

One of the most rapid improvements in China's sporting world is its rise as a football nation.

Primary school students in Wuhan city, playing football

1. Use the table of statistics and information in the text to compare the housing conditions for the three families of different incomes.
2. Describe the differences between city life and life in the countryside in China.
3. What changes in the communes have been encouraged by the Chinese Government?
4. How are very young children looked after in China while their parents are working?

Social Progress

Case Study 1: A Commune Family

Wang Shu Ying lives in the Evergreen People's Commune outside Beijing. Aged 72, she is one of the oldest members of the commune. She lives with her son, aged 46, daughter-in-law, aged 44, and two grandchildren, aged 21 and 18. The family live in a terraced brick house in this fairly prosperous commune. Wang's husband was killed in 1948 during the Civil War with the Nationalists.

Wang often remembers the harsh life before 1949, when conditions, especially for peasant women, were very hard. If food was short, as it often was, the man, as the main breadwinner, would receive the best there was. If the family were destitute, it might sell its girl children as child-brides, servants or prostitutes. In extreme cases, a man would even sell his wife. Wang also remembers the practice of 'foot binding', when from about the age of six, girls had their feet tightly bound with bandages so that over several years, the bones were gradually broken and the much-admired but extremely painful 'lily feet' resulted.

Wang's daughter-in-law, Wenhui Bao, benefited from the law passed in 1950 which forbade foot binding, arranged marriages, child marriages and wife beating. Women, in law, were now the equal of men. Wenhui works with her husband in the fields and is paid on the basis of equal pay for equal work.

Wang, although now too old to work, need not fear for welfare, because like everyone in China she is entitled to the 'five guarantees' of food, clothing, housing, medical care and a decent burial. The commune provides her with these welfare services and last year when she became seriously ill, she was first treated by the commune doctor – one of the '**barefoot doctors**' – and then she was sent to the nearest hospital. Her family accompanied her and prepared her food in hospital. Their wages were made up for them by the other members of their production team. In hospital she was given a successful operation using acupuncture.

In the evening Wang's grandchildren read to her, for she was born too early to benefit from the basic education which all Chinese now receive. Her eldest grandson is planning to marry next year when he reaches the legal age of 22 and he has told his grandmother that he plans to have only one child. He was shocked when she told him that when she was young, families were much larger and parents would continue to have children until a boy was born. But of course a great deal else was different then.

A country doctor giving regular physical examination to an old peasant

Case Study 2: A City Family

The Yang family live in Nanking. Yang Hung-chi is 32 and works in a factory which makes engineering equipment. His wife Huan Su-ching is a supervisor in a textile mill, in charge of a department employing over 100 workers. Their son and daughter are still at school.

A loom worker at a textile mill

The family live in a three-roomed apartment in an eight-year old block of flats for factory workers. The flat has no kitchen – the family usually eat in the factory canteen – but they can cook on their balcony. They have no running water and share a toilet with several other families.

When the children were younger, Huan was able to continue working because nurseries are very common in Chinese cities. She was also grateful for the canteens at work, for this meant that she did not have to prepare full meals at night for her family after a hard day's work. Before they moved into their new flat the Yang family lived in an older part of the city in a block of two-storeyed buildings. Accommodation there was very crowded, for the flats were much smaller and Yang Hung-chi's father had also lived with them until he died.

The grandfather had been a rickshaw 'boy' before the Revolution but such employment had been forbidden by the new **communist** Government. He was sometimes invited into the children's school to tell the children about life before the Revolution. This was known as 'recalling the bitterness and thinking of the sweetness'. The old man was pleased to tell of his early life and then would help the children in their work session when they would test and pack small flashlight bulbs.

Although life was very crowded in the old flat, great care had been taken to avoid the disease which had been common when the grandfather

The Yang family
in their apartment

had lived there as a young man. The community set up a neighbourhood committee to keep streets, lanes and courtyards clean. The committee was responsible for supervising hygiene and eliminating the breeding grounds of flies and mosquitoes. The new block of flats also has a street committee to ensure cleanliness.

The Yang family are happy with their life and think that as China becomes more modern their standard of living will get even better. Above all they would like to be able to buy more of the goods which they see advertised in the streets nowadays. They were very pleased when they were able to buy a television set.

These two case studies of families in China highlight the major social improvements which have been carried out since 1949. The position of women has improved greatly, welfare services and primary education have been introduced, famine has been eradicated and living standards have improved for all. Life expectancy has improved and illiteracy has been greatly reduced. Compared with pre-1949 China or many other developing countries, China's record in social achievement is impressive.

A LONG WAY TO GO

However, China still has a long way to go to catch up on the other two Superpowers. Housing, particularly, is a major problem for many Chinese and in many small urban streets or tiny villages living conditions are very poor. China has made major advances, which have applied to all sectors of society, but an important feature of her new modernisation programme will be to overcome those areas of backwardness which still exist.

Questions

1. In what ways did Wang Shu Ying's early life differ from the present life of her daughter-in-law?
2. What health and welfare rights are guaranteed to Chinese people today?
3. What do the lives of Chen Su-ching and her daughter reveal about women in present-day China?
4. Why would the children of the local school be interested in the grandfather's life?
5. In what ways have the Chinese improved public hygiene?
6. Summarise the achievements in social life in China as revealed by the two case studies.

Birth Control

As we have seen in the first unit of this chapter, China is the world's most populous nation. At the end of 1979 its population was officially reported to be around 975 million people. Since the world's population is about 4000 million, this means that China has about one quarter of the world's population. To deal with this problem of over-population, China has been making major efforts to reduce its population growth rate. In the 1950s it was 2.2%. In the 1970s it was down to below 1.5%. It is hoped to reduce it to 1% and eventually to zero by the end of the century.

A variety of methods are being adopted to bring about the fall in the birth rate which will be necessary to reduce China's population growth rate.

1. *Marriage age.* The legal age for marriage has been raised from 20 to 22 for men and from 18 to 20 for women. Although it is legal to get married at these ages, the 'recommended' ages for marriage are 28 for men and 25 for women.

2. *'One is enough'.* A massive propaganda campaign has been started to encourage families to have only one child. This policy is backed up

A 'One is enough' street poster, encouraging families to have one well-fed child

by a number of benefits to couples who carry it out and by a number of penalties for couples who ignore it. A monthly bonus of 5 yuan (8% of the average town wage) has been offered to all single-child families who pledge not to have further children. They will also receive preference in the allocation of housing and in educational opportunities for the child.

These privileges are automatically withdrawn on the birth of a second child. If a third child is born, the family begins to suffer penalties. Wages can be reduced by 5-10% after the third child and up to 20% after a fifth. The press has reported cases of couples holding official positions who have been penalised financially for having third and fourth children.

3. *Family planning*. Article 53 of the Chinese Constitution 'advocates and encourages family planning'. Birth control pills are distributed free of charge and other methods of family planning are also freely available.

ACHIEVEMENTS AND PROBLEMS

China's annual birth rate is calculated to be 16.5 per thousand. This compares with 15.3 per thousand for the USA and with 34 per thousand for India. This reveals that China's population policy has been achieving results and that China is approaching the population growth rates of Western industrialised nations.

However, it is believed that China's population policy is more successful in the cities than in the countryside, where most of the population lives. In the countryside the peasants have tended to stick to the old saying of 'more hands mean more work and more income'. Children are also seen as being important to help care for parents in old age. And there still exists a tradition of continuing to have children until the birth of a son.

To try to overcome these problems, the Chinese Government are offering families with one child a private plot of land equal to that of families with two children. In addition pensions are being linked to family size. Parents with one or no children will receive the highest pension.

Even if China manages to achieve its population plans and reduce its growth rate to zero by the end of the century, this will still leave it with a population of 1200 million. If this fails and women of child-bearing age continue to have children at the current rate, it is calculated that within a century there will be over 4000 million Chinese, equalling the present population of the world. This shows the importance of the population policy now being adopted.

Questions

1. Why is China's population growth a source of great concern to its leaders?
2. Outline the various methods introduced in China to reduce the birth rate.
3. What success has China had in this?
4. What difficulties have been encountered in the Chinese countryside over reducing the birth rate and why is this so important for the long-term success of the whole programme?

Education

CHANGES IN EDUCATION

When Mao Zedong came to power in China in 1949, the chance of getting an education was limited to a privileged few. Most Chinese people were unable to read or write. Mao, however, gave official encouragement to education for all young Chinese, and thousands of schools were built.

The **Cultural Revolution** of the late 1960s brought changes in education because Mao wanted young people, especially those in the cities, to experience 'manual labour', so that they would appreciate the value of farm work and factory work. Millions of school, college and university students were sent to the countryside to work. Another change at this time was that university and college entrance exams were abolished to allow more people to attend.

After 1976 there were new changes when Chinese leader, **Deng Xiaoping**, encouraged the 'Four Modernisations' to advance China's economy. For these 'modernisations' to take place it was necessary to train people to be capable of making and operating complex technical and scientific machines and equipment. Entrance examinations were again encouraged, standards in colleges were raised, and many teachers and professors returned to education jobs, after years in the countryside. The study of foreign languages, especially English, was seen as one of the keys to understanding imported foreign technology.

An English class in progress at the May 7th School, Shanghai

PROBLEMS FOR CHINA'S EDUCATION PROGRAMME

All children in China attend primary school, and most go on to middle school. There are now ambitious plans to expand education for older teenagers and adults. The education plans, however, face serious problems:

1. *Shortage of teachers*. Owing to the various changes in education policy in the 1970s there is a shortage of skilled experts in many areas of education.

2. *Qualifications*. The need for qualifications and entrance exams has led to huge numbers of people applying to sit exams. In 1977 millions sat the first entrance exams for university but only a few got to college because of the shortage of places available. Even by 1982 only one-tenth of the three million students who sat the college entrance exams were accepted.

3. *'Lost generation'*. Many of those students previously sent to the countryside now wish to complete their college education. Some television education courses are available to try to help overcome the shortage of college and university places and staff, and night-school classes are also provided.

4. *Language*. China's own language has recently been simplified, but learning a foreign language is difficult because of the large number of characters in the Chinese language.

The system of education

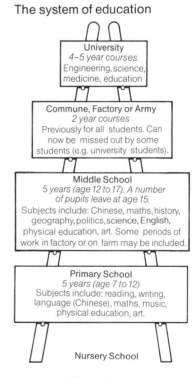

Questions

1. What changes were made in China's education system during the Cultural Revolution of the 1960s?
2. What changes have taken place in the 1980s?
3. Describe the four problems facing China's plans to develop its education system.
4. What is meant by the 'middle school' in China?

139

2. The Economy

China's Economic Development

Understanding the path of economic development followed by China since the 1949 Communist Revolution is not an easy task. Between 1949 and 1976 the greatest single influence on economic development was 'The Great Helmsman', Chairman **Mao Zedong**. But the path he chose was full of twists and turns which sometimes led to confusion and uncertainty. Since Mao's death in 1976 his successors, led by **Deng Xiaoping**, have found themselves on the same difficult road and have had to change direction at least once.

There are two main reasons for the difficulties which Mao and his successors have encountered. The first lies in the fact that China is unique in the modern world: a major Power of great potential strength but still basically an agricultural country. In many ways China is more similar to the developing countries of the **Third World** than to the other two major Powers. The second reason lies in the influence of the example set by the Soviet Union: the only example of development towards a socialist economy available to the Chinese leaders in 1949. These two factors and the changing attitudes towards them on the part of the Chinese leadership were responsible for the changes outlined below.

THE ECONOMY AFTER MAO

Following the death of Mao in 1976, and the removal from power of the **Gang of Four**, China began an ambitious programme of economic modernisation. Under the effective leadership of Deng Xiaoping, Vice-Premier and Vice-Chairman of the Chinese Communist Party (**CCP**), China began to move towards economic progress along the road favoured by the right wing of the CCP (or Moderates). The emphasis in China today is on efficiency and the growth of the economy, on competition between factories and on profit. In industry, more decision-making power has been given to people at local levels. Collective ownership of small factories by local **communes** is encouraged, and in the factories 'the workers are the masters' and their rights are given more importance. In agriculture, incentives

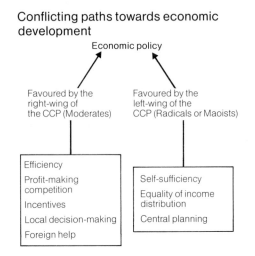

Conflicting paths towards economic development

Economic policy

Favoured by the right-wing of the CCP (Moderates)

Favoured by the left-wing of the CCP (Radicals or Maoists)

Efficiency
Profit-making competition
Incentives
Local decision-making
Foreign help

Self-sufficiency
Equality of income distribution
Central planning

are offered to peasants to increase their production and earnings from private plots.

The main part of the post-Mao economic policy is the emphasis on the 'Four Modernisations': an attempt to improve agriculture, industry, science and technology, and defence.

In February 1978 a ten-year plan (1976–85) was presented to the Fifth National People's Congress (see page 152). This plan was very ambitious and called for more investment in the following eight years than in the previous twenty-eight. The output of coal and steel was to be doubled; 120 large-scale industrial complexes were to be completed; industrial production was to increase by over 10% each year from 1978 to 1985; agricultural output was to be almost doubled. To help achieve this programme China embarked on the 'Great Leap Outwards', encouraging foreign investment in the Chinese economy. Japanese, American, British and other foreign companies were invited to invest in China following visits by Deng and his colleagues to the USA and Europe.

Within a year, however, the plan ran into problems. Deng and his followers had tried to do too much too quickly and it soon became clear that the Chinese economy could not cope with the rapid changes being introduced. Larger yields in the fields led to problems in providing enough irrigation; there were shortages of energy and building materials; too few machine tools were being produced; too much crude steel and not enough high-quality finished steel was

The four modernisations

 Agriculture	Industry	 Science & Technology	Defence
Increases in grain production	Increased steel production	Rehabilitation of scientists	Modernisation of tanks, aircraft, ships and submarines
Great improvements in mechanisation	Introduction of modern technology	Re-establishment of research institutes and academies	Increase and improvement of nuclear missiles
Improved drainage and irrigation	Greater efficiency, productivity and profits	Research into the 'Five Golden Blossoms' atomic science, semi-conductors, computers, lasers and automation	New links with Japan, Western Europe and the USA

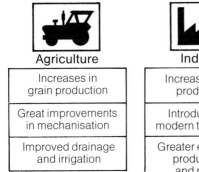

A steeet poster to emphasise the importance of the Four Modernisations

being produced; and the large quantities of imports flowing into China could only be paid for by massive foreign borrowing.

As a result, the over-ambitious plan was shelved by the end of 1979 and China began a three-year period devoted to 'readjusting, restructuring, consolidating, and improving the national economy'. Deng did not completely abandon the chosen road, but advanced more slowly along it. Most of the previous targets were revised downwards to make them more realistic. Many foreign contracts were cancelled and the whole pace of progress was slowed down so that the Chinese people might understand and accept the changes being made. The slower pace would also help to prevent some areas of the economy developing too fast for other more backward areas such as transport and energy supplies. Any imbalance in the developments in the various areas could only lead to major economic problems.

Readjusting the Economy

This involves changing the priorities in economic growth so that the imbalances in the economy are reduced.

China's Economic priorities in the 1980s

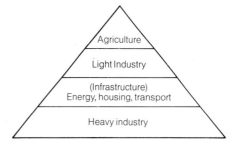

Agriculture

Light Industry

(Infrastructure) Energy, housing, transport

Heavy industry

Restructuring the Economy

Several policies have been introduced to direct China towards a system of 'market socialism'. These are:

1. greater freedom to make decisions at local level (but central planning remains important);

2. incentives (for example, private plots and 'sideline' industries) for production teams in agriculture;

3. increased prices paid by the State to agricultural producers;

4. the profit motive: factories to increase sales, even by means of advertising, to increase income and profits;

5. bonuses and piece-work rates introduced to stimulate production in factories;

6. workers encouraged to form their own cooperatives to produce any goods in short supply, and keep the profits for themselves.

Consolidating the Economy

Effort is to be concentrated in those high-priority investment projects which are profitable. Lower-priority projects such as small-scale State-owned factories are to be delayed or cancelled. Profitable enterprises will survive and be encouraged, unprofitable enterprises will disappear unless they are vital to the State.

Improving the Economy

Through the introduction of new technology it is hoped to improve efficiency and profits. This involves importing modern technology from abroad to bring the typical factory up to the standards of the most advanced 'model' factories which are shown off to foreign visitors.

When this period of reassessment is completed China will probably press ahead with a new **five-year** economic **plan**. This plan will probably continue the progress made during the early 1980s. The use of 'misguided' agricultural policies left over from the past coupled with a continuing food problem means that rapid change is unlikely. In industry, the twin policies of changing priorities away from heavy to light industries, and of decentralisation of decision-making, are likely to remain important. Progress is being made, but a Chinese 'economic miracle' is unlikely in the next few years.

THE LEGACY OF MAO ZEDONG

Phase 1 (1949–56): Following the Soviet Example

The economic organisation developed in China in the years immediately following the Communist Revolution was greatly influenced by the Soviet Union, with whom China signed an economic cooperation agreement in 1949. The agricultural system was gradually reorganised, from a large number of privately owned farms and smallholdings to collective farms and eventually communes. In terms of industrial development, China was very backward in 1949 compared with the USA and the Soviet Union. The method adopted to achieve industrial progress largely followed the Soviet model of centralised State planning through a series of five-year plans. In the early post-Revolution years the USSR gave China huge loans, helped to train Chinese workers, and helped to establish many new factories. The emphasis, as it had been in the USSR, was on heavy industry, with little investment in industries producing consumer goods or in agriculture.

During this period China made considerable economic progress, but by the mid 1950s the Soviet model began to seem unsuitable for China.

Phase 2 (1956–9): A Change in Direction

By 1956 the Chinese economy appeared to be developing in a lopsided way. There was too much emphasis on heavy industry; too few factories were making light machinery and farm implements. Industrial development was also concentrated in a small area along the coast. The lack of investment in agriculture was leading to difficulties in food production. In addition, the Soviet system of centralised planning was found to be unsuitable in a country with less developed transport and communications systems.

Mao now moved away from Soviet influence and in 1958 China entered the stage in her development known as the '**Great Leap Forward**'. During this period there were spectacular efforts made to increase agricultural and industrial output, and Mao tried to achieve greater balance in the economy. This was done by increasing investment in agriculture, improving the country's infrastructure (roads, bridges, irrigation and reservoir schemes etc) and setting up large numbers of small factories to produce much-needed implements and small tools.

Great numbers of peasants were sent out to modernise the countryside by laying new roads, building canals, dykes and reservoirs, and planting new forests. The People's Communes became the basic economic, social and political units of China, and remain so today.

The Great Leap Forward was not a complete success: mistakes were made, food shortages continued, and the withdrawal of Soviet aid almost proved disastrous. But China had begun to develop along lines more suited to her own people and circumstances, and moved away from the inappropriate aspects of the Soviet model of development.

Phase 3 (1959–76): Reassessment

In the early 1960s many of the achievements of the Great Leap Forward were changed or abandoned. Peasants were allowed to own private plots and to produce goods for sale in local markets. Black-marketeering grew, prices rose, and private production grew rapidly. Industrial workers received bonus payments for good results, and personal gain became more important than national progress.

This change of direction led to a great debate about the road China should follow in the future. Some leaders wanted to follow the Soviet example: offering incentives to workers and employing experts to establish efficiency in the economy. Others, the supporters of Mao, were opposed to any system likely to produce divisions in society by offering privileges and status to a few, and which might lead to a return to capitalism (as they claimed had happened in the USSR).

This debate culminated in the period known as the **Cultural Revolution** (1966–9), during which the people of China were encouraged to criticise old ideas and overturn them and throw out the people responsible for them if necessary. This developed into a major political upheaval which had disastrous effects on the economy. After a long struggle, which at times came close to a major conflict, Mao and his supporters emerged in a very powerful position.

Mao now adopted the slogan 'Agriculture the foundation, industry the leading sector' to indicate that China has basically an agricultural economy and could not aim at rapid industrial development immediately. The Soviet model was finally abandoned and Chinese workers encouraged to 'Serve the People' by producing good-quality work. Equality was more important than efficiency and speed.

The death of Mao had many implications for China, its people, and its economy. The debate over which road to take was once more at the forefront of Chinese politics.

Questions

1. Describe the main policies contained in the 1976–85 ten-year plan.
2. Why was the 'Great Leap Outwards' slowed down after 1979?
3. What are the main economic priorities for the 1980s? (Refer also to the table on p. 144.)
4. How important has Mao's influence been in the economic development of China?
5. Study the cartoon below. What is the cartoonist trying to illustrate about Chinese economic development?

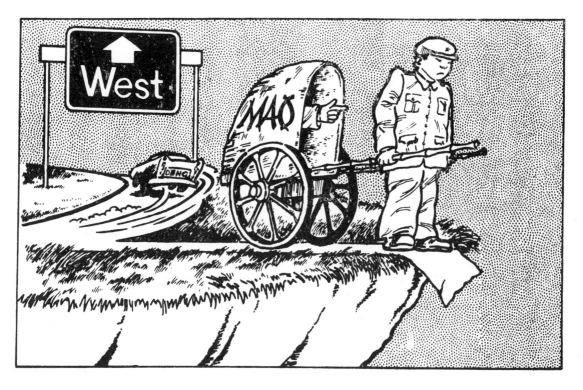

Growth trends in the Chinese Economy, 1957–78 (average annual growth, as a percentage)

	1957–70	1966–9	1969–73	1974–5	1976	1966–76	1977	1978
Gross national product	5.1	2.5	10.1	5.1	0.0	5.7	8.2	11.6
Industrial production	9.3	4.7	13.1	7.3	0.0	8.0	14.3	13.4
Agricultural production	1.8	0.0	6.1	2.1	0.0	2.8	2.7	8.3

Main industries

Chinese industrial growth was high throughout the late 1970s: heavy industrial output increased 10% in 1979, while light industrial output increased 15%. Steel output continues to rise, and reached 32 million tonnes in 1978. Oil output is not rising as hoped although it reached 100 million tonnes in 1978. Present plans look to the expansion of the industrial base: iron, steel, other metals, mining and transport infrastructure. A major petro-chemical industry is being established based on China's oil and natural gas resources. Light industry currently takes only 6% of State investment funds, while heavy industry gets 55%. Future expansion of light industry, especially textiles, is planned.

Agricultural sector and main crops

The growth of agricultural output was low in the late 1970s. In 1978 grain output totalled 300 million tonnes. A record grain harvest in 1979 was insufficient to prevent continued imports. The predominance of food grains seems to be falling in some areas as communes diversify into cash crops such as tea and cotton. Cotton output has remained constant at around 20 million tonnes since 1970. Current policy is concerned with improving irrigation and water supply infrastructure, and with the mechanisation of larger-scale holdings.

Main exports

Over half of exports are manufactured goods such as textiles. The rest are oil, coal and footstuffs. The main markets are Japan (18%), Hong Kong (22%), COMECON States (15%), the USA and Germany.

Main imports

Imports on new technology and complete industrial plants, such as power plants, petrochemical works and steel works are of growing importance. Other imports include grain, fertilisers, televisions, wrist watches. Main sources are Japan (29%), COMECON States (16%), Germany (8%), the USA, the UK, Canada and Australia.

Scope for additional investment

Foreign investors are actively sought in the provinces as well as the capital for joint ventures with municipalities and corporations. Free-trade zones are being established to encourage the entry of foreign enterprises (in Fujian and Sechou). There seems to be no restrictions as to the industries in which foreign enterprises will be welcomed. In general the interest is in the acquisition of modern technology. Most interest has been shown in ventures relating to textiles and light industry, development of natural resources (especially oil) and the tourist industry.

(Adapted from *Problems of Communism*, September–December 1979)

The Economy in Action

INDUSTRY

Much of China's industry is organised in large-scale works situated in city areas, and run as State enterprises. Since 1978, however, Vice-Premier Deng Xiaoping has been encouraging changes in how the economy is run. Firstly, some of the large-scale enterprises have been trying new management methods. Secondly, some small-scale 'sideline' industries are being allowed. Thirdly, a few 'enterprise zones' have been set up.

Case Study: A Large Industrial Works, Number 12 cotton mill, Shanghai.

This mill turns out cotton twill material and is part of the huge Shanghai textile industry which has over 400 000 workers. Before 1949 the owner of the mill was also the manager, making most of the decisions. From 1949 till 1980, a board of directors was appointed by the Government. In 1980, the Number 12 mill was given more 'self-management' when the workers' congress at the works was given more say in the managing of the factory. They can now produce goods beyond the State quota limit, and

Free enterprise market in main square of
Huangling, Shaanxi Province

can sell them at a profit, which can be used for new machinery or benefits. Recently the factory bicycle shed was enlarged, and a paved road was laid along the front of the mill. The new system of management also includes staff for planning and for sales, and closer inspection of goods produced in the factory.

(Adapted from *China Reconstructs*, May 1981)

Case Study: Chengdu Market

Chengdu, a rudimentary free market, operates along the main street from dawn until dusk. A good woollen suit, made to measure in a few hours, costs £25–30 – a lot of money to a Chinese but a bargain for the western tourists who are now being lured to Sichuan. Most of the local trade is in food. Pigs reared in private plots at a nearby commune are killed and sold in joints hung from a clothes-line strung between two trees for 30–35p a pound, with the price falling towards the evening. Stalls are packed with cabbages, corn cobs, huge Chinese radishes, tangerines, poultry and rabbits. They are usually run by retired men and women. If you are young you can lose work points and pay for being absent from your commune, although the takings from a good stall more than make up for this.

(*Economist*, 18 October 1980)

Case Study: Jiang Guoliang, Watch repairer (small-scale enterprise)

Jiang Guoliang left school in the city of Shanghai in 1977, but no job was available for him. He had a sprained arm and was therefore not sent to work on a rural commune. Instead, he spent a few years doing odd-jobs, such as repairing furniture.

In 1980 he sat and passed a test as a watch repairer. This allowed him to get a licence to set up as an 'individual industrial business', mending and cleaning clocks and watches.

Jiang works in a small entry porch in his parents' flat and deals with about 15 customers a day. He works 12 hours a day, so some people come to him for watch repairs rather than go to the State repair shop because they can go on their way to or from work. He also trys to mend old watches that the State shops turn away. He earns about £50 a month and hopes to learn soon how to repair digital watches.

(Adapted from *US News and World Report*, 23 March 1981)

Jiang Guoliang

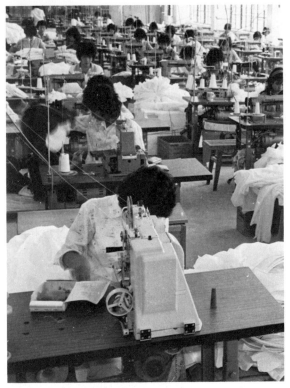
Xiamen garment factory

Xiamen Special Enterprise Zone

In an attempt to hurry along the economic progress in China, a few 'special' enterprise zones have been set up. With fewer planning restrictions and more financial incentives offered, it is hoped that foreign businesses will be attracted to set up. The Xiamen Zone is in Fujian Province in Southern China, near to Hong Kong, Macao and Taiwan. It is hoped that business people from these areas will set up industries in the zone, on land which can be rented but not bought. The zone was set up in 1979, and by 1980 had made some increase in its exports and economic growth.

Questions

1. What economic changes have been encouraged by Deng Xiaoping?
2. How do these changes affect some industrial works, such as the Number 12 cotton mill in Shanghai?
3. How does the small-scale watch repairer manage to compete with the State watch repair shop?
4. What is 'special' about the Xiamen special enterprise zone near Hong Kong?

AGRICULTURE: THE COMMUNE

Most of China's population live and work in rural communes: the basic unit of rural organisation in China today. The communes are communities of between 10 000 and 25 000 people and, although their main purpose is agricultural, they provide many other functions. According to Mao, they combined 'industry, agriculture, commerce, education and military affairs'. The commune is therefore the major unit of political organisation in the countryside, the militia is based on it, welfare services such as the care of the old and the education of the young are based on it, and the commune is also responsible for developing small-scale industry.

Development of the Commune

When the communists came to power in 1949, most of China's agricultural land belonged to a small group of landlords. One of the first acts of the new communist Government was to put into effect the Agrarian Reform Law in 1950, whereby the land was taken from the landlords and redistributed to the peasants.

Shortly after this the peasants were encouraged to farm cooperatively. This was done in a series of gradual steps. Mutual aid teams were set up. A number of farmers shared their work, animals and equipment, but they still owned their own land. The mutual aid teams were then encouraged to join together to form cooperative farms. By the middle of 1955 there were about 650 000 of these cooperatives, with a membership of about 17 million households out of a population of some 110 million. The success of these in increasing crop yields encouraged others to form and by 1957 practically the whole of rural China was organised in cooperatives. During the Great Leap Forward, the cooperatives were organised into large units which were to be more than just large farms: these were called People's Communes. Gradually, during the 1960s, they settled down into their present form.

Organisation

Each commune is sub-divided into a number of **production brigades.** There are from five to ten brigades in a commune, depending on the size of the commune. The brigade is responsible for medium-sized projects such as small industries or building schools or clinics. The commune itself is responsible for larger-scale industry (such as a small hydro-electric power station)

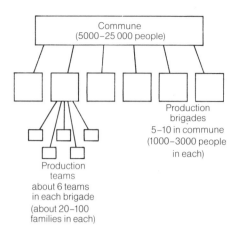

Commune
(5000–25 000 people)

Production
brigades
5–10 in commune
(1000–3000 people
in each)

Production
teams
about 6 teams
in each brigade
(about 20–100
families in each)

and for organising major projects such as flood control.

Each brigade is split into about six **production teams**. The team is the unit responsible for agriculture and for day-to-day work. Individual incomes are worked out at team level. After the State has taken its share of produce in taxation and in purchases, the remainder is distributed to the team members as wages. The rest of their income is made up in cash, according to how many 'work-points' they have built up during the year. A certain percentage of the team's gross income is set aside for welfare purposes and a further percentage goes towards financing those communal projects that need large-scale investment.

Present Priorities

During the Cultural Revolution, a great deal of emphasis was placed on the communes. This was not just done for agricultural reasons but also for political purposes. The communes were to represent the socialist ideal. Students and others from the towns were sent to the communes to work and to learn the political importance of this type of work. Private plots were discouraged and often work-points were allocated for political 'correctness' as much as for hard work. The ideal to be copied was the Dazhai Brigade which was setting a lead in 'self-reliance' in a very poor agricultural area of China.

The new leadership of China have, however, moved away from trying to make every commune copy the Dazhai example. Instead, the production teams have been encouraged to specialise in whatever income-earning activities are available to them. Instead of encouraging

peasants to work harder by political slogans and the 'Thoughts of Mao Zedong', a large number of material incentives have been introduced, according to the principle of 'more pay for more work'. Finally private plots are once again encouraged and each peasant has a small plot on which to grow vegetables and keep some animals. The produce of these plots can be used by the peasants themselves or sold in the nearby market.

Since each commune is now encouraged to produce what it is best suited for, some communes will do better and have a higher standard of living than others. The communes on the outskirts of large cities such as Beijing (Peking), Shanghai or Nanking will have good incomes, and electricity in their new-built brick houses, while more remote communes will have poorer incomes and still be made up of traditional peasant houses of mud walls and thatched roofs.

The Dazhai production brigade at work

Workers on a richer commune near Shanyang, preparing to deliver fresh vegetables to city markets

Case Study: Family Life on a People's Commune

'Ch'en Ho-Kuang, 39, and his wife Wang Yen-liu, 36, are field hands on the Ta Li People's Commune near Canton. They have quite a good standard of living, since this is a fertile farming area. Like all other peasants in Hao Mei village, the Ch'ens own their own house, a fairly new whitewashed brick building in a row of ten attached tile-roofed dwellings on a narrow lane. Their home which they share with three daughters, 11, 9 and 4, consists of a small entry hall, large living room and sizeable bedroom, small kitchen and back court with privy; they bath in a communal facility. The tile-floored high-ceilinged rooms are hot in summer, but they have an electric fan. Among other coveted 'things that go round', as the rural Chinese put it, they have an electric clock, a sewing machine and two bicycles. The rooms are adequately furnished: three beds, a desk, a large table, nine chairs, . . . , two big jars for storage of rice and a small glass-topped dresser on which sits a bowl of fruit. After deductions for their oil and rice allotments, the Ch'ens earn around $29 [£15] a month, though this depends on 'work-points', earned on performance in the field. They also raise some food – and possibly some extra cash – on a small private plot.'

Although earnings seem very low, the Ch'ens pay no income tax, housing costs are very small and medical care and education are virtually free.

Questions

1. In what ways are the People's Communes more than just 'large farms'?
2. Outline the steps in agricultural reform which led to the setting-up of the communes.
3. Describe how a commune is organised.
4. Explain how commune members are paid.
5. What changes in agricultural policy have there been since Mao's death?

A domestic scene on a Chinese commune in Sichuan Province

Economic Problems and Potential

PROBLEMS

'The Chinese people's march towards the great goal of the Four Modernisations echoes from foothills of the Yenshan Mountains to the shores of the Yellow Sea. We are setting out on our new Long March to conquer the mountains, seas, plains, oil fields and mines of our motherland. We want to scale the heights of science and technology. We want to develop normal trade relations with other countries of the world.'

(Chinese *People's Daily*, 1979)

Before these aims can be achieved in the changed priorities of the Chinese economy, a number of problems have to be overcome.

Economic problems

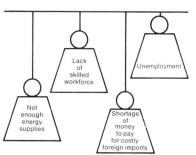

1. *Energy supplies*. Although China already produces large quantities of energy (third largest producer in the world) there is not enough available to meet the rapid modernisation demands. At present, coal is the main energy source while many oilfields are still being developed.

2. *Lack of skilled workforce*. Owing to former education policy which removed many city students to the countryside, there is a lack of specialised people in factories. Because qualifications were previously not required, there is now a great shortage of skilled labour of many kinds: scientists, technicians, managers and engineers.

3. *Shortage of money for foreign trade*. Until recently China was not much involved in foreign trade, but because there is now a rush to trade, to build up China, this has led to a shortage of money for the many trade deals promised. Over-optimism has led to a number of deals being cancelled with foreign companies. In other cases, such as the huge Baoshan Steel Works by the Chang Jiang (Yangtze River), some cutbacks have been made and West German and Japanese steel companies have been affected.

4. *Unemployment*. As modernisation and mechanisation continue, fewer jobs are available. There are several million unemployed, especially young people in the cities, yet many people leave the countryside to move to the cities.

5. *Slowness to adopt change*. Many officials and civil servants do not agree with the changes in how the economy is run. Both Vice-Premier Deng Xiaoping and Premier Zhao Ziyang in 1981 criticised the slowness of some officials. The cartoon below appeared in *China Reconstructs* in 1981 and illustrates the view that some officials are slowing the programme of the Four Modernisations.

ECONOMIC POTENTIAL

Much of China's future potential depends on how well the 'Four Modernisations' policy works. Even if there is only a small improvement, for example, 3% as in 1981, China still has the potential to be an economic Superpower in the future.

What's your hurry?

Modernization

He's in no hurry.   *Liu Yong*

Economic potential

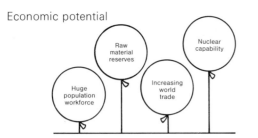

1. *Large workforce*. With a large supply of people who will work for low incomes, China could attract foreign firms. The Government are encouraging foreign firms to set up in China and many companies are interested in a future possible market of 1000 million people.

2. *Mineral reserves*. China has a great variety of mineral reserves. Huge coal, oil and natural gas deposits have still to be developed. Uranium is plentiful and in 1982 China offered to sell uranium to the European Community (EEC).

3. *World trade*. Earlier policies of trying to make China as self-reliant as possible have been set aside and China is interested in opening up trade links with Japan, the USA and the EEC. This trade will bring China much-needed technical and mechanical industrial 'know-how' and equipment to modernise China's industries, railways and agriculture.

4. *Nuclear capability*. China is already a nuclear power in both military capability and electric power generating. In 1980, Chinese technologists were able to launch two intercontinental rockets over a distance of 10 000 kilometres. With help from France, China is now building more nuclear power stations to supply energy for industry.

Questions

1. Describe the general aim of the 'Four Modernisations' as outlined in the quotation.
2. What problem does the cartoon of the Four Modernisations illustrate?
3. What difficulties have to be overcome before China's economy can improve greatly?
4. Why could China be described as an 'economic Superpower' of the future?

China as a Model for Developing Countries

Although China is seen as an emerging world Superpower, it must also be seen as belonging in many respects to the so-called Third World. With so much of its population living in the countryside, its dependence upon agriculture is obvious. However, unlike many Third World countries, China has been remarkably successful in coping with and even solving those problems which in many other developing countries seem insurmountable. China's success in feeding, clothing, housing and educating a population of about 1000 million, its success in slowing down its population growth rate and its success in developing an industrial base has given it an enviable reputation and suggested that it can in many respects provide a working model for other Third World countries.

When the communists came to power, China was known as the 'land of famine'. Today, although periodic disasters can occur, the standard of living in the countryside provides a marked contrast to countries like India. A great deal of the credit for this can be traced to the development of the People's Communes. The gradual **collectivisation** of agriculture which led to the foundation of the communes, has helped to increase food supplies and improve living standards. The communes have allowed peasants to farm cooperatively in large units, to share labour and equipment and to develop a means of rural society in which social welfare can be promoted.

Along with the communes have gone the two important principles: self-reliance and 'walking on two legs'. During the Great Leap Forward, the Chinese began to carry out the idea of self-reliance to avoid becoming dependent on outside foreign aid. Along with this went the idea of combining the large-scale and small-scale, modern and traditional, methods: called 'walking on two legs'. Although errors were made in carrying out these ideas too rigorously, this did allow China to develop ideas and technology suitable to her own needs and to avoid the dangers of over-reliance on foreign aid. Throughout China, people were encouraged to 'do-it-themselves' rather than depend on sophisticated technology. An example of this can be seen in the production and use of energy. The Chinese are encouraged to develop their own local energy where appropriate, and many communes have built small hydro-electric generators. In addition some villages use a form of 'biogas production'. Air and watertight drums produce methane gas from the bacterial decomposition of organic material. The gas is used for cooking and lighting and to power small internal combustion engines. Also, the 'sludge' remaining after the gas has been produced makes an excellent fertiliser.

Medical care in the countryside has been greatly improved thanks to the development of **'barefoot doctors'**, clinics and county hospitals. Education in the countryside still lags behind the cities but in most places elementary education has been established. Living standards are also poorer in the countryside but the gap is not as great as in many Third World countries and this has been due to deliberate Government policy to make rural life more attractive. The policy of small-scale and medium-scale industry located in the countryside has also helped to prevent the mass migration to the cities which is a major feature of developing countries.

China has actively encouraged other Third World countries to follow her lead by offering them friendship and economic aid. An excellent example of this was the building of the Tan-Zam Railway between Tanzania and Zambia. The railway was completed in 1975 thanks to Chinese financial help and technical advice. What was particularly important about this scheme, however, was the way in which China provided this aid. The loans were interest-free and no political concessions were demanded.

The Chinese approach to Third World aid can be seen in the following extract from an article in *The Times*, at the time of the completion of the Tan-Zam Railway in 1975. It shows how the Chinese, as a result of their own experiences, can provide the kind of development that poorer countries require.

'Promoting development' rather than simply providing aid, is a more accurate description of China's position than of any other country's. For China is itself part of the Third World, grappling with its most typical problems on its own soil and gradually transforming the very conditions that have given rise to world confrontation between rich and poor. A condition of Chinese aid is that both specialists and other workers who do a tour of duty in a foreign country are paid according to the standards in force in that country. As the standards of living in most developing countries is low, this reduces costs considerably.

FUTURE DEVELOPMENTS

China can provide in many respects a working model for developing countries. But it must be remembered that much of what has happened in China came about as a result of a major social and political revolution. Such conditions may not exist in other countries.

Finally mention has to be made of the new economic policies being followed by the present leadership of China. The old policy of self-reliance is being replaced by a greater involvement in the outside world, new emphasis is being placed on economic and industrial progress. To what extent will this open up a gap between city and countryside and perhaps strain the working model of Third World development which China has given the world? This is a major question for China's new leadership.

Questions

1. What major feature of China's economy suggests that it is similar to a Third World country?
2. In what social and economic measures has China been more successful than most other Third World countries?
3. Explain the importance of the following in making these achievements:
   (a) the communes,
   (b) the policy of self-reliance,
   (c) the policy of 'walking on two legs'.
4. How has China shown its identity with the developing countries through its programme of foreign aid?

The Tan-Zam Railway

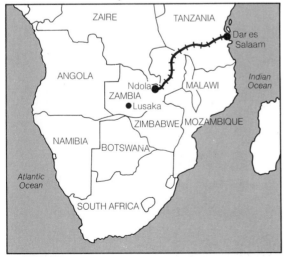

3. The Political System

The Political System in Action

The formal political system of China is based upon a **Constitution** dating from 1954, a Constitution which has been much modified over the years. The State Council in Beijing (Peking) is the nearest equivalent to the British and American Cabinets and is headed by the Premier (at present Zhao Ziyang) and various Vice-Premiers who head Departments of State such as Defence, the Economy, Industry, Agriculture and so on.

Below the State Council, at national level, are the Provincial Councils. These govern the provinces and major cities of China, such as Beijing and Shanghai, according to directives from the State Council. Beneath this, at county or city level, are the Hsien Councils and below these, at commune and town level, are the Hsiang Councils. At each of these levels Congresses elect the councils for the areas they serve.

ELECTIONS

In 1980 there took place for the first time in over 20 years elections for county and municipal governments. These elections were carried out as follows: any elector, with the support of three others, was able to nominate a candidate and this list of candidates was then inspected by an electoral commission and reduced to a number slightly greater than the number of places to be filled; for example, in Beijing there were 592 approved candidates for 350 places. The elections took place according to a secret ballot.

To the rest of the world these elections were seen as evidence that the new leadership in China wished to make the political system more democratic, but still within the limits of control by the Communist Party.

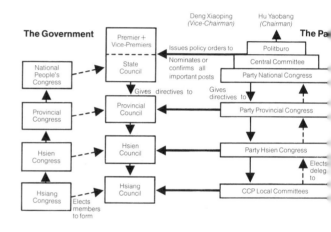

The first municipal elections in more than 20 years draw a massive turnout at a university ballot box.

THE PARTY

The most important feature about the political system in China, however, is that, as in the USSR, there exists only one political party – the Chinese Communist Party (**CCP**) – and it is the Party which effectively controls government at all levels, from the State Council to the committees which run the **communes** and factories.

The CCP is not open for anyone to join. Membership is a great honour and involves hard work and considerable responsibility. Membership is small compared with the overall population of China; there are some 26 million full-time members, about 2% of the population. Young people under 15 can join the Young Pioneers and those of 15–25 years join the Communist Youth League.

At all levels of government, Party officials or **cadres** influence and direct policies and decisions. At the head of the CCP is the Central Committee whose leading members form the **Politburo**. The person who leads the Party is the Chairman, a position held by **Mao Zedong** till his death in 1976. He was succeeded for a period by **Hua Guofeng**. Then in 1981 **Hu Yaobang** replaced him as Chairman. As we shall see, real power in China lies, at present, in the hands of **Deng Xiaoping**, Vice-Chairman of the Party. The activities and manoeuverings of the leaders in the Politburo determine the policies and direction of China. Below the national scene, at the local level in the communes and factories, the local Party officials are key figures in explaining current Government policy and in encouraging people to follow this policy.

Case Study: A Local Party Official

Teng Jiayun is the Party Secretary of the Tsao Kang production brigade of the Yun Men Kou People's Commune near Chengdu, capital of Sichuan province. He is 29 years old and is in charge of the 450-household production brigade. In an interview with an American journalist he described his responsibilities:

'Most members of the brigade (work unit) have no fear of me at all. I do my work by trying to reason things out. But if any brigade members do bad things, then they might be afraid of me .... I spend a lot of my time working in the fields', says Teng, but as party secretary, a post for which he receives a small salary ($22 a month), he must also mediate conflicts, punish

misdemeanors and even try to persuade couples to have only one child, in accordance with Peking's hope of limiting population growth ... . 'Whenever the leader talks to the offender, usually that is sufficient', Teng says. 'But if the leader chooses, he may also call a meeting to criticise the offender in public. If the person does not work hard, it is very easy to penalise him because of the new system of more pay for more work.'

Questions

1. Explain the importance of the Communist Party in the government of China.
2. What is the Politburo and who has held the post of Chairman of the Communist Party?
3. What responsibilities do members of the Communist Party have? (You should refer to the case study of Teng Jiayun.)

Political Developments

On 1 October 1949, from the top of the Gate of Heavenly Peace in Beijing, Mao Zedong announced the foundation of the People's Republic of China. Since then, China has undergone a series of dramatic political upheavals. These major changes in political development reflected important divisions among the leaders in the CCP over what kind of communist society China should become and how it should reach that kind of society. This was later to become known as the 'two road struggle'.

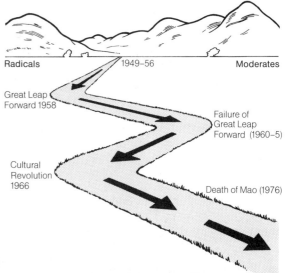

Radicals — 1949–56 — Moderates
Great Leap Forward 1958
Failure of Great Leap Forward (1960–5)
Cultural Revolution 1966
Death of Mao (1976)
Present leadership

The principal stages in this 'two road struggle' were:

1. the **Great Leap Forward**,

2. the **Cultural Revolution**,

3. the power struggle after Mao's death.

The dispute often centred on personalities but it was always about ideas. The two groups in the CCP can be termed the 'Radicals' and the 'Moderates' and the political and economic development of China can be traced according to whichever group was in control of the Party.

Both the Radicals and Moderates believed in a communist society led by the Communist Party but they disagreed about the kind of society that should be and about the way of creating that society. Their main points of difference can be seen over their approaches to the economy, to education, to the role of politics and to the place of the Party in society. We can see these differences in this chart.

Radicals	Moderates
Main priority should be given to politics, to continual revolution and to the creation of a classless society.	Main priority should be given to economic progress. China needs to develop economically to join the advanced nations of the world.
Workers are to be encouraged by political incentives. The Thoughts of Mao Zedong are to be the main source of inspiration.	In industry there should be bonuses and production incentives to encourage people to work harder.
Industrial growth should not be followed at the expense of the ideals of the revolution.	In agriculture there should be more encouragement of peasants to produce more and to benefit directly from this, even if it means encouraging private plots in the communes.
In education, politics are to be all-important. Exams create elitism and should be abolished. Education should mix theory and social practice. Students should work in factories and communes as well as study in school and university.	In education, examinations are necessary to select people to be trained as technical experts needed by China's industry.
Above all else there should not exist a privileged elite of Party members and technical experts.	To avoid economic chaos, Party leaders, teachers and technical experts have to be encouraged and rewarded.

THE GREAT LEAP FORWARD

By 1956 the first part of China's Communist Revolution was over. The communists had secured their power and had laid the foundations of a socialist economy. The next stage in China's political development was to bring to light the split in the party between the Radicals and Moderates. Mao felt that the first five-year plan, which had closely followed the example of the USSR, had not been fully successful. He wanted China to follow its own road, concentrating more on the peasants and leading to a more classless society.

As a result, in 1958, China was launched upon a new pattern of economic development: the Great Leap Forward. This was a major attempt to increase dramatically production in agriculture and industry. It was also a political move to change China into the kind of society Mao wanted. Emphasis was placed on developing small-scale as well as large industry. This was to become known as 'walking on two legs'. In the countryside the communes were set up. The spectacular targets would be met by using China's vast population: the so-called 'blue ants'. People were encouraged to work hard by Party cadres exhorting them with political slogans: 'Work for China', 'Serve the People', 'Politics in Command'. All were expected to pitch in and work for China.

The Great Leap Forward soon began to run into difficulties. The period 1959–61 was one of dreadful weather and disastrous harvests. In

1960 the Soviet Union, in protest against the Great Leap, withdrew all technical aid from China. In terms of the spectacular targets set, the Great Leap was not a success. It did have important results for the Chinese economy: it encouraged 'self-reliance' and it set up the communes. It was, however, a political set-back for Mao. It led to a loss of personal power for him and as a result a loss of power for the Radical cause within the Party. From 1961 onwards the Moderates began to show their influence, and moves were made to make the economy more stable. Mao seemed to be in danger of losing control in the party to the Moderate wing, led by *Liu Shaoqui.*

THE CULTURAL REVOLUTION

On 16 July 1966, Mao, at the age of 72, swam 9 miles (14 kilometres) down the Chang Jiang (Yangtze River). This much-publicised event was a signal to his supporters that he was in excellent health and that he was back in place as leader of his nation. This came at the end of many months of internal dispute within the Party between the Radicals led by Mao and the Moderates led by Liu Shaoqui. Mao was to settle this struggle by appealing to the masses of China to help him win the ideological struggle against the 'Party persons in authority taking the Capitalist road'. These people were described as 'revisionists' who wanted to revise true Marxism–Leninism for their own purposes, just as the USSR had done under **Khrushchev**.

The Cultural Revolution – as this massive upheaval in China became known – was launched when Mao addressed millions of young schoolchildren and students in massive parades in Beijing during August 1966. These young Red Guards were to become the leaders in Mao's new revolution against those who wanted to turn China back along the capitalist road. Mao

Poster of Khrushchev and Lin Shaoqui

felt that the young in particular needed to learn the importance of revolution for they had never known the old China of **imperialism** and **capitalism** before 1949.

The *Beijing Review* in September 1966 reported the following statement by the Red Guards of a Beijing School:

All present day reactionaries say: exploitation is justified, oppression is justified, aggression is justified, and revisionist rule is justified: but it is unjustifiable for the proletariat to rebel. It is Chairman Mao, our most respected and beloved leader and the greatest revolutionary teacher, who turned this pig-headed theory right side up. Chairman Mao has said: 'In the last analysis, all the truths of Marxism can be summed up in one sentence: to rebel is justified'.

Red Guards renaming East Yangwei (displaying pomposity) Road, as Fanhsiu (anti-revisionism) Road during the Cultural Revolution

The Red Guards were encouraged to 'struggle' against 'those in authority who have wormed their way into the Party and are taking the Capitalist road', to 'criticise' revisionist ideas and to 'transform the old educational system' and all other aspects of 'bourgeois ideas, culture, customs and habits'. Armed with the *Little Red Book* of the 'Thoughts of Mao Zedong', they were sent out into China to carry out this revolution. They attacked anything and anybody connected with old China, they criticised and humiliated teachers, factory managers, party officials, they replaced street names and even changed traffic signals so that red became the signal for 'go'. Above all they praised Mao to god-like status.

In December 1966 the workers in China became involved and the economy began to fall into chaos with industrial and agricultural production being disrupted. During 1967 the Red Guards began to·get out of control and the People's Liberation Army (PLA) was used to restore order. By 1968 the Cultural Revolution was over and the millions of Red Guards returned home or to the countryside to help the peasants.

What did the Cultural Revolution achieve?

1. It restored Mao to full control of the Party. Liu Shaoqui and other Moderates throughout the Party at all levels were disgraced and removed from positions of power.

2. In the economy it re-established the importance of agriculture and the importance of politics rather than technical expertise.

3. In education it led to a reduction in the amount and importance of exams. It also re-established the idea of mixing theory and practice. Students, teachers, doctors, scientists had to mix book-learning with practical work in factories and fields.

The Cultural Revolution was undoubtedly a time of massive upheaval and turmoil in China. Since Mao's death it has become clear that there was a great deal of personal suffering during this period and that the Chinese economy was greatly set back.

The following extract comes from an article printed in *The Scotsman* in 1981. It details the upheavals caused during the Cultural Revolution:

Hsai Tzu-ching is the distinguished Professor of Modern History at Beijing University. He is also an ex-cowboy.

'I was not a real cowboy of course. But like so many others I was upbraided by students and junior staff for being what they called a capitalist roader. The Red Guards said I was poisoning my students' minds. So they sent me to a farm for a year and put me in charge of cattle.'

An Gang is deputy editor-in-chief of the People's Daily . . . The Red Guards found special work for senior editors. An Gang and his colleagues were forced to clean the People's Daily toilets for a year or so as radical youths occupied the newspaper.

Chen Shao-min is head of a large general hospital in the city of Harbin, Manchuria. He too became victim of youthful revolutionaries and was forced to do farm work. At his hospital some of the nurses decided that they would like to be doctors, and that the doctors should be nurses.

The life of the nation was disrupted for an entire decade, and that for a society already economically backward is the kind of handicap that cannot be afforded. Only now is the hospital in Harbin moving back to normal. As in the rest of China, the hospital is suffering from the fact that an entire generation of students wasted its time.

(*Scotsman*, 27 May 1981)

Questions

1. What is meant by the phrase the 'two road struggle'?
2. Summarise the main policy differences between the two factions in the Chinese Communist Party (the Moderates and Radicals) with regard to
   (*a*) the economy,
   (*b*) the role of the Party and of politics and
   (*c*) education.
3. Describe the aims of the Great Leap Forward, showing how it can be seen as part of the Radical development in China.
4. What important political results did the failure of the Great Leap Forward have for Mao?
5. Why did Mao decide to launch the Cultural Revolution?
6. Describe the main features of the Cultural Revolution and explain its importance in the political development of China.
7. What effects did the Cultural Revolution have on China's social and economic development?

The Power Struggle

Following the dramatic events of the Cultural Revolution, the major political issue of the early 1970s was that of who was to be Mao's successor. This was of course not just a question of personalities but also of policies, of which road China was to follow.

An early candidate for successor was *Lin Biao*. He had been Defence Minister and Mao had come to rely upon him during the Cultural Revolution, when he was in fact named as successor to Mao for leadership of the CCP. In 1971, however, Lin died in a mysterious air-crash over Outer Mongolia, apparently trying to escape from China after a failed plot to assassinate Mao.

As Mao's health began to deteriorate, the effective leadership of China was undertaken by Mao's life-long comrade, **Zhou Enlai**. Zhou began to act as a moderating influence and gradually began to restore some order and stability to China after the excesses of the Cultural Revolution. In 1973 Zhou arranged for the return to office of *Deng Xiaoping*, a leading Moderate, who had been disgraced during the Cultural Revolution as 'Liu Shaoqui's henchman'.

During 1975 Zhou himself fell ill and Deng began to emerge as the person most likely to succeed him and as a result to succeed Mao himself. In early 1976 Zhou Enlai died but once again, as during the Cultural Revolution, Deng became the victim of a Radical campaign, led by Mao, and he was expelled from office. Instead of Deng, the CCP announced that Zhou Enlai would be succeeded by **Hua Guofeng**.

Five months later, on 9 September 1976, Mao Zedong died and Hua took over as Chairman.

A Guide to the Power Struggle in China

Mao Zedong
The great revolutionary leader – but who would succeed him?

Lin Biao
Named Mao's successor during the Cultural Revolution but died in 1971 escaping from China after failing in plot to kill Mao.

Zhou Enlai
Effective leader of China during Mao's last years. Died shortly before Mao.

Deng Xiaoping
Most powerful politician in China today.

Hua Guofeng
Became Chairman in 1976 on Mao's death. Resigned 1981.

Hu Yaobang
Present Chairman of the CCP. Appointed 1981.

The Gang of Four,
led by **Jiang Qing**, Mao's widow. Arrested in 1976 on charge of plotting to seize power after Mao's death.

Demonstration against the Gang of Four, 1976

Shortly after this it was announced that a group of extreme Radicals had been arrested for plotting to seize power. This group became known as the **Gang of Four** and were led by Mao's widow, *Jiang Qing*. The Gang of Four were accused of being extreme followers of Mao, of being interested only in power and of being responsible for all the terrible things that had happened during the Cultural Revolution and after. Jiang Qing herself became the object of extreme abuse, being described as 'savage as a mad dog'. The arrest of the Gang of Four showed that the Radical faction in the CCP was in retreat. Hua owed his position as Chairman to Mao and he was loyal to many of Mao's policies. But by rejecting the extreme radicalism of the Gang of Four, he was able to act as a moderating influence and opened' the way for the new economic policies of the Four Modernisations.

THE PRESENT LEADERSHIP

With the arrest of the Gang of Four the position of Chairman Hua seemed secure. Pressure from Moderates in the CCP forced him to accept the return to office in 1977 of Deng Xiaoping. In the period which followed it became increasingly clear that it was Deng who was behind the development of the new economic policies. One of the famous sayings of Deng had been, 'it doesn't matter whether a cat is black or white as long as it catches mice'. This had been taken as evidence of following the 'capitalist road' before the Cultural Revolution. Now it could be seen to summarise the new policies of China: that most things were acceptable if they worked.

In November 1980 the Gang of Four were put on trial for 'counter-revolution'. The trial was used as a means to finally discredit the Radicals and emphasise that the new leadership was firmly in charge. The trial also implied that if the Gang of Four were guilty, then Mao himself must also have been guilty. It was suggested that a fifth empty chair should have been put in the dock to remind the people of Mao's unseen presence. The trial also indirectly affected Chairman Hua, since he had been chosen by Mao. During 1981, criticism began to appear of Hua's leadership and Hua was often absent from important Party meetings. Later that year it was announced that Hua had resigned as Chairman of the CCP and that he was being replaced by **Hu Yaobang**.

These events confirmed the position of Deng Xiaoping as the undisputed leader of China, since Hu was a loyal supporter of Deng. With the

Jiang Qing on trial, 1981

trial of the Gang of Four and the demotion of Hua, Deng had completed a long struggle for control in China for his Moderate policies.

Questions

1. Why was the issue of Mao's successor so important for China's political future?
2. Make a list of the following names and briefly describe the part each played in the power struggle over Mao's succession:
   Lin Biao; Zhou Enlai; Hua Guofeng; Jiang Qing and the Gang of Four; Deng Xiaoping.
3. In what ways did Deng Xiaoping show that he had become the new leader of China?

De-Maoification

ISSUE

When Mao Zedong died in 1976, millions of Chinese mourned the death of their greatest leader, the father of communist China. Known to his people as 'The Great Helmsman', he had been revolutionary leader, Chairman of the Chinese Communist Party from 1935 to 1976, world statesman, philosopher, poet and political thinker. His body was embalmed and placed in a Mausoleum in Tienanmen Square in the centre of Beijing: a fitting tribute to someone who had been worshipped like a god during his life.

Mao was born in 1893, the son of a peasant. He first became involved in politics in 1911 when the Chinese royal family was overthrown. By 1921 he had become a communist and helped found the Chinese Communist Party. In 1927 the ruler of China, **Chiang Kai-shek**, turned against the communists and opened up a period of civil war which did not end until 1949, with Mao's victory. During that period Mao emerged as a great **guerrilla** leader, forming the Red Army, ensuring their survival with the epic Long March into the Chinese interior and finally winning success by leading the national struggle against the Japanese who had invaded China in 1937. When the Japanese surrendered in 1945, the civil war between Mao and Chiang resumed until in October 1949, Mao was able to proclaim the People's Republic of China. Chiang fled with his supporters to Formosa (now called Taiwan) where he set up a rival government to the communists on the mainland.

From 1949 to 1976 Mao continued to dominate China. His vision of a revolutionary China reached its peak during the Cultural Revolution. At this point, worship of Mao was raised to the level of a cult and the *Little Red Book* of the Thoughts of Chairman Mao became like a bible.

THOUGHTS OF MAO ZEDONG

On the need for revolutionary war: 'Every Communist must grasp the truth, "Political power grows out of the barrel of a gun".'

On guerrilla war: 'The revolutionary war is a war of the masses; it can be waged only by mobilising the masses and relying on them.'

1. When the enemy advances we retreat.

2. When he escapes we harass.

3. When he retreats we pursue.

4. When he is tired we attack.

On reactionary foreign powers: 'All reactionaries are paper tigers. In appearance, the reactionaries are terrifying, but in reality they are not so powerful. From a long-term point of view, it is not the reactionaries but the people who are really powerful.'

On the People's Army: 'Our principle is that the Party commands the gun and the gun must never be allowed to command the Party.'

On revolutionary youth: 'How should we judge whether a youth is a revolutionary? How can we tell? There can only be one criterion, namely, whether he is willing to integrate himself with the broad masses of workers and peasants and does so in practice.'

On study: 'In order to have a real grasp of Marxism, one must learn it not only from books, but mainly through class struggle, through practical work and close contact with the masses of workers and peasants.'

On revisionism: 'After the basic victory of the socialist revolution in our country, there are still a number of people who vainly hope to restore the capitalist system and fight the working class on every front, including the ideological one. And their right-hand men in this struggle are the revisionists.'

On the USA: 'Riding roughshod everywhere, US imperialism has made itself the enemy of the people of the world.'

On the USSR: 'The revisionist leading clique of the Soviet Union is a mere dust heap'.

REASSESSING MAO

Since Mao's death, China has started to develop along a road which, in many respects, is against what Mao believed in. The trial of the Gang of Four was used to discredit the Radical ideas that Mao had himself advocated. This has meant that the new leadership in China have had to present Mao in a different image. They have had to begin a process of 'de-Maoification'. Of course this could not proceed too quickly, for you cannot treat someone like a god and then suddenly make major criticisms of all that he stood for.

Instead there has been a gradual process by which it has been officially admitted that Mao made mistakes. Many of the worst excesses have been blamed on the Gang of Four but Mao is blamed for putting too much emphasis on the class struggle. Deng Xiaoping has suggested that Mao was 70% right and 30% wrong. His mistakes were made during the Great Leap Forward and during the Cultural Revolution. The honourable part covers his career up to 1949, his role as a political thinker and his part in ensuring that after the Revolution there would be no return to the corruption of the past. Despite the removal of Mao's posters, despite the drop in

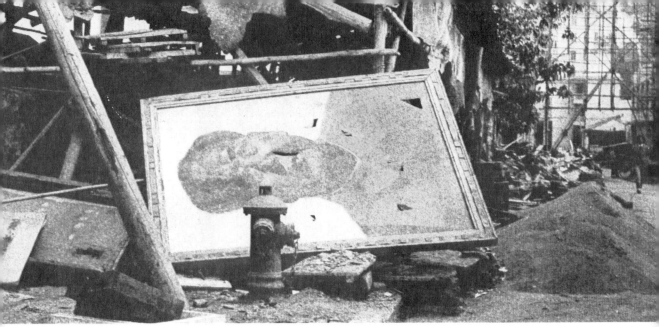

The downfall of Mao: picture on Guangzhou garbage heap, 1981

popularity of the *Little Red Book*, the Chinese will still remember Mao as an extraordinary leader. But this will be in the context of an ordinary mortal who made mistakes and not as a god.

Questions

1. Write a short biography of Mao Zedong, showing why he was such a major figure in modern Chinese history.
2. Explain what is meant by 'de-Maoification' and explain why the new leaders of China felt it necessary to undertake this.

Democracy and Human Rights

In 1957 Mao Zedong launched the Hundred Flowers Campaign. He encouraged writers and artists to enter into free discussion, to criticise and comment on communism in China: 'let a hundred flowers bloom and a hundred schools of thought contend'. This invitation led to a flood of criticism, much of which was directed against the Communist Party and even against communism itself. This experiment in free discussion seemed to have backfired and the Hundred Flowers Campaign was halted. China reverted to the process of Thought Reform to transform people's thinking. To many in the West this seemed like brainwashing. It seemed to be

re-inforced with the later devotion to the Thoughts of Mao Zedong. Children especially appeared to be exposed to political indoctrination in school. Undoubtedly, during the height of the Cultural Revolution, there was great pressure on the Chinese people to follow the Party line.

A NEW FREEDOM?

The new leadership which came to power after the death of Mao and the arrest of the Gang of Four seemed to be promising a new era of greater freedom and democracy. They criticised the Cultural Revolution because, although it had started out with the intention of making the Party more answerable to the people, it had ended up in a cruel and harsh tyranny.

The Constitution, revised in 1978, stated:

'Citizens enjoy freedom of speech, correspondence, the press, assembly, association, procession, demonstration, and the freedom to strike, and have the right to "speak out freely, air their views fully, hold great debates and write big-character posters".'

People were encouraged to petition for the reversal of judgements made against them during the Cultural Revolution. In addition a new formal legal system was set up which guaranteed the rights of defendants. Finally direct elections were to be held for county-level (Hsien) Congresses.

Democracy Wall, Beijing

The response to this official democratic movement was enormous. Wall posters appeared in huge numbers. Democracy Wall in Beijing became the central place for these posters. In them people called for democracy, human rights and free elections. Leading Party officials were criticised. In January 1979 a large number of peasants came to Beijing to protest about living conditions. Many young people converged on cities protesting about having been sent to the countryside during the Cultural Revolution.

RETREAT

Faced with this overwhelming response, the Government began to take a firmer line. By March 1979 posters began to be pulled down and Democracy Wall was moved from the centre of Beijing to the outskirts of the city. This was repeated in other cities. At the same time two leading dissidents, Wei Jingsheng and Fu Yuehua, were arrested, put on trial and given harsh prison sentences. Wei, editor of a political journal which had been posted on Democracy Wall, was sentenced to 15 years in prison for allegedly giving military secrets to foreign journalists.

In 1980 the 'four big rights' – to speak out freely, air views freely, hold great debates and write big-character posters – were removed from the constitution. Did all this merely repeat the pattern of the Hundred Flowers Campaign? Had the authorities released forces which they feared could get out of hand? Certainly any further democratisation will only come about with Party approval and direction. The decision to hold elections and to introduce new law codes do show a desire to introduce a more democratic system, but the tougher line on dissidents emphasises that this will be within the limits of Party control.

Questions

1. What was the Hundred Flowers Campaign?
2. What evidence was there of greater political freedom in the period after Mao's death?
3. In what ways and for what reasons were limits placed on this political freedom?

4. International Involvement

Foreign Policy

AIMS

'It is our hope in China that not only the United States, but Japan and Western Europe and the Third World will unite to deal with Soviet hegemonism (expansion).'

(*China's Vice-Premier Deng Xiaoping, 1980*)

In recent years much of China's aim in foreign policy has been to oppose and obstruct the aims of the Soviet Union.

China: Foreign policy aims

To oppose the USSR, for example in Afghanistan, Kampuchea

To build up China's military defences by, for example, modernising military equipment

CHINA

To support Third World countries, for example in Africa

To increase trade rapidly with other countries such as Japan, the USA

BACKGROUND

After the Chinese communists, led by **Mao Zedong**, gained power in China in 1949, China relied on help from its **communist** neighbour, the Soviet Union. Like the USSR, China was very critical of the USA and other Western **capitalist** countries. In the **Third World**, China aimed to show by aid and example that Chinese communism was a good model for other developing countries. Mao gave his support to 'peoples' wars against oppression'. During this time, however, Mao was also concerned to build up China as a self-reliant country, not depending too much on outside help.

This aim of self-reliance by China was given even more emphasis by Mao after the Sino-Soviet split in the 1960s, when the Soviet Union cut off aid to China. Since the death of Mao in 1976, however, the new leaders of China have aimed to obtain closer links with Western

Europe, the USA, and Japan. These links help China to increase its potential threat to the USSR, and to obtain much-needed modern technology and equipment for its ambitious 'modernisation' programme (see page 140).

AREAS OF INTEREST: RELATIONS WITH NEIGHBOURING COUNTRIES

Troops at the Chinese borders

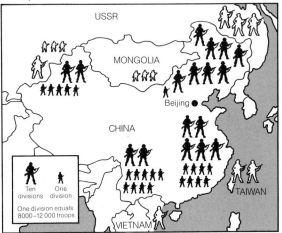

(*Newsweek*: Greg Kauffman)

The USSR

China's relations with her largest neighbour, the Soviet Union, are the most important part, in China's view, of the whole of its foreign policy. From being communist allies in the 1950s, the relationship has changed completely by the 1980s to one of hostility to each other. The reasons for the change and the development of Sino-Soviet relations are covered in the unit on pages 125–6.

Vietnam

After the American forces withdrew from Vietnam, and North and South were united into one, the Soviet Union supplied aid and advisers, and its warships were allowed to use harbours in Vietnam. China was highly critical of this, seeing it as Soviet expansion in South-east Asia. In 1978, Vietnam signed a treaty with the USSR and then invaded Kampuchea. The Chinese Government decided this was too much of a threat, so Chinese troops invaded Vietnam in January 1979 'to teach Vietnam a lesson'.

> Just before sunrise last Saturday, tens of thousands of Chinese troops, backed by fighter planes, tanks, and artillery, invaded Vietnam. The assault began with a relentless barrage of artillery fire directed at Vietnamese villages and military outposts, and it stretched across most of the 600 mile border. Radio Hanoi described it as a large scale invasion, and stated that Chinese troops had penetrated six miles into Vietnam.

The Chinese invasion of Vietnam, 1979

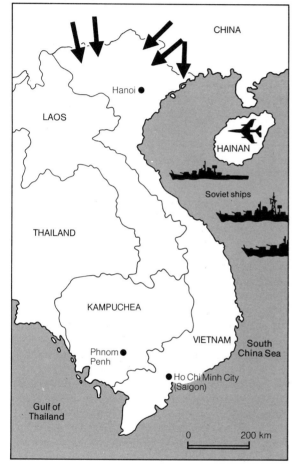

After about one month in Vietnam, the Chinese forces pulled back, stating that they did not wish to hold any Vietnamese territory.

Taiwan

In China's view there is only 'one China' and Taiwan (formerly Formosa) belongs to China, as part of the People's Republic. 'There should be no "Taiwan question" at all, either historically, legally, or internationally.' (Chinese

Taiwan

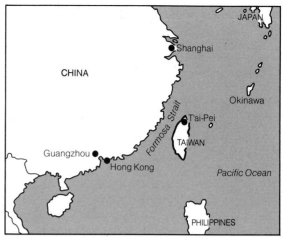

Government spokesman 1981) When Nationalist leader **Chiang Kai-shek** fled to Formosa in 1949 and set up a non-communist Chinese government there, the USA undertook to defend Formosa as 'the real China'.

Since the USA recognised communist China in 1979, however, its support for Taiwan, although continuing in terms of aid and weapons, has not been at full diplomatic level.

China's present policy is to seek the re-joining of Taiwan with mainland China, although recent Chinese plans for such a move have been rejected by the Taiwan Government.

Hong Kong

Since 1832, when two Scotsmen set up business near Canton, the city of Hong Kong has become a busy overcrowded seaport. It is a British colony, but the lease on most of the area runs out in 1997 by which date it must be given back to China. Although China does not recognise the lease, it has never tried to take over Hong Kong by force. In 1984 China and Britain signed a 'hand-over' treaty.

At present, China is offering Hong Kong housing space on the mainland and is interested in good relations with Hong Kong to help its own 'modernisation' plans.

About 150 000 Chinese refugees cross the border into Hong Kong each year, some legally, some illegally. Most settle in Hong Kong and this increases its already excessive population. Extra British troops were sent out in 1980 to help police patrol the border so that many of the illegal immigrants could be caught and sent back to China.

Tibet

Chinese troops took over Tibet in 1951 and Dalai Lama, the religious leader, fled. Since then Tibet has been ruled as an 'autonomous' region of China. Recently there have been moves by China to encourage more Tibetans to become **cadres**, and, in keeping with China's new policies, to encourage some privately owned land and animals.

India

In the 1962 border war, Chinese troops captured areas of disputed mountainous Himalayan border territory from India. China's relations with her large neighbour have been poor since then, and the India–USSR friendship treaty in 1971 did not improve Chinese–Indian relations. By 1981, however, China was interested in improving relations and the Chinese Foreign Minister Huang Hua became the first Chinese leader to visit India since 1962. Part of his discussion with the Indian Prime Minister, Mrs Indira Gandhi, included the disputed border areas.

Huang Hua in India

Japan

China's desire for closer links with Japan in recent years has two main aims. By encouraging Japan to increase its military spending, China will further threaten the USSR. Also, Japan has many of the high-technology items that China needs to develop its modernisation programme.

In 1978 China and Japan signed a Friendship Treaty. This restored full diplomatic recognition between the two countries and led to trade agreements worth about $20 billion over several years. In 1980 Japan gave China a $200 million loan, while Japanese firms such as Sanyo Electrics, Hitachi Engineering and Canon Cameras have all agreed to set up factories and cooperative works in China.

RELATIONS WITH OTHER PARTS OF THE WORLD

The USA

Since the exchange of ambassadors between China and the USA in 1979, China has eagerly accepted US trade and US support against the Soviet Union. In that year, **Deng Xiaoping** visited the USA, and several trade agreements have been made since then. China has agreed to sell cotton goods to the USA while US firms such as Kodak, Coca Cola, Inter-Continental Hotels, and Macdonald Fast Foods (Hamburgers) have all gained trading and production footholds in China. Total US trade with China was about $4 billion in 1980; it is expected to increase to $10 billion by 1985.

Deng Xiaoping meets Alexander Haig, 1981

'Drink Coca Cola' advert in Guangzhou

164

Europe

China, in the 1980s, has been interested in Europe for two main reasons. Firstly, China encourages the **NATO** military alliance to be more aggressive towards the Soviet Union, and to build up its military strength. Also, China is interested in EEC trade, especially in electronics, engineering, radar, and military equipment.

By 1980 Chinese exports to the EEC had increased to about £700 million but EEC exports had reduced slightly to £650 million. The goods bought by China included two nuclear power stations to be built by France, and coal-mining equipment to be supplied by Britain's National Coal Board. Britain is interested in supplying a wide range of goods to China. For example, Britain hopes to sell Harrier Jump Jets to China, although the Chinese consider them too costly. Also Chinese agricultural experts have visited Britain and, in 1981, over 6000 pedigree chickens, hatched at Dumfries, were sent to China by Ross Poultry Breeders of Newbridge, near Edinburgh.

EEC trade with China

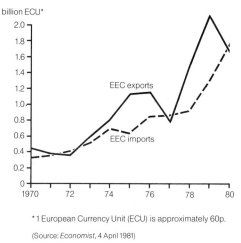

billion ECU*

* 1 European Currency Unit (ECU) is approximately 60p.

(Source: *Economist*, 4 April 1981)

Third World

China's aim is to be a friend and leader to the countries of the Third World. This aim is mixed with the desire to block moves by the Soviet Union in the Third World, where possible.

In South-east Asia, China would like closer support from ASEAN countries (Thailand, Malaysia, Singapore, Indonesia, and the Philippines) to oppose the USSR's ally, Vietnam, and its intervention in Kampuchea since 1978. In Africa, China gained the support of several African States by helping their economies after they gained independence. In the 1960s China gave aid to Mali and Guinea, and China supplied technical help and money to build the Tanzania–Zambia railway. In 1981, China supported a Third World candidate, Mr Salim of Tanzania, as the new Secretary General of the United Nations, despite strong opposition from both the USSR and the USA.

FOREIGN POLICY PROBLEMS IN THE 1980s

1. *Anti-USSR policy*. This has not only cut China off from much-needed Soviet technical and scientific aid but has also led China into military confrontation and competition with the USSR in terms of developing nuclear weapons and modernising its army.

2. *Support for other governments*. As part of its policy of opposing the USSR, China finds itself supporting some governments who have little respect for communism. For example, China has trade links with Chile, supports NATO and EEC governments, and Chinese leaders went to meet the Shah of Iran.

3. *'One China' policy*. The continuing support for Taiwan (formerly Formosa) by President Reagan and his advisers has led China to threaten a reduction in US relations if the USA does not accept, as China maintains, that Taiwan is part of China.

Questions

1. Outline the main aims of China's foreign policy.
2. What difficulties do China's foreign policy aims face in the 1980s?
3. What is China's policy towards Taiwan?
4. What signs are there in China of the closer Chinese–US trade links?

Military Strength

QUANTITY WITHOUT QUALITY

If military strength were measured simply in terms of numbers of troops and quantity of equipment and weapons China would be more powerful than either the Soviet Union or the United States. The People's Liberation Army (PLA), with its $4\frac{1}{2}$ million troops and vast numbers of tanks, aircraft and ships, appears on paper to be very strong. These bare statistics are, however, very misleading. Because so much of the equipment is out-of-date, China's military machine bears no comparison with the strength of the other two Great Powers.

The People Liberation Army: Major Mission Forces

Nuclear War

2 CSS-3 (limited-range Inter-continental
  Ballistic Missiles 3500 miles)
30–40 Intermediate-range Ballistic Missiles
30–40 Medium-range Ballistic Missiles
90 1U-16 bomber aircraft
102 submarines (questionable)
Urban tunnel systems
Electronic warning systems (obsolescent)

Conventional War

Ground forces
129 combat divisions (including 11
  armoured and 3 airborne)
150 independent regiments
56 support divisions: artillery, engineer, etc.
Sizeable regional forces

Air forces
Over 4000 jet aircraft: dedicated to air
  defence and ground support
300 light bombers
350 helicopters
AA artillery, surface-to-air missile units,
  warning network

Naval forces
68 submarines: snorkel, diesel-powered
4 advanced submarines (including 1
  nuclear-powered)
11 destroyers with surface-to-surface
  missiles
14 frigates
19 patrol escorts
Large numbers of patrol craft, many well
  suited to close-in and coastal operations
Amphibious elements of the navy,
  composed largely of very old vessels of
  World War 2 vintage

Mobility forces
Airlift for 1 division at light scales
Amphibious lift for short-range lift of 30 000
  troops
Trucks and armoured cars in modest supply
Improving but still modest railroad and road
  transport systems

(From Angus M. Fraser,
'Military Modernisation in China',
Problems of Communism,
September–December 1979, p. 40)

EMPHASIS ON DEFENCE

China's armed forces are designed almost exclusively for defence although they are also capable of fighting limited wars in South-east Asia. The principal enemy is the Soviet Union, and fear of the USSR's ambitions in Asia has led to efforts to raise the level of defence to deter this potential enemy from attacking.

The main strength of the PLA is in the infantry, but even here there is a shortage of the equipment necessary to make a modern army mobile and effective. Trucks, armoured cars and helicopters, for example, are in short supply. The air force and navy are both more suited to local defence than to attack. The fighter and bomber aircraft used (which are mainly modernised versions of old Soviet models) have a short range and are generally too slow and inadequately armed to pose a threat to any country with modern systems of air defence. Similarly, the patrol boats and destroyers are effective within limited areas, but would be ineffective in any major confrontation. China's apparent submarine strength is a myth: the submarines it possesses are obsolete diesel-powered models which urgently need replacing.

However limited China's strength in conventional forces, in terms of nuclear capability, it is even further behind the USA and the Soviet Union. China's very modest nuclear force would only be of use as a retaliatory weapon. If used as a 'first strike' force, China would be inviting total devastation from a well-equipped enemy.

Questions

1. What is
   (*a*) the main strength, and
   (*b*) the main weakness, of China's military forces?
2. Describe the main purpose of China's armed forces.

Military Modernisation

THE NEED FOR MODERNISATION

Even before the death of Mao Zedong in 1976 there was considerable debate among Chinese leaders about the need to modernise and improve China's military forces. Some leaders wanted new weapons immediately while others wanted to concentrate on the development of industry and saw the People's Liberation Army (PLA) as adequate for its main job of defending China.

The description of China's present military strength in the previous unit indicates the reasons why some leaders thought improvement was needed. But why did China's military forces become so outdated in the first place? The leaders who came to power after the Communist Revolution in 1949 had very little experience in the design of weapons: most of the PLA's weapons had been captured from the Nationalist forces. The Korean War in the early 1950s gave China no time to build a modern army, and the Chinese relied heavily on the Soviet Union as a supplier of military equipment. With the emphasis on defence, China produced sturdy and reliable weapons during the 1960s and 1970s – gunboats, destroyers and aircraft – but they were far behind the United States and the Soviet Union in performance and capability.

By the mid 1970s an increasing number of Chinese leaders had become concerned at their country's slow rate of military progress, even although China had by that time experimented with its own nuclear weapons. With the death of Mao and the introduction of the Four Modernisations the improvement of China's military forces became an important priority. Although Deng Xiaoping looks upon the other three modernisations as being more urgent than military modernisation, the strengthening of China's military capability is likely to continue steadily throughout the 1980s.

THE PATTERN OF MODERNISATION
(What weapons does China want?)

The items described in the next table show that China's main aim in updating her military forces is to improve the strength of her defence against any potential enemy. The concentration on anti-tank weapons, nuclear shelters, anti-submarine equipment, etc illustrates the defensive emphasis of the military modernisation programme. There is no sign of a major move on the part of the Chinese to increase their arsenal of nuclear weapons as a destructive threat to the USSR or any other potential enemy. China appears to be steering a middle course between complete lack of nuclear deterrent on the one hand and hostile attacking capability on the other.

Types of weapons, equipment and technology in which China has expressed interest since 1 January 1977

Type	Percentage of sample
Whole aircraft (26) and spares	34.1
Anti-tank weapons	17.6
Shelter, nuclear attack	9.5
Anti-submarine warfare gear	7.1
Computers with military applications	5.9
Reconnaissance and communications satellites	5.9
Anti-aircraft weapons	4.7
Tanks and armoured personnel carriers	4.7
Nuclear weapons and missiles	3.6
Naval engines	2.3
Submarines	1.2
Equipment for ships of over 10 000 tonnes	1.2
Laser applications	1.2
Bridging equipment	1.2
	100.1*

*Discrepancy due to rounding

Sources: 85 press reports from 23 separate press and journal sources and 3 discussions with military visitors to China.

(From Angus M. Fraser, 'Military Modernisation in China', *Problems of Communism*, Sept.–Dec. 1979, p. 40)

Further evidence of the defensive nature of these developments came in a speech by Ye Jianying, Vice-Chairman of the **CCP**, in 1978 when he urged the Chinese people to 'dig tunnels deep'. A number of major cities including Beijing and Shanghai have built anti-nuclear tunnels around their perimeters to protect the people from possible nuclear attack. Effort has also gone into setting up an efficient radar tracking system and an early warning system against Inter-continental Ballistic Missiles attacking from the direction of the USSR.

The kind of Harrier Jump Jet that the Chinese are interested in

THE AIMS OF MODERNISATION

There is little evidence that China is likely to become more aggressive towards the other Superpowers as a result of the recent military policy. Defence is the key-word. There have, however, been signs recently that China is more prepared to become involved in international affairs, particularly in Asia. Military assistance has been given to a number of revolutionary **guerrilla** forces as well as to Tanzania and Pakistan. In 1979 China went to war with Vietnam in what was an important 'learning experience' for the PLA. But modernisation to such an extent that China could present a military challenge on a world scale is still a long way away.

CAN CHINA CATCH UP?

In some vital areas – satellite communications, lasers, and space technology – China is trying hard to catch up with the USA and the USSR. In a sense, however, the Chinese have to run fast to stay in the same place because the rapidly developing technology of the other two Superpowers means that they too are pushing further and further ahead with military developments.

Representatives of the PLA have discussed their needs for modern weapons with Britain, West Germany, France, Sweden, and Italy as well as with the USA. With the new economic policy of reassessment, however, some of the large-scale military contracts negotiated in 1978–9 have been cancelled. The enormous cost of modernisation looks likely to mean a slowing down of the rate of progress desired.

Questions

1. Why has there been growing concern among Chinese leaders about their country's military strength in recent years?
2. What new weapons would they like to acquire?
3. How are these weapons likely to be used in future?
4. Explain the meaning of 'the Chinese have to run fast to stay in the same place'.

Changing Relations with the USA and the USSR

ISSU

The world could be described as the arena ('wrestling ring') in which the Great Powers struggle with each other for superiority. Over the past few decades, the most important change in the Great Power line-up has been the move by China to break relations with the Soviet Union and to seek closer links with the USA.

Why did China make this change and what effect has it had on China?

A Chinese delegation in the UK, investigating pilot training in the Royal Air Force.

CHINA'S RELATIONS WITH THE USA AND THE USSR IN THE 1950s

After the Chinese Revolution in 1949, when the new Communist Government of Mao Zedong came to power, China was desperately in need of aid to rebuild. For this aid, China turned to the USSR, its 'Communist friend and neighbour', and in return Soviet military aid, advisers, technicians and industrial equipment were given.

During this time China's view of the USA was that it was an **imperialist** power threatening China over Korea and Formosa, and was a 'capitalist hyena'.

1950s

Young People's Republic of China + powerful friend, Soviet Union

Imperialist paper tiger, USA

WHY DID THIS LINE-UP CHANGE?

There are a number of reasons why China chose to change the Great Power line-up. There were disputes over border territory between the USSR and China, with China claiming parts of Mongolia as Chinese territory. The two leaders, Mao and **Khrushchev**, did not have much respect for each other. The two countries also quarrelled over which was the 'true' communist follower of **Karl Marx**, and over which was the leader of world communism. By the 1960s the disputes became serious and China gradually moved away from the USSR's friendship to establish, in the 1970s, closer links with the USA (see pages 13 and 164).

EFFECTS OF THE CHANGE ON CHINA

'It is our hope in China that not only the United States, but Japan, West Europe and the Third World will unite to deal with the Soviet Union's expansion.'

(*Chinese Vice-Premier Deng Xiaoping, 1980*)

China is now very critical of the Soviet Union and encourages the USA and Western Europe to build up their military strength to oppose the USSR. China has criticised Soviet intervention in Afghanistan and Angola. China also now finds itself confronted directly across the border, by almost a quarter of the USSR's much better equipped army and airforce. The Chinese have moved to closer diplomatic and business links with the USA to help China's modernisation of its army and its economy. Over 60 US firms have set up in China, and US-Chinese trade increases each year.

1960s–1980s

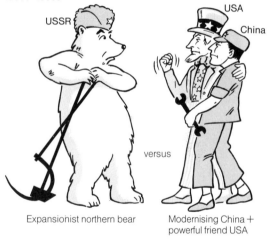

Expansionist northern bear

Modernising China + powerful friend USA

Questions

1. Describe China's relations with the USA and the USSR before the 1970s.
2. Why did China change from support of the USSR to support of the USA?
3. What was Deng Xiaoping's view of the Soviet Union in 1980?
4. What criticisms of the USSR have recently been made by China?

USA: Time chart

Date	Social and economic	Political	International affairs
1945		Truman becomes President	United Nations formed End of World War 2
1948	Marshall Aid Plan for Europe		Berlin Crisis
1949			NATO formed
1950			USA enters Korean War
1952		Eisenhower becomes President	
1953			Korean War ends
1954	Courts declare racial segregation in schools		US H-Bomb tests SEATO formed
1955			Baghdad Pact formed (later CENTO)
1958	US Space Satellite	Alaska joins USA	
1959		Hawaii becomes 50th State	
1960	Civil rights protests begin	Kennedy becomes President	
1961			US becomes involved in Vietnam
1962			Cuban missile crisis
1963	Civil rights march in Washington	Kennedy assassinated in Dallas, Texas. Johnson becomes President	
1965	Riots by blacks start in several US cities		
1968	Martin Luther King assassinated. Civil Rights Acts passed	Nixon becomes President	USA and USSR begin SALT
1969	US Astronauts land on moon		
1972		Watergate break-in	Nixon visits USSR and China
1973			USA signs ceasefire in Vietnam War
1974		Nixon resigns. Ford takes over as President	
1975	US and Soviet spacecraft link up space		American troops leave Vietnam
1976		Carter becomes President	
1979			USA-China diplomatic relations begin
1980		Reagan becomes President	USA protests over Soviet action in Afghanistan
1981	Public spending cuts. Increase in US inflation and unemployment figures		USA protests over military rule in Poland
1982	12 million unemployed (10.8% of workforce)		US advisers and increased aid to El Salvador. Reagan visits Central and South America. Plans for M-X missile
1983			US troops invade Grenada
1984	Los Angeles Olympic Games	Reagan re-elected President	US troops leave Lebanon

USSR: Time chart

Date	Social and economic	Political	International affairs
1945			End of World War 2
1948			Berlin Crisis
1950			Friendship Treaty with China
1953		Stalin dies	
1954	Virgin Lands scheme		
1955		Khrushchev emerges as Soviet leader	Warsaw Pact formed
1956		Policy of de-Stalinisation	Policy of peaceful coexistence. Hungarian Revolution
1957	Launch of Sputnik I		
1960			Ending of Soviet aid to China
1961			Berlin Wall built
1962			Cuba missile crisis
1964		Brezhnev and Kosygin emerge as Soviet leaders	
1968			Invasion of Czechoslovakia. SALT begin with USA
1969			Sino-Soviet border clashes
1970	Ninth five-year plan		
1972			Nixon visits USSR (detente)
1973			SALT 1 agreement. Brezhnev visits USA. Soviet aid to Egypt and Syria
1975	Five-year treaty with USA to buy grain. US and Soviet spacecraft link up in space		Aid to Angola
1976	Tenth five-year plan		
1977		New Soviet Constitution announced	Aid to Ethiopia
1979			SALT 2 agreement (not ratified by USA). USSR invades Afghanistan
1980	Moscow Olympic Games		
1981			Arms reduction talks with USA begin in Geneva
1982		Brezhnev dies. Yuri Andropov becomes Soviet leader	Martial law in Poland
1983			Soviet fighter plane shoots down South Korean airliner
1984	BAM railway completed	Andropov dies. Konstantin Chernenko becomes Soviet leader	

China: Time chart

Date	Social and economic	Political	International affairs
1949		Foundation of People's Republic of China	
1950	Agrarian Reform Law		Friendship Treaty with USSR. China enters Korean War
1953	First five-year plan		Korean War ends
1956		'Hundred Flowers' Campaign	
1958		Great Leap Forward begins	
	First commune set up		Beginning of Sino-Soviet dispute
1959		Liu-Shaoqui Replaces Mao as President of China	
1960	China in economic crisis		Soviet advisers withdrawn from China
1961	Reversal of Great Leap Forward policies		
1964			China explodes first atomic bomb. USA increases involvement in Vietnam
1966		Beginning of Cultural Revolution	
1968		Liu Shaoqui dismissed	
1969		Cultural Revolution brought to an end	Sino-Soviet border clashes
1971		Lin Biao dies in plane crash after failing to seize power	US Table-tennis team invited to China. China admitted to UN
1972			Nixon visits China
1976		Death of Zhou Enlai. Death of Mao Zedong. Hua Guofeng succeeds Mao as Chairman of CCP. Gang of Four arrested	
1977		Deng Xiaoping returns to power	
1978	Four Modernisations programme put into action	Democracy Wall provides focus for dissidents	Great Leap Outwards: Beginning of greater contact with foreign business world
1979			Deng visits USA. China invades Vietnam
1980	Four Modernisations programme scaled down	Gang of Four put on trial	
1981		Hua Guofeng replaced as Party Chairman by Hu Yaobang	
1982			Chinese Foreign Minister visits Moscow.
1984	Prime Minister Zhao Ziyang calls for a mixed economy in China		President Reagan visits China. Agreement over Hong Kong. China to buy US military equipment.

Who's Who

Yuri Andropov (1914–84) Former head of KGB. First Secretary of the Communist Party and leader of the Soviet Union from 1982 to 1984.

Menachem Begin (b. 1913) Prime Minister of Israel from 1977 to 1984.

Leonid Brezhnev (1906–82) First Secretary of the Communist Party of the Soviet Union and leader of the Soviet Union from 1964 to 1982.

Jimmy Carter (b. 1924) President of the USA (Democrat) from 1976 to 1980.

Fidel Castro (b. 1926) Revolutionary leader of Cuba since 1959.

Konstantin Chernenko (b. 1911) First Secretary of the Communist Party and leader of the Soviet Union after the death of Andropov in 1984.

Chiang Kai-Shek (1887–1975) Became leader of the Nationalist Government in China in 1928. Led the Civil War against the communists. In 1949, when Mao Zedong and the communists gained control of China, Chiang and his army fled to Formosa (now Taiwan). President of Taiwan from 1950 onwards.

Deng Xiaoping (b. 1904) Vice-Chairman of the Chinese Communist Party. Formerly Vice-Premier of the People's Republic of China (1977–80).

Gerald Ford (b. 1913) President of the USA (Republican) from 1974 to 1976.

Gang of Four Main opposition to Chairman Hua after the death of Mao Zedong in September 1976. Led by Mao's widow Jiang Quing. Arrested and imprisoned in October 1976.

Hu Yaobang (b. 1916) Succeeded Hua Guofeng as Chairman of the Communist Party in China in 1981.

Hua Guofeng (b. 1920) Became Chairman of the Chinese Communist Party in 1976 after death of Mao Zedong. Resigned as Chairman in 1981.

Lyndon B. Johnson (1908–73) President of the USA (Democrat) from 1963 to 1968. Became President after assassination of President Kennedy.

John F. Kennedy (1917–63) President of the USA (Democrat) from 1960 to 1963. Youngest, and first Roman Catholic, President. Assassinated in Dallas, Texas, 1963.

Ayatollah Khomeini (b. 1900) Leader of the Islamic Revolution in Iran which overthrew the Government of the Shah of Iran in 1979. Religious and political leader of the new Islamic Republic of Iran.

Nikita Khrushchev (1894–1971) First Secretary of Communist Party of the Soviet Union after death of Stalin. Leader of USSR till dismissal in 1964.

Martin Luther King (1929–68) Baptist minister, leader of the peaceful campaign in the 1960s for civil rights for blacks in the USA. Awarded Nobel Peace Prize in 1964. Assassinated in 1968.

Lenin (1870–1924) Revolutionary leader of the Bolshevika. Became leader of the Soviet Union after seizing power in 1917 Revolution.

Mao Zedong (1893–1976) Became leader of the Chinese Communist Party in 1935 and led communists to victory in 1949. Leader of People's Republic of China from 1949 until his death in 1976.

Karl Marx (1818–83) German philosopher. Founder of communism.

Richard Nixon (b. 1913) President of the USA (Republican) from 1968 to 1974. Resigned in 1974 as a result of Watergate affair.

Ronald Reagan (b. 1911) US President (Republican) 1981–

Anwar Sadat (1918–81) President of Egypt from 1970 till his death in 1981 as a result of assassination.

Joseph Stalin (1879–1953) Became leader of the Soviet Union after death of Lenin. Dominated the history of the USSR until his death in 1953.

Lech Walesa (b. 1943) Leader and founding member of Polish Solidarity union.

Malcolm X (1925–65) Real name Malcolm Little. Leading spokesman of the Black Muslim Movement. Assassinated 1965.

Zhou Enlai (1898–1976) Premier of communist China from 1954 onwards. A close associate of Mao Zedong. Also served as China's foreign minister.

Glossary

AWACS Air Warning and Control System. A type of American aircraft fitted with radar scanners which can pick up, over a wide area, information about military, naval, and aircraft movements.

Balance of payments The difference between the total amount of goods and services which a country exports compared with the total amounts of goods and services it imports.

Barefoot doctor Term used in China to describe people trained in basic primary health care.

Cadre A specially trained member of the Communist Party who can operate as a leader and political adviser in local situations.

Capitalism A socio-economic system based on private ownership of property and means of production.

CCP The Chinese Communist Party. The sole and leading political party in the People's Republic of China.

Civil Rights Movement The campaign by black Americans during the 1950s and 1960s to gain equal rights with white Americans. Lead by Martin Luther King.

Cold War The rivalry and hostility between the USA and USSR following the end of World War 2.

Collective farm One of the two main forms of agricultural organisation in the USSR. Large farm owned by the State but run by elected committee of farm members.

Collectivisation The process, under communist States, where peasant farmers give up their private plots of land to State control to be grouped into larger collectively-owned farms.

COMECON Council for Mutual Economic Assistance. A trade grouping set up in 1949: the communist equivalent of the EEC. Includes the USSR and most East European countries.

Commune (People's Commune) The large communities in which most Chinese people live and work. The basic unit of organisation in the Chinese countryside: responsible for agriculture, small-scale industry, welfare, local government and defence.

Communism A classless social system in which private property is abolished and all the means of production are publicly owned.

Congress The legislature of national government in the USA, composed of the Senate and House of Representatives.

Constitution The body of rules which determine how a country is governed.

CPSU The Communist Party of the Soviet Union (the sole and leading political party).

Cruise missile An American nuclear missile which can be launched from land, ship or plane. It flies just above ground level and has great accuracy.

Cultural Revolution The period in Chinese politics (1966-9) when China was cast into upheaval by Mao Zedong. People were encouraged to criticise established ideas in a process of continual revolution.

Democratic Party One of the two main political parties in the USA, supported mainly by 'the ordinary people'.

Detente The relaxation of international tension between the USA and the USSR and their respective allies.

Dissident One who disagrees with and opposes the ruling political group or the political ideals of a country.

Domino theory The theory put forward by some American politicians that if one country in an area such as Central America becomes communist then others will 'fall' also, like a row of dominoes falling over.

Electoral College The institution which formally elects the President of the USA.

Federalism The political system in which power and responsibility are shared between a national (Federal) government and regional governments.

Five-year plan The means used by the governments in communist countries to set production targets for various areas of the economy.

Gas-guzzler Large US automobile with high fuel consumption.

Ghetto An inner-city area of great poverty and deprivation, usually containing a large proportion of one ethnic group.

Great Leap Forward That period in Chinese politics (1958-61) when there was a campaign to make great advances in the Chinese economy. Largely unsuccessful.

GOSPLAN The State Planning Commission which has responsibility for economic planning in the USSR.

Guerrilla warfare A 'hit and run' form of warfare favoured by an irregular army against the regular armed forces of a government or invader.

Hispanics The term used to describe Spanish-speaking Americans.

Imperialism The process by which one country dominates another, either by military or economic strength.

Komsomol The young Communist League in the Soviet Union, with a membership of millions.

Kremlin The group of buildings in Moscow which houses the centre of Soviet Government.

Ku Klux Klan The semi-secret organisation in the USA which is militantly anti-black. It is also anti-communist and anti-semitic.

Legislature The body of people who make laws in a country.

M-X missile Missile Experimental: a system of land-based missiles on underground tracks, designed to be moved between silos in order to confuse the enemy.

Multinational A massive business or industrial organisation with branches in many countries throughout the world.

Nachalstvo The elite ruling class in the USSR composed of senior officials of the CPSU, the Government and the military.

NATO North Atlantic Treaty Organisation. Military alliance of the USA and Western European Powers formed in 1949 with the aim of preventing communist expansion.

Neutron bomb A special nuclear bomb with a high-energy radiation explosion. The radiation kills living organisms but there is no huge blast to destroy buildings.

NORAD North American Air Defence Command. Agreement set up in 1958. Cooperation between the military forces of Canada and the USA to defend North America.

OPEC Organisation of Petroleum Exporting Countries. Set up in 1961 by leading oil-producing countries such as Saudi Arabia to safeguard their oil interests.

PLO Palestine Liberation Organisation. An Arab movement whose aim is to replace the State of Israel by a new State in which Palestinian Arabs and Israelis would have equal rights.

Pravda The official Communist Party newspaper in the Soviet Union. It is the most widely read newspaper in the Soviet Union and has a circulation of over ten million copies daily.

Politburo The leading politicians in the communist parties of the Soviet Union and of China.

Primary election The process in the election of the President of the USA in which party members can decide among different candidates which should eventually stand as candidate for their party.

Production brigade/team The different parts into which a commune is divided for work purposes.

Racism The political theory which regards certain groups of people as inferior to others because of their race or ethnic grouping.

Republican Party One of the two main political parties in the USA, supported mainly by 'the rich and business world'.

SALT Strategic Arms Limitations Talks.

Solidarity The trade union which emerged in Poland in 1979.

State farm One of the two main forms of agricultural organisation in the USSR. Very large farm owned and run by the State, with employees paid as in factories.

Supreme Court The leading court of law in the USA.

Supreme Soviet The legislature of national government in the USSR.

Third World The term used to describe the developing countries of the world.

UNO The United Nations Organisation. Set up in 1945 to encourage the ideal of world peace and cooperation. Most countries in the world are members. The headquarters is in New York.

Warsaw Pact Military alliance of most communist States in Europe, formed 1955.

Acknowledgements

The publishers wish to thank the following for permission to reproduce the photographs (or cartoons) on the pages listed:

Sally and Richard Greenhill (16); Philadelphia Inquirer, the Washington Post Writers Group (17, 65); Andrew Sacks (19); John Topham (20, 22, 24, 26, 32, 50, 55, 79, 114, 122, 124, 125, 130, 161, 164, 168); Popperfoto (22, 25, 39, 45, 50, 60, 65, 66, 119, 157, 160); Keystone Press Agency (22, 50, 51, 87, 113, 114, 157, 164, 165); Rex Features Ltd (22, 70); Camera Press (29 Sarah Webb Barrell; 32 Tom Hanley; 72, 85, 102; 139 Paul Raffafle; 147 Richard Harrington; 148; 155; 164 Harry Redl); Associated Press (32, 40, 109); Library of Congress (33); St Louis Post Dispatch (44); Ford Motor Company (47); *Punch* (54); JAK *Evening Standard* 7/8/74 (57); Novosti Press Agency (76, 77, 79, 81, 92, 93, 95, 97, 113); *Krokodil*: no. 27, 1978 (87); no. 34 1977 (93); *Soviet Union* no. 3 1977 (100); Lada Cars Ltd (103); Society for Cultural Relations with the USSR (107); John Gittings (133, 145); Society for Anglo-Chinese Understanding (134, 136, 155, 157, 160); Xinhua News Agency (134, 135, 146, 148); Chinese Visual Aids Project, Polytechnic of Central London (137, 141); *US News and World Report* (145); *China Reconstructs* January 1981 (149); Patrick Booz (152).

The publishers also thank all those who gave permission to reproduce extracts from their publications, or to use their material as the basis for illustrations. Acknowledgement is given beneath each extract in the text.
The extracts on page 12 are from *The Observer*, *The Times* and *The Scotsman*.
Although every effort has been made to trace copyright owners, the publishers apologise for any ommissions.

Picture research by Procaudio Limited, London.

Illustrated by Stephen Gibson

Oliver & Boyd
Robert Stevenson House
1–3 Baxter's Place
Leith Walk
Edinburgh EH1 3BB

A Division of Longman Group Ltd

ISBN 0 05 003298 4

First published 1983
Third impression 1985

Produced by Longman Group (FE) Ltd
Printed in Hong Kong